MAJOR THEMES
IN MODERN
Philosophies
OF JUDAISM

MAJOR THEMES
IN MODERN
Philosophies
OF JUDAISM

ELIEZER BERKOVITS

KTAV PUBLISHING HOUSE, Inc.

NEW YORK

Library of Congress Cataloging in Publication Data

Berkovits, Eliezer, 1908-
 Major themes in modern philosophies of Judaism; a
critical evaluation.

 Includes bibliographical references.
 1. Judaism—20th century. 2. Cohen, Hermann, 1842-
1918. 3. Rosenzweig, Franz, 1886-1929. 4. Buber, Martin, 1878-1965. 5. Kaplan, Mordecai Menahem, 1881-
6. Heschel, Abraham Joshua, 1907-1972. I. Title.
BM195.B47   181'.3   74-3024
ISBN 0-87068-264-4

MANUFACTURED IN THE UNITED STATES OF AMERICA

TABLE OF CONTENTS

FOREWORD

As its title indicates, this volume deals with several major themes in the modern philosophies of Judaism as they emerge from some of the key writings of the authors discussed.

The analysis is critical. I believe that in my criticism I have given illustrative expression to the conviction that at this time we have neither a theology nor a philosophy of Judaism that does justice to the essential nature of Jewish teaching about God, man, and the universe as expressed in the classical sources of Judaism, nor one that can be maintained with contemporary philosophical validity.

In my opinion, we have reached a stage that requires a great deal of rethinking of the nature of the Jewish position in the history of human thought and commitment in the light of contemporary philosophical problematics and existential experience. Judaism is awaiting a reformulation of its theology and philosophy. It will, however, be accomplished by means of an intellectual strength that draws its creative inspiration as well as its contents from the classical sources of Judaism—Bible, Talmud, and Midrash.

The chapter on Buber was previously published by Yeshiva University, New York, in 1962, under the title, *A Jewish Critique of the Philosophy of Martin Buber*. The critique of Reconstructionism appeared in *Tradition,* in the Fall, 1959 issue, under the title, "Reconstructionist Theology." The essay on Heschel was also published by *Tradition,* in the Spring-Summer issue of 1964. The essay, "Faith and Law" was previously published in *Judaism,* in the Fall issue, 1964. Our thanks are offered to the publishers for their kind permission to reprint these essays in their present form.

ELIEZER BERKOVITS

The Hebrew Theological College
Hol Hamoed Succot, 5734

CHAPTER 1

Hermann Cohen's Religion of Reason

In the closing quarter of the nineteenth century and during the opening years of the twentieth, the brilliantly shining star in the sky of philosophy in Germany was Hermann Cohen. As one of the founders of the Neo-Kantian School at the University of Marburg he enriched the philosophical treasures of his native land with the creations of his genius. After a life of estrangement from Judaism, the grand old man of German idealism who had started out in life as a rabbinical student at the Breslau Rabbinical Seminary, returned to the faith of his fathers, the faith of his youth. The fruit of this return was a rediscovery of religion that, in a philosophical interpretation of Judaism, Cohen considered to be the religion of reason. The final results of the rediscovery were in the process of formulation in numerous essays during the years of Cohen's retirement from his chair in Marburg, and have been collected in three representative volumes as *Hermann Cohen's Jüdische Schriften.* Our attention, however, will be concentrated on two works in which Cohen's religion of reason found its final statement: the one entitled, *Der Begriff der Religion im System der Philosophie* (The Concept [Idea] of Religion in the System of Philosophy), published in 1915, and the other, *Die Religion der Vernunft aus den Quellen des Judentums* (The Religion of Reason from the Sources of Judaism), published posthumously in 1919. Franz Rosenzweig, Cohen's faithful disciple during the master's Berlin years, wrote of *Die Religion der Vernunft:* "In this work, that will still be read when the language in which Cohen wrote it will only be understood by scholars, was harvested the entire Jewish yield of this life and thus, indeed, the yield of this life in its entirety." [1] To us, it would seem that the essence of *Die Religion der Vernunft* is contained in *Der Begriff der Religion.* On this subject, not unlike Philo

1

in his days, Cohen wrote in one format for the philosophically schooled gentile reader, and in another for the believing Jewish intellectuals. *Der Begriff der Religion* is the version of *Die Religion der Vernunft* for the gentiles, whereas *Die Religion der Vernunft* is the Jewish version of *Der Begriff der Religion*.

I. ETHICS AND RELIGION

During the years that Cohen was creating his great system of philosophy in his works on logic, ethics, and aesthetics, he could find no place in it for religion. He regarded the particularism of all religions to be all the more dangerous since it was falsified by a pretense to universalism. Cohen's chief ethical concern was universalism; the goal of ethics was the totality (*Allheit*) of mankind. Only if religion would be willing to surrender its particularistic principles of faith, could it make mankind, in its universality, the goal of its teaching. But then it would have to submerge itself in ethics.[2]

Ethics cannot recognize the independence of religion. It sees in religion a *Naturzustand,* a state of nature, that in its cultural maturity must dissolve in ethics. Religion may be a handmaid to ethics, helping to transmit ethics into the stream of general culture; but its goal must be self-immolation through the fulfillment of its culture function on behalf of ethics.[3]

In one respect, however, ethics must grant recognition to the idea of God. This is necessitated by a methodological problem of ethics itself. It is characteristic of the ideal of morality that it is not realizable in time. Every phase of ethical realization is momentary; the striving and the progress must continue in eternity. This is the law of the ethics of the pure will. Ethics requires eternity. One must never waver in one's trust in eternal progress, that alone can bring about the full triumph of the idea of the Good. But how does one get the certainty of eternal duration? The eternity of the ideal is not to be separated from the eternity of Nature. For without Nature as its foundation the ideal is not realizable. One cannot strive for the realization of the ethical ideal in a void. The monotheistic God idea is introduced into the system in order to guarantee the eternity of the ethical ideal by securing its indispensable parallel, the eternally continued existence of Nature.

"God means that Nature has continued existence as certainly as morality is eternal. The ideal (of morality) can as little provide this certainty as it can be provided by nature." The surety of this parallelism is the truth that Cohen calls God. "And now the eternity of the ideal is secured through the divine providence over nature for the sake of morality." [4]

What we get here is, of course, a reformulation of Kant's idea of God as "a postulate of practical reason." It is incorporated into the system as a solution to a methodological problem. Cohen acknowledged its importance for his ethics in later years when he wrote that without it, his *Ethics* would have remained a "torso." [5]

This was how far Cohen went in admitting religion into his ethics. But when his long road of *t'shuba,* of return to Judaism, was about to be accomplished intellectually too, he found that there were other problems of man as he lived with himself as well as with his fellow man that remained unresolved in his system and, with regard to them, ethics was helpless. In the *Ethik* man is not the individual human being as he exists in his biological reality and social and historical context. There, man is defined by what he ought to be; that means that he is understood through the ideal of *Allheit,* the ideal of the universality of man, that of mankind. Man, one might say, is mankind. "Therefore, without (the idea of) totality (*Allheit*), and that means without *beginning* with totality, the idea of man cannot only not be completed, but it can absolutely not be developed and established."[6] In *Der Begriff der Religion,* Cohen recognizes that this idea of man is inadequate. It does not take cognizance of the day-to-day reality of the human condition. And, now, he asks what for the author of the *Ethics* is the surprisingly bold question: "What is man and what is he lacking, if he is *only* mankind?" [7] What is he indeed, in his own private situation? There are times of human weakness, of human failure. Above all, there is sin—"sin that overwhelms man; through it he loses his human dignity. He is diverted from the path of mankind and shrinks into *Individuum,* an individual." [8] If we wish to use a more apt term for what he wishes to say, we might exchange Cohen's *Individuum* for Kierkegaard's "single one." What can ethics do for a man, who is conscious of his guilt and cannot free himself from it? Here is the boundary line between ethics and religion, according to Cohen; here is the "birthplace of religion." How strange that only at this late hour in his life did it occur to Cohen to raise the basic question of human existence in all seriousness! There is, of course, a trace of it already in the *Ethik*. He quotes the fateful words of Ezekiel of the "soul that sins," that were to play such an important part, years later, in *Die Religion der Vernunft,* that the soul is the "person," the *Individuum,* that is discovered in the sin.[9] However, nothing comes of it in the *Ethik*. There it leads into a *cul de sac* and it is soon forgotten. Is it possible that there was present in Cohen much more of the affirmations and commitments of his youth as an observant Jew than the Herr Professor permitted to well up into his full consciousness?

There is yet another problem of man with which ethics, as conceived by Cohen, cannot cope. It arises, not from the life of man as he struggles with his own conscience in the solitude of his heart, but from the life of man in society, together with other human beings. A fundamental concept of ethics is the idea of honor, of human dignity. The essence of man, says Cohen, is his dignity—his human dignity, he adds significantly. He means by the addition, a dignity that is his, not because of his individual or particular status, but an honor and respect that is due to him simply because he is man. Therein is grounded the idea of the equality of all men.[10] However, as Cohen puts it in *Der Begriff der Religion,* this respect refers to the moral dignity of man. It does not consider the particular situation in which each individual human being finds himself. It has no eye as to whether a man is poor or rich, miserable or happy. In the equality of their dignity because they are all human, one perceives the individual as an abstract humanity. Just as the individual cannot emerge unto himself with the help of ethics alone, neither can the other man claim my attention as an individual, as "a single one." [11]

Cohen formulates the problem somewhat differently in the introduction to *Die Religion der Vernunft*. We saw earlier in our discussion, that in his ethics the "I" is really mankind. But from this follows, that so also is the "He" or "She." And, indeed, on the basis of the *Ethik* there is no difference between the "I" and the "He." Whatever is due to him is also due to me. What is missing in this scheme is the "Thou." The "Thou" comes into being when I behold the man beside me in his individual circumstances that may lay claim to my pity. But while there is room in Cohen's ethics for universal honor and dignity, there is none for individual pity or sympathy.[12]

Because of these insufficiencies, ethics has to call on religion for the solution of its unresolved problems. This does not mean that ethics now recognizes the sovereign independence of religion, but only its specific character, a character which is not distinguished by some other source of knowledge and truth—which is impossible—but only by its specific contents. Ethics does not here turn into religion. However, by the broadening of its problems, by the completion of its concept of man through the idea of the individual, and by an enriched self-awareness, the compass of ethics is expanded to include the contents of religion.[13] But how is the complete harmony between the two to be achieved while preserving the unity of their methodological validity? The answer to the question is provided by Cohen's religion of reason, as presented to us in the two volumes, *Der Begriff der Religion* and *Die Religion der Vernunft*.

II. THE RELIGION OF REASON

1. *Being and Becoming*

As Cohen puts it, "reason is the organ of the laws," meaning that it is the instrument that provides the rules that validate the speculations of man, the laws of logical thinking. The religion of reason, accordingly, is under the authority of such speculative lawfulness. It disregards all historical factuality as purely incidental. It is based fully on this lawfulness of logical thought. This is, in essence, reason's share in religion.[14]

In the opening pages of *Der Begriff der Religion* Cohen had already given an indication of the significance of his position when he stated that logic and religion have one basic idea in common, i.e., the idea of Being. Being is no less a problem of religion then a problem of logic.[15] According to Cohen, "logic is the thinking of the origin";[16] thus, the understanding of all movement requires the thinking of rest as its origin, the grasping of all Becoming demands the thinking of Being as its logical precondition. Heraclitus' "All flows" had to be corrected by Parmenides' idea of Being. This, of course, leads us to the Kantian theory of Substance as the idea of relation, that is the logical point of rest to which all changes must be related and without which the processes in time remain inexplicable.[17] The same problems and similar solutions are also the preoccupation of religion. Religion must find the origin of Becoming, and finds it in Being that is identified as God. God is the precondition of Becoming, which is the world of nature and of man. God as Being is the explanation of Becoming. However, it is important to note that there is no material relation between God and the world. Becoming is not emanation of Being. It does not issue from Being, nor is it contained in it. Just as the Kantian Substance has logical significance for change, so religion's God as Being has logical significance for Becoming. Just as in logic thinking is the thinking of the origin, in religion thinking is the thinking of God as the thinking of origin. "Nature is the Becoming that demands that Being be given to it as its foundation." [18]

God is Being, Becoming is existence (*Dasein*). One discovers existence through the senses; God, however, is nonperceptible Being grasped by reason. Thus, God is not only one, but unique, the only Being. Nothing has being apart from him. Nature has existence, but not being. Nature is nothing compared to the Being of God. Uniqueness, therefore, excludes all pantheism, which identifies Being with Becoming. It also renders impossible any idea of mediation, be it dualistic like Philo's thought of the logos, or trinitarian, like the Christian belief in a triune God. God alone has being.[19]

2. *Creation and Revelation*

Since God is thus conceived as the origin of Becoming, he is of necessity the source of all activity. This yields us the idea of creation. But we have seen that God's significance for Becoming is logical, therefore creation must not be understood as an activity added to Being. That would establish a material relation between Being and Becoming which was excluded. Cohen says that creation is not an activity but the precondition of causality and of all activity. Thus, creation is called the essence of Being as uniqueness, or as Cohen says, "The uniqueness of divine Being is accomplished in creation." [20] We assume that what he means is once again the direct result of the logical significance of Being for Becoming. One can only speak of the uniqueness of Being as a distinguishing characteristic from the Non-Being of Becoming. Since Becoming demands Being for its ground of necessity, Being has to include creation, not as an act in time, but as the basis of all acts in time. Thus Cohen would say, "Creation is the ground attribute (*Urattribut*) of God . . . not as a consequence of uniqueness . . . But identical with it." [21] Although it is somewhat difficult to see how an attribute, however fundamental, could be identified with God, what Cohen had in mind was to make sure that creation should not be understood as a physical act in history, but as the origin of the space-time dimension as required by his logic. From this he derives the idea of the continuity of creation. If creation were a physical act on the part of the deity one such act would suffice and Becoming, too, would be such an individual event. But since creation is the ground of all activity, it must continually remain that ground. Thus Becoming itself is forever renewed. Cohen identifies this thought with the traditional formulation in the daily prayer of the Jew that maintains of God that "he renews in his goodness the works of creation daily." [22]

Man is part of nature. But man is not only nature, says Cohen; he is also reason. Creation of man was his creation as a rational being. This Cohen calls revelation. Revelation is the creation of reason. It is through reason that man discovers God, that he discovers truth. Thus, revelation should be understood as the continuation of creation. Revelation completes creation. [23]

The contents of revelation are "the statutes and laws" of Judaism. But they have their foundation in reason. They are revealed to man rationally. This changes revelation from a fact in history to a spiritual event occurring in human consciousness. What happens now to the historic revelation at Sinai? It, too, has to be spiritualized. Cohen thinks that he has found support for his theory in the Bible itself. The Bible warns against any "corporeal" visualization of the experience at Sinai. When the Bible says: "And the Eternal One spoke unto You out of the midst of the fire; ye heard the voice of the words, but ye saw no form," [24] Cohen maintains that even to hear would still be too much of a "materialization" of the divine. He interprets, therefore, the phrase, "ye heard," as: "you understood and obeyed," which the Hebrew, *shom'im,* permits. The strangest support for his rationalistic interpretation of revelation Cohen finds in the biblical statement: "It is not in heaven, that thou shouldst say: Who shall go up for us to heaven, and bring it unto us, and make us to hear it, that we may do it? But the word is very nigh unto thee, in thy mouth, and in thy heart, that thou mayest do it." [25] According to Cohen, this removes revelation from history. If tradition does associate revelation with the history of Israel, it is due to the fact that for the sake of the establishment of monotheism—which in its essence is fully universalistic—it was necessary to make it the purpose of national existence, to fill with it the national consciousness. Revelation is universal, it is addressed to man and not specifically to the Jew.

Its association with Israel, one might say in view of Cohen's interpretation, was a mere expedient, a kind of accidental monotheistic politics to introduce monotheistic universalism into history.

In conclusion of the theme Cohen writes: "If this spiritual process [of revelation] in the course of political events was nevertheless given the distinction of a historic act in order that it might have the character of a national one, so—as we have seen—the critique and the correction entered at the beginning of the genuine, the literary history and have transferred Sinai into the heart of man. That which is eternal, removed from all sense experience and thus also from all history, is the ground and the guarantee for that which is innermost to the national history. It preceeds it, because it is its foundation." [26]

3. Correlation and Attributes

Cohen asserts that the creation of man in reason establishes a link between God, the Creator, and man. Revelation is revelation to man; thus God enters into relation with man. This link by way of reason Cohen calls correlation. "The uniqueness of God (as the Creator) conditions His relation to the reason of man. The reason of man as creation of God, conditions his relation of reason to God." [27] The result is correlation. One is probably justified in saying that the idea of the correlation is the most important concept in both works, *Der Begriff der Religion* and *Die Religion der Vernunft*. It is given the task of solving the problems of human existence that, as we saw, ethics cannot solve.

Reason is twofold, theoretical and practical. Since reason is the basis of the correlation between God and man, the correlation, too, has to be twofold. It may reveal to man the answers to the purely theoretical question of "whence?". In this sense, man discovers in the correlation Being as God who is unique and, as we saw, because of that, the Creator. And as he knows God, free of matter and life, as all Spirit, so does he recognize himself, because of the correlation, also as spirit similar to God, though of course not identical with or equal to him.[28] But as reason is also practical, in the correlation man will be enlightened also on the ethical question: what for?

The question, "what for?", is answered by purpose. Theoretical reason is revelation that provides the ground to the realm of nature, i.e., causality; practical reason reveals the ground to the realm of man, it completes causality through purpose. But purpose is accomplished through action. Thus we reach the divine attributes of action, whose theory was developed by Maimonides. Cohen, however, places his own interpretation on them. How can action be an attribute of God? Being is at rest within itself. It is not subject to question of purpose. Yet Being as God is the ground, the origin, of the dimension of purpose. We have therefore to say that the question of purpose points beyond Being into a new phase of the correlation. "Action" with God is the foundation of the possibility of action in Becoming as it is represented by man. Action is always under the aspect of purpose, but purpose is for man. Therefore, attributes of action are not so much attributes of God as paradigms, norms for human action. God as Being is not only the origin of Becoming, he is also the *Urbild,* the arch-idea for human action. That the rabbis ascribed "modesty" to God, for example, proves that attributes are such norms (*Musterbilder*) for human morality. Cohen maintains that "what is called divine attribute is not at all an attribute in the logical, but only in the ethical sense. The attribute does not stand in logical relation to the Substance, but rather in ethical relation to the substance of man.[29] The same idea was expressed by Cohen in a different context, when he said: "Only those attributes should be ascribed to him [God] which serve as the ground for man's morality and favor his drawing near to God."[30] Through the divine attributes man should learn to act in accordance with them, and only those which serve this purpose are attached to God. In essence, it is the same idea that Cohen had already formulated rather succinctly in the *Ethik.* Having declared that it was God who taught man what morality was, he added: "Not what God is has God to teach me, but what man is."[31] In keeping with his religious phase, we ought to say: "What man should be." It is important, however, to realize that as a result of all that, "Being once again marches out of its boundaries into correlation with Becoming in man."[32]

We have now gained two forms of the correlation, corresponding to the two forms of reason by which God enters into relation with man. One is as Being as the origin of all causation; the other as Being as the ground of all ethical purpose. This helps us to establish the meaning of God for man. "Only in correlation with man should the essence of God be determined."[33] This is most elaborately demonstrated in the realm of purpose, the realm of ethical action for man. God is his attributes for man; God is the *Urbild,* the arch-idea. The one and unique God has no "reality." He has the reality of the Idea, the idea of the holy God, the idea of the holy spirit, which, according to Cohen is identical with the idea of morality.[34] "Holiness is morality" says Cohen. Holiness matures into all the ramifications of correlation, it embraces justice and love. "Holiness is altogether only morality. And with God, too, it has only that meaning of morality which the correlation with man demands."[35] God, whose essence is determined by the correlation, is therefore the idea of holiness, the idea of love and justice.

4. Love, Forgiveness, and Reconciliation

The idea of God as the paradigm of ethical action points to man's purpose in his life with other human beings. The other man is at first "man beside me" (*Nebenmensch*). Ethics by itself knows only him. As we saw, it cannot consider him in his specific situation, whether he be rich or poor, happy or miserable. However, one cannot isolate oneself from society and, since poverty is the general lot of man, one dare not separate oneself from the social suffering of poverty. In the *Begriff der Religion* Cohen already stated that it is through sympathy that one overcomes the distance that prevails between one man and another if their relation is based on the sole demand of ethics, i.e., respect. "And where once sympathy has entered, there love for mankind must also blossom. . . . Love for mankind is the religious form of the social relation between man and man."[36]

Later on, in his work on the religion of reason, Cohen also said that, as man considers the human misery of "the man beside him," he responds with sympathy. Thus, through sympathy he transforms "man beside him" (*Nebenmensch*) into "fellowman" (*Mitmensch*). It is something that ethics cannot do, maintains Cohen. Sympathy is the original form of man's love for his fellow human being. "God has created man, but his fellowman he [man] must create himself." Of it Cohen says that it is religion that has to bring about this new creation. "Thus God has to become the creator for a second time in that he forms man into fellowman through man himself, through the share of reason in religion."[37]

It should now be clear how it is the share of reason in religion that brings this new creation of the fellowman about. In the ethical correlation between God and man, God is revealed to man as the paradigm of God's love for man. In the social legislation of the Bible regarding the poor, Cohen sees God's love for man made manifest. They are limitations of property rights for the sake of the poor. Especially in the law of the *Shabbat* he finds the idea of equality expressed. Thus we have found the meaning of God's love for man. "The sympathy with the poor which God awakens within us through His commandments, becomes for us the understandable ground for the meaning of God's love." [38]

Closely related to God's love for man is man's love for God. At first, Cohen sees a serious problem here. It would seem that from the point of view of monotheism one should take objection to the very idea of man's love for God. God is the Being for which only the thought of man may search and whom only the understanding can establish. However, the intellectual task is an infinite one. It is not "a quiet possession, a gift complete." How can this restless search for God be called love?[39] The answer is that since God, as we saw, is never "reality" for man since he is Idea—the idea of morality—in loving Him we love the idea, the norm, the paradigm. If I want my thinking of God to be love of God, I have to think of the moral universe of man's social existence, I have to direct my concern to it and love it. Therefore, asserts Cohen, man's love of God is not a form of anthropomorphism, for the problem is resolved by the paradox that to love God means that one should love man.

As man changes "man beside him" into fellowman, he transforms the "He" or "She" into "Thou." In fact, it is only through this act that he himself becomes a fellowman; and as he becomes a fellowman, he becomes "I." It is only through "thou" that we become "I." Thus, a new correlation is established, the correlation of I-Thou between man and man. Yet, man does not exist only in the social context. What of the "I" in the absolute? in separation? What of man as he exists by himself and for himself? With this question, of course, we have arrived at the second problem of man, that as we heard, ethics alone could not solve.[40] Man exists by himself by recognizing his guilt, by realizing that he is a sinner. Thus he becomes the individuum, the individual being in separation. However, the realization of sin is not the ultimate goal; the goal is liberation from sin. Only through such liberation does the individuum become the "I," the person in full reality. Sin is—in a sense—a transit station from individuum to the "I."

Other stages along the journey are redemption and reconciliation. God liberates man by forgiving his sin. It is man alone who has the task of bringing about forgiveness. His is the responsibility of *t'shuba,* of return, of renewed stirring for self-sanctification after every failure. The goal of his stirring and self-uplift is God. Man alone cannot accomplish his liberation. God alone can take his sin from him, God alone is his redeemer. "The sin before God leads us to redemption through God. Redemption through God leads us to man's reconciliation with himself. And it is this that ultimately leads the "I" to reconcilation with God. It is reconciliation with God that brings the individuum to feel maturity as "I." [41] Man is turning away from the old and beginning on a new road. Through his liberation from all his sins he gains new strength. Now man is able to create a new heart for himself and a new spirit. With his new "I" he steps into life and proves himself.[42]

With the help of religion we have now deepened our understanding of man and, thus, also our understanding of God.

This is now the third facet of the correlation between God and man; it is forgiveness and redemption. "It is the essence of God to forgive the sins of man. This is the most important content of the correlation between God and man." [43]

5.   *Ethics and Messianism*

In one more respect has ethics to broaden into religion. At the beginning of our analysis we have seen how, even at the time Cohen believed that religion would have to submerge in ethics he still needed the idea of God in order to complete the ethical system which he had erected. At that time, all he said was that the eternity of ethical striving and realization was guaranteed by the preservation of Man and Naure parallel to each other. However, that guarantee was provided by the God idea of monotheism. While not discussing it explicitly, as he did with the other two problems about which ethics was helpless, it would appear that at a later time Cohen realized how inadequate his God-idea in the *Ethik* was to fulfill the task he had allotted to it.

The God-idea of the *Ethik,* as we have pointed out, was a reformulation of one of Kant's postulates of practical reason. Now, a postulate of practical reason may be a methodological requirement in order to complete a system, as the God postulate, indeed, completed Kant's critique of practical reason and as, in its new formulation, it was intended to complete Cohen's ethical system of the pure will. But one thing a postulate cannot do—it cannot guarantee anything. It may methodologically smooth out some ruffled spots in thinking, but it can do nothing for the reality of existence. And thus the God-idea of the *Ethik* could not accomplish that for the sake of which it was originally introduced; it could not guarantee the continued existence in fact, in history, of man and nature.

At a much later time, Cohen realized that ethics may define, for its own purposes, God as the guarantor of the ever-continuing realization of morality on earth. "Yet its means fail beyond the definition, beyond the postulate of this idea." It is religion alone, out of its own specific nature, that can provide trust in God and confidence in Him that, indeed, man and nature will endure as needed by the task of never-ending ethical fulfillment. This trust and confidence found its expression in the messianism of monotheism. The messianic God guarantees the preservation of nature and its connection with the infinite task of morality.[44]

III. GOD—IDEA OR MORE THAN AN IDEA

1.

Having analyzed the main points in Cohen's philosophy of religion, the question that forces itself to our attention is: Who or what is this God of the religion of reason? Readers of Cohen, and also those who studied his works, thought that in the final reckoning He was not a personal God, but only an idea. It is true that in the very beginning of *Die Religion der Vernunft* Cohen states that, in religion, the Being of philosophy changes from a *neutrum* into a person, yet they felt that in the further disquisition of the subject matter, there was little to support the statement. Franz Rosenzweig, in his introduction to the *Jüdische Schriften* of the master, defended Cohen against such an interpretation. He maintained that there could be no worse misunderstanding of the thinker as well as his thought than to assume that with Cohen God was only an idea. He continues the explanation:

> With the word 'idea' is expressed of what kind our statements are that can be made about God. One cannot—and that is what the word [idea] says—describe God, one cannot figure him out, one cannot grasp him. For an idea is neither an object, nor a logically [*gesetzlich*] complete unity, nor a concept. But one can say what, without God, could not be; or differently expressed, what it is for which God lays the ground. By indicating this "ground-laying,"

the content of an idea is exhaustively stated for Cohen. However, it is not yet done merely with the indication of the contents. With it begins what Cohen calls its [the idea's] inexhaustible fruitfulness. And this fruitfulness philosophy can only establish by individual examples, and only as a fact.

We believe we have shown how the God-idea is used by Cohen as "the ground-layer." We have seen how it lays the ground for Becoming, for creation and revelation, for love and forgiveness, for the continuity of nature parallel to the eternal ethical striving of the pure will, for messianism. We shall yet see how philosophy has been imposed upon to accept the "fruitfulness" of the idea as a fact. But does Rosenzweig's explanation meet the criticism of those who maintain that the God of the *Religion of Reason* is a mere idea? Obviously, this religious philosophy has nothing to do with the God that cannot be described, that cannot be grasped, with the *deus absconditus*. Cohen emphasizes again and again that God can never become a reality, that —for instance—even His holiness is for man only, and what it is for God is not only unknown to us but is none of our concern. Nor is there any possibility of any kind of an emotional or affectional relation to God. In loving Him one loves the idea of morality for which he is the norm, one really loves man.[46]

However, let us see whether Rosenzweig's interpretation of the idea as *Grundlegung* (ground-laying) does indeed give us a God that is more than an idea. Fortunately, Cohen himself gave ample explanation for what he meant by an idea. Thinking, of course, is not sense perception. What for the eye is seeing is, for thinking as it deepens, vision. Such a vision of thought is the idea, which as a *hypothesis* precedes all scientific thought, it forms its ground, it indicates its outline and gives indication of its content. Thus, Cohen can say: The idea is the hypothesis and the hypothesis is the idea.[47] In other words, the idea is a methodological principle with which all scientific and philosophical thinking must begin.

In another place Cohen writes clearly, "The idea as such can only be methodological ground-laying." A problem arises when one moves from the realm of logic into that of ethics, for instance. There one meets with the justified desire that the idea of the good should be more than just a methodological principle. This is understandable, says Cohen, since the spirit attaches a value to the idea far beyond all nature and its scientific interpretation. Nevertheless, even this problem cannot be solved in any other way but by the idea as a principle of ground-laying.

Ethics and logic may differ from each other in their content, but in the unity of thinking they must not be separated from each other. Nature and ethics must remain united in the unity of methodology. This means, then, just as the idea of Being is the methodological ground for logic and science, so can the idea of the Good be no *more* than the methodological ground for ethics.[48] But how does it stand with the God-idea in the religion of reason? In another context, in which Cohen describes the God-idea of Being as the ground of existence (*Dasein*) identical with Becoming, he adds the significant words: "Here the spiritual association reveals itself (*Gemeinschaft,* literally "community") with the fundamental thought (*Grundgedanken,* literally, ground, or basic, thought) of the logic of pure reason."[49] What he is saying here is that just as Being in logic is a methodological principle of origin, so it is also in religion. In yet another context, comparing the God-idea of ethics with that of religion, Cohen affirms: "Here too, the identical nature of the idea for both ethics and religion has been maintained."[50] There is no getting away from it, the idea in logic is identical in its nature with the idea in ethics and with that in religion. In all these disciplines it has the significance of the methodological ground, without which no thinking can even begin. This unity in the methodology of thought is, indeed, what Cohen repeatedly calls the share of reason (*Vernunftanteil*) in religion. Without it, the religion of reason would be impossible. This, however, means that the God-idea in Cohen's religion of reason is, strictly speaking, no more than the fundamental hypothesis.

The concept of God as an idea receives its strangest emphasis when Cohen discusses man's love of God. The question that proffers itself for immediate consideration is: How can one love an idea? If Rosenzweig's interpretation were correct, there would be little reason for the question and much less need for the surprising answer: "How can one love anything else but an idea!" Cohen believed that "even in sensuous love one loves the idealized person, only the idea of the person."[51] The meaning of the statement is that in the love of God one loves only the idea of God, as indeed in the religion of reason, man knows nothing more about God than the idea of Him. In ethics the idea becomes the ideal, so that Cohen says in conclusion: "The love of man for God is the love for the moral ideal. Only the ideal can I love and the ideal I can only grasp through loving it. The ideal is the paradigm (*Urbild*) of morality. . . . However, only as an object of understanding can I make the paradigm an object of love." [52]

2.

One might, perhaps, suggest that the concept of correlation proves that God is much more than a mere idea for Cohen. It seems to indicate that some kind of a personal relation exists between God and man. Franz Rosenzweig, in the introduction to the *Jüdische Schriften,* sees in the correlation "the new fundamental concept" (*der neue Grundbegriff*) which Cohen discovered in his religious philosophy. He describes it as "a relation of mutuality between man and God." He relates his effort to bring Cohen and Buber together, feeling that there was an approximation in Buber's thinking at the time toward Cohen's position. Buber was about to make his own discovery of "relation' as the basic word (*Grundwort*) of religion. Rosenzweig understood that there was more than a "terminological closeness" between Buber's "relation" and Cohen's "correlation." In our opinion, it was not just incidental that he did not succeed in bringing the two men closer together.

The truth is that nothing could be further from Cohen's idea of correlation than Buber's concept of relation. Cohen would have shuddered intellectually at the thought of an I-Thou relation with God. For him it would have been "materialization," which he equated with pantheism, or "personalization," which was the Christian aberration. That correlation was nothing of an existential nature between the individual human being in his full humanity and God, one could have guessed from the fact that in its original form it is not between God and man, but between God and Nature. According to Cohen, religion would have no use for God in his uniqueness, "if his correlation with man, and that means first with Nature, could not be secured." The correlation with nature is necessary as a precondition to that with man.[53] Since man is part of nature, without which man could not be, God's correlation with nature must precede his correlation with man. On the other hand, in its ultimate form, correlation exists between God and mankind. We have seen how, according to Cohen, the God-idea preserves for ethics the possibility of eternal realization by guaranteeing the continuity of Nature. In view of this Cohen maintains: "In order that mankind may be effective according to the eternity of the ideal, ethics requires the God-idea. The correlation means here that between God and mankind." [54] All this shows how thoroughly Rosenzweig must have misunderstood on this point *both* his master and his friend. Just as Buber's I-Thou relation with God would have been intellectually anathema for Cohen, so would Buber have thought it meaningless to see his "relation" in the image of correlation between God and nature and God and mankind. Cohen also says that God is Being but has no existence (*Dasein*).[55] His existence is absolutely beyond the reach of man. Quite obviously the dialectical situation that relates man to God involves God in existence. Buber does indeed say that while God is the Absolute and as such not a person, there is a personal aspect to his absolute Being.[56] By denying existence to God's Being Cohen excludes every possibility of a "personal" aspect of the Absolute. But man can have no relation whatever with Absolute Being on the level of his own personal existence.

3.

What then is Cohen's correlation? In *Die Religion der Vernunft* Cohen warns us against "materializing" or "personifying" the correlation. The correlation has to be understood conceptually, it is an abstract link between God and man. Spirit alone is the connecting link of the correlation; but he hastens to add that the function of the "holy spirit" has "only logical meaning." We have to recognize the union (*Vereinigung*) with logical strictness, but not visualize it in the manner of some vague connection." [57] Now, what is this abstract, logical link of the correlation? Nothing is given explicitly in the form of an explanation in *Die Religion der Vernunft*. On the other hand, in *Der Begriff der Religion* Cohen takes pains to explain what is meant by "the logical union." Only in the light of what is said there is it possible to understand his theory of the correlation as it appears in his later work. Far from being a new fundamental concept (*der neue Grundbegriff*) as Rosenzweig thought, Cohen states explicitly, "the correlation is a scientific 'basic category' [*Grundform*] of thinking in our terminology of judgment." Indeed, it has its place in his *Logik*. The general name of the "ground category" of correlation, says Cohen, is purpose. Two entities may be related to each other by a purpose that binds them to each other. The purpose is a purely logical one, a logical requirement. Thus, for instance Cohen defines the relatedness between past and future. According to him, time is always future-directed. Out of this future-directedness emerges the past, backwards. Every moment is a relation point of anticipation. It exists "in this correlation" says Cohen.[58] Correlation is a logical principle that relates two ideas in such a manner that their meaning is determined in logical mutuality. This is the ultimate meaning of correlation also in Cohen's philosophy of religion. With this meaning in mind does he say: "We posit a relation of purpose between God and man as well as between God and Nature."

Cohen's philosophy demands the idea of God for the creation and preservation of Nature and man; it demands it as the idea of purpose; ". . . what one wants with creation or preservation is brought to its determination in the positing of this purpose, the correlation between God and Nature."[59] We may now be in a better position to understand what Cohen meant when he said that God was holy for the sake of man. So is He also the paradigm of action for the sake of man. Becoming is related to Being by correlation, i.e., the idea of purpose. The continuity of nature is guaranteed so that the eternity of ethical endeavor may be possible. This is the meaning of the correlation between God and nature. This guarantee of infinite ethical realization is the correlation between God and mankind. Thus Cohen would say: "If, accordingly, I want to formulate the idea of God, I have to establish an intended purpose between God and man."[59] This means, then, that the idea of man is contained in the God-idea, just as the idea of God is contained in the idea of man. God defines man and man defines God because of the bond of purpose between them. In essence this is a ramification of the fundamental idea of creation. We heard Cohen describe creation as the arch-attribute of God, contained within the very concept of God's uniqueness. God's uniqueness is conceived with the purpose of providing the ground for Becoming. Without uniqueness of Being, Being and Becoming would merge into each other and the result would be pantheism. In the light of such an understanding of the idea of correlation could Cohen write that God was determined by His correlation to man as man was determined by his correlation to God. The mutuality of the correlation is achieved by the bond of purpose between them. But the correlation must not be "materialized" or "personalized." It is only abstract and logical.

One might wonder how this meaning of the correlation can be maintained in its specifically religious significance in the correlation in which man, realizing his sin, awaits God's forgiveness. Yet, even here Cohen insists on its logical character. Only man is to be thought as the active factor in the correlation. "God, on the other hand, is thought of as the goal, at which man's own moral activity is directed. . . . All activity lies with man." [61] Even in this specific religious form of the correlation, mutuality consists in man's directedness at God as the goal; in the realization of his failure and in the activity of *t'shuba,* "return," man in the correlation is all alone. Cohen exclaims: "How could God enter into association (*Gemeinschaft*) with man!"

We have to reach the conclusion that in Cohen's religion of reason God is nothing more than a methodological idea. Even in the correlation man remains all by himself with his ideas and thoughts, though they are God-directed as the goal of his relatedness. Man is forever alone; God is only the object of his thinking. Or if we wish to use Buber's terminology, this God is an It.

IV. THE RELIGION OF REASON AND JUDAISM

1.

The religion of reason has universal validity and cannot be limited to the Jews. That it was developed from the sources of Judaism was merely a coincidence. Yet, since it does claim to be an interpretation of the sources of Judaism, the question, to what extent may this interpretation be accepted, is inescapable. It would seem to us that Cohen's religious philosophy, as distinct from his personal religion (about which see later), is not a philosophical reinterpretation of his personal religion but its philosophical rejection.

The inescapable truth about Judaism is that it sees God as personal and as involved and acting in history. Whatever its philosophical validity, creation in Judaism is a volitional act and not a mere logical precondition for all activity. And so, also, does God act in history, in the life of people and of nations. Revelation is not just the truth that human beings perceive through their rational ability, but—however it may be interpreted—an actual event occurring between God and this human being or this people. Independent of the problem of whether the good is good because of its own intrinsic nature or because it is commanded by God, it is not true to say of Judaism what Cohen says of the religion of reason, namely, that it speaks of the laws of God because it considers the will of reason as the law of God.[62] This may be consistent if one sees, as Cohen did, revelation in man's reasoning faculty. It is, however, not true of Judaism, whose concept of revelation is fundamentally different from his. The autonomy of the will does indeed raise a serious problem in any philosophy of a religion that recognizes a law of God, but this problem cannot be solved by simply declaring the will of reason to be the revealed law of God.

As we have seen, in Cohen's religious philosophy God has only Being but not existence. Whatever its philosophical or theological interpretation, in Judaism God is so intensely present that his existence practically conceals his Being. The genuine religious concern is much more with His existence than with His Being. His presence in history is the source of all religious problematics. It is, of course, correct to say, as Cohen does, that the revelation at Sinai has been spiritualized by the Bible itself, but it is simply not true that with this spiritualization Sinai has been placed in the heart—or, as he should have said more consistently, in the mind—of man. Notwithstanding all spiritualization, Judaism remained inseparable from Sinai as an event in space and time. Eliminate Sinai from the mountain and the desert and you have lost Judaism's share in life and history.

It is rather significant that Cohen never makes mention of the exodus. Now, any kind of rationalism may have its problem with the exodus story. It is, of course, possible to spiritualize it. But no matter what one's personal attitude to it may be, it is not possible to eliminate the exodus from Judaism as an actual awareness of divine concern with the destiny of the Jewish people become manifest in the actuality of a historical situation. The very first of the "Ten Words" states: "I am the Eternal, your God, who has led you out from the land of Egypt." Here lies one of the vital roots of Judaism. A religion of reason that disregards its importance in the self-understanding of Judaism and in its world view is just not drawn from the sources of Judaism. In the Introduction to which we have referred repeatedly, Rosenzweig mentions a *seder* (the Passover festive meal) that the young "Dr. phil.," at the time completely estranged from Judaism, attended in his father's house. The bright young man was most appreciative of his father who, in order to make his son more comfortable at the family table, went over the first part of the *Haggada* (the telling of the Passover story) in only twenty minutes "without referring to a single Jewish emotion." It would seem to us that even at the conclusion of his intellectual return Cohen still did not know what to do with the Passover story philosophically.

Cohen was convinced that in numerous ways his religion of reason was anticipated by medieval Jewish philosophy and especially by Maimonides. Cohen already made the observation in the *Ethik* that Maimonides, in true religiosity, presented us with the thought that God was an idea. His argument there was that a person is determined by life, and Maimonides dared to exclude life from the essence of God.[63] It is surprising how a man of the philosophical genius of a Hermann Cohen could have misunderstood Maimonides so thoroughly. The author of the *Guide for the Perplexed* excluded not only life from the essence of God, but dared to go even further in a statement in which he said that God was one without oneness and existing without existence.[64] This, too, of course, could be misinterpreted as meaning that he was unique and not just one, that he had Being, but not existence (*Dasein*). But quite obviously, it is not what Maimonides meant to say. He was saying that none of the terms derived from human experience apply to God. He cannot be described in human language. The "one" of our experience is part of a series, God is not. "Existence" is always created, or as Maimonides would say, it is *efshar hamziut,* it is a possibility relative to a cause; God is *m'huyab hamziut,* he is absolute and exists of his own uncreated intrinsic necessity. In the same sense does he exclude life from the essence of God. Life as a matter of human experience is created, it is relative to a cause. Not such is the "life" of God. Following his own characteristic formulation, Maimonides could have said: God has "life" without life; He is "person" without being a person.

It never occurred to Maimonides to suggest that God was an idea. There is no trace of it in all his work. On the contrary, Maimonides' God, like that of the Bible, acts in history. Maimonides, in the analysis of his theory of the negative attributes, explains omnipotence as not lacking in power to produce the universe. Cohen sees in it an affirmation of his own idea of creation as the logical category of the "ground." He believes Maimonides says that God being self-sufficient to create the All, is the logical origin of all activity.[65] Nothing of the kind! Anyone who is familiar, for instance, with Maimonides discussion of the idea of creation cannot miss the fact that for Maimonides creation is an act performed by divine power and not just the logical ground for all activity of Becoming. One may recall here his argument against the Aristotelian concept of an uncreated world. According to Aristotle God is not free to as much as be able to lengthen the wing of a fly.[66] One would have to say that he could not do that according to Cohen's God-idea either. It is significant that there is no room for miracles, for direct divine intervention in the destinies of man, in the religion of reason. Now, however rationalistic one may be regarding this matter, still the truth is that with Maimonides the biblical record of the miracles was the ultimate reason for his espousing the idea of creation *ex nihilo*.[67] This is true of all rationalistic Jewish philosophers of the Middle Ages. Notwithstanding their rationalism, they accepted God as reality of Being with personlike actual involvement in the world and the affairs of man.

Cohen reinterpreted Maimonides' attributes of action as a paradigm for human action. According to Cohen, as we saw, Being does not act. But undoubtedly what Maimonides means by attributes of action are actual volitional deeds of God within the space-time continuum. In innumerable passages in the *Guide* God appears as an intelligent being that acts freely and with choice and discretion. Whether one is personally able to accept the idea is irrelevant. This is Maimonides and such are the medieval Jewish philosophers.

Cohen also says that the fact that in medieval Jewish philosophy the *muskalot rishonot,* the innate categories of thought, were accepted as equal in authority to the contents of revelation proves that revelation was understood as correlation by way of reason.[68] It is just not so. Because the content of revelation was true, therefore all truth, even the not revealed one, was equal in its truth value. Yet, reason remained reason and revelation was revelation. Saadia and Maimonides both believed that the contents of revelation—or part of it, according to Saadia—could be discovered by reason alone. This presented them with a serious problem: if this were so, what need was there for revelation? [69] Their preoccupation with the problem proves that they did not identify revelation with correlation by way of reason but saw in it an actual event of history. Maimonides was of the opinion that as to the first two of the "Ten Words" the people and Moses were on the same level, for they express purely rational truth, which was grasped by the people by the same intellectual method as by Moses himself. This might be seen as supporting Cohen's view of revelation. Yet, Maimonides also believed that the other eight words were revealed to Moses alone, while the people were actually hearing the divine voice, which however reached them without intelligible articulation.[70]

Finally, let us consider what Maimonides has to say about man's love for God. "What is the way of loving Him? As man meditates on His wondrous and great deeds and creatures and beholds in them His wisdom, which is incomparable and infinite, he will be overwhelmed immediately by love and he will praise and exalt. He will greatly desire to know the Great Name, as David said: My Soul thirsteth for God, for the living God!" [71] This is rather different from Cohen's love of God as the love of the ethical ideal, as different as is the God-idea of the religion of reason from Maimonides' "living" God. Rosenzweig tells us in the Introduction that when Cohen, in the early days of 1918, showed him the first pages of *Die Religion der Vernunft,* he praised it in terms similar to those in which the circle around Virgil praised the appearance of the *Aeneid;* he made special reference to Maimonides, to which Cohen answered: Yes, I have been thinking the same: "The Rambam (the traditional way of referring to Maimonides, Our teacher, Moses the Son of Maimon) will be satisfied." How moving the blind loyalty of the disciple! How melancholy the old man's desire to return!

2.

The universalism of the religion of reason is also applied to the people of Israel. Israel, the people of monotheism, is a universalistic people, for monotheism itself is universalistic. The one God is the originator of the one mankind. Only in monotheisn is mankind one. The purpose of Israel is to strive for the unity of a monotheistic mankind. Its goal in history is to dissolve itself into the unity of all nations. Messianism is the promise that this all-embracing unity will be achieved. Messianism is the religious concept of the guarantee of nature as a lasting correlate to continuous ethical realization which must end in the triumph of the good. The Jewish state of old was too narrow a compass for monotheistic messianism. It had to go. The state soon fell apart. It had little significance for this people, says Cohen. In the *Ethik* he even declared that the state was not just lost; it was given up by the prophets. Already there Cohen stated that the meaning of the religion of the prophets, upon which the continued existence of Judaism rests, was to prepare mankind's union of states through the messianic idea.[72]

The people of Israel was needed for the establishment of monotheism. This is the meaning of the chosenness of Israel. It symbolizes God's love of mankind.[73] The idea is also formulated somewhat differently. The election of Israel has a twofold meaning. Historically, it served the purpose of arousing the national consciousness for the historic mission. Its higher symbolic significance lies in the fact that it prepared Israel for its messianic mission, for its elevation into mankind.[74] Election and chosenness are, of course, traditional terminology. With Cohen they cannot mean a divine act in history. Since revelation is rational enlightenment, to be chosen means to recognize and accept the idea of monotheism as one's truth and mission.

How far removed Cohen's ideas on the subject of Israel and messianism are from the way the Jewish people understood itself and its historic way one may judge by the fact that the word exile does not occur once in his discussion. Of course, if the state is an unnatural framework for monotheism, statelessness is not exile; on the contrary, one might say it is the ideal situation for the Jew.[75] There is Jewish isolation, but it is enforced upon Israel from without because of the, as yet, unrealized ideal of worldwide monotheism. The isolation, the unrealized idea of mankind, brings suffering upon Israel. Israel suffers as the symbol of mankind, it suffers for the sake of mankind. And this is another aspect of its chosenness.[76] Cohen also says that suffering became Israel's life force. With others it is an indication of decline and the end; but Israel's world mission begins with its martyrdom. Suffering is a means of self-sanctification. It is a symbolical expression of reconciliation with God. Suffering is the precondition of redemption. It liberates man from the "sediments" of his empirical humanity. It is his ascent to the ideal moment in which he becomes himself. Redemption need not be postponed to the end of days; it is attached to every moment of suffering. Every moment of suffering is also a moment of redemption. Thus, suffering is no contradiction to Jewish survival; it is its very basis.[77]

In the various discussions of the subject of suffering, Cohen becomes almost poetic in its praise. He practically offers a philosophical ode to it. Yet, notwithstanding some significant words he did say about Jewish martyrology through history, one wonders whether he had a personal realization of what was involved in it for the untold masses— and not just individual saints—of the martyrs of Israel. How much understanding did he have of the vitality and staying power of the Jew and his faith, if he saw in Jewish suffering the life force that secures its survival? He does acknowledge that Israel is a priestly nation, not a nation like any other, it is a people of faith; not as Israel, but as an anticipation of mankind. Israel is unique—for the time being—because the others have not yet become what they are supposed to be, mankind. One might say, in accordance with Cohen, that Israel is a negative nation; its uniqueness is imposed upon it by the inadequacy of others. In essence, there is no such thing as a Jewish identity. His universalism is so world-estranged that he thinks it necessary to disclaim any trace of anything specifically Jewish even in Jewish martyrology. He writes: "Jewish bravery is . . . simply a virtue of history, of the historical man and not of the individual. And messianism breaks the backbone of nationalism so that the bravery of the Jews not be degraded to a mere national virtue. The human bravery of the Jew is as historical virtue, the virtue of bravery, human bravery, the bravery of the truth of the religious ideal of mankind." [78] Poor Cohen! How afraid he was that he might find in his Jewish people something specifically Jewish.

Cohen's interpretation of Judaism and Israel is, of course, a philosopher's attempt to lend scholarly dignity to the typical assimilationist ideology of German reform Jewry of his generation. We might forgive him his time-boundness. Nor is there any need, at this late hour in history, to discuss with any seriousness the assimilationist fervor of a former reform Jewry. All that is by now, at least intellectually as well as ethically, dead as the dodo. Yet, even at this hour he should be taken to task for his scholarly and philosophical inadequacies and inconsistencies.

But for one vague reference to a complete dissolution of all national distinctions, Cohen sees as the goal of the messianic idea not the disappearance of all states but their organization in a union of states. In this respect, however, he did exempt Israel from the universal order to be. From the viewpoint of messianism history is the future. "The future becomes the reality of history. Therefore, only a spiritual world can fulfill this national existence," meaning the national existence of the Jewish people.[79] Cohen understood very well that just as man does not live by bread alone, neither can he live by the spirit alone. It was for this reason that in his *Ethik* he introduced the idea of God in order to guarantee the continuity of nature, full well realizing that without nature the ethical deed was not possible. Later on, in *Die Religion der Vernunft* he very wisely stated that man required the connection with nature. "He is not just spirit of holiness." In his "spirtualization" of religion Cohen had some trouble explaining how one could pray for such mundane things as bread to eat, clothes to wear, for health and bodily well-being. He solved the problem by the ingenious idea that the religious demands the empirical foundations of the I, as the "negative conditions" of its existence. It needs the biological and historical individual. Thus man is given care for his empirical, biological, and historical ego. Thus, he may pray for the earthly blessings of life without shame.[80] It is rather strange that having recognized all this, he still wanted only a spiritual world for Israel alone, as if man, and especially a people, could live in the realm of the purely spiritual. How little understanding he had for the essential feature of Judaism one may judge by his comment that in prayer the concept of God becomes the Kingdom of God. The praying community is the forerunner of the messianic kingdom of the future. It accepts the yoke of the Kingdom daily, thus preparing the future.[81]

It is rather strange to receive such an interpretation from a knowledgeable Jew who considers himself a socialist at that. He even makes reference to the majestic *Alenu* prayer, in which the Jew expresses his hope for the establishment of the world as a Kingdom of God. The truth is that in prayer the Jew prays for it, hopes for it, but it is not in prayer that the Kingdom is established. It is not the praying community that builds the Kingdom but the doing community, the active one, the living, historical, community. Even though a people may forsake all hedonism, all power history, even though it may seek as its goal some form of ethical and spiritual realization, it needs "nature," it demands for its "negative condition" the empirical foundation of its spirituality, as long as it desires to remain on this earth with the goal of establishing the real world as a Kingdom of God. The entire problematic of Jewish existence, its authenticity, derives from it. Cohen's Kingdom of God, realized in prayer is Christian, not Jewish. Reserving the spiritual world for Israel, he proved that he did not understand the historical Israel. His Israel is a construct of his private predilection.

Cohen senses that his radically universalistic interpretation of messianism does not fully harmonize with the sources from which he has drawn it. He cannot help confessing that "but of course messianism is forever burdened with the providence for the believing people (*Glau-*

bensvolk), for the servant of God. And thus this conflict continued to remain in the prayers too. The return to Zion, the rebuilding of the Sanctuary, together with the sacrifices, is most intimately associated with messianic universalism. Therefore, the latter had inevitably to spiritualize and to broaden the former." [82] This, of course, is quite an understatement for the rejection of the idea of return to Zion. More important than that many prayers of the synagogue are for return to Zion and for the restoration of Jerusalem is the fact that all the writings of the prophets are saturated wih the hope and the promises of Israel's return to Zion. There is no biblical prophetism without the promise and the assurance of return to the ancient homeland. Universalism and affirmation of a particular Jewish destiny inseparable from the land of Israel are the main themes of the prophets. Most important of all, however, is to understand that the two are found in the Bible together most naturally, without the slightest notion of a conflict between them.

It is not messianic monotheism that contradicts the idea of return to Zion, but the assimilationist interpretation of it. There is authentic universalism in messianism, as there is in it also, not as a burden but as an enthusiastic espousal, the vindication of the people of Israel, redeemed in Zion and Jerusalem. He who sees only the universalism does not understand its messianic version; he who sees only particularism does not understand Judaism and its people of Israel. The unique character of Jewish messianism lies in the fact that in it universalism and Jewish reality on empirical, biological and historical foundations, dwell together harmoniously. When one asks the question how that is possible, one is just trying the door handle to the antechamber of Judaism. [82]

V. PHILOSOPHY AND RELIGION

1.

We believe that our discussion of the religion of reason shows that Cohen has not developed any new philosophical insights in order to establish "reason's share" (*Vernunftanteil*) in religion. He uses some of the basic concepts of his *Logik* for the purposes of establishing his philosophy of religion. We have seen how Being is thought as God as a *logical* requirement for the origin of Becoming—a thought which conforms to the thesis of Cohen's *Logik* that thinking is the thinking of origins. As he also says: "All pure knowledge (*Erkenntnis*) must be

variations of the principle of origin." [83] Whatever he says about creation
(that includes also revelation) as the "arch-attribute" of Being and
"inherence" in it, and whatever else follows from the idea of the philosophy of religion, is the application of Cohen's interpretation of Kant's
category of the substance as a precondition of all relational concepts.
There is clear indication of that in *Die Religion der Vernunft*.[84] We shall
quote here the relevant passage from the *Logik*. "The substance now
becomes analogous to the subject. As the subject has to await its predi-
cates if anything is to become of it, this also happens to the substance.
The nimbus of the absolute is taken from it. It leads the dance of the
[concept] of relation. It has to await the relations which alone can make
anything of it. It has its correlate in the [concept] of inherence. The
accidents and modi are within it; and only insofar as they are in it, can
anything come of it. It is only the precondition for the relations, which
though in need of it as precondition, have yet to develop the precondition to its contents and significance (*Inhalt und Gehalt*)." [85] In this passage is contained the gist of "the share of reason" in Cohen's religion of
reason. As the substance, so too Being as God lost its "nimbus of the
absolute." This God is nothing without its attribute of creation, which
as creation of nature and creation of man in reason gives us all the
other attributes. As we saw, the "arch-attribute" of creation inheres in
the uniqueness of the God. Thus, this God also leads "the dance of all
relation." He is the precondition of Becoming, but it is Becoming that
develops "the contents and meaning" of God as precondition, for it is
through Becoming that we know what is posited by creation, the in-
hering fundamental attribute.

Needless to say the idea of correlation which plays such an important
part in the religion of reason has been lifted from here. The substance
and its accidents and modi are logically related to each other. The substance is the precondition that is, in its turn, defined by the accidents
and their modi that develop its contents and significance. That is the
essence of the correlation that Cohen described as established by the
concept of purpose. The purpose is the purely logical one of mutual
dependence and definition. In the same way, Becoming is the correlate
of Being; God and Nature, God and Man are in correlation. This is the
ultimate meaning of the statement that correlation is neither material, nor
personal, but purely logical.

Even when Cohen believes that he is affirming the phrase from the daily prayers of the Jew that states of God that in his goodness he renews daily the works of creation, he is only dressing up in religious language a principle of logical thought as he understands it. In the *Logik* Cohen maintained that the law of the principle of origin has to accompany every phase of pure thinking. He gives the following example to prove his point: "If mathematics as the mathematics of science is to determine motion, which runs in restless progression, it has to fix the origin of this motion. This origin is not only valid for the beginning of the motion, but every progression of it has to emerge anew from the same origin." [86] Since "the origin" is a principle of thought, it can, of course, not stand only at the beginning of the motion which is logically interpreted. The origin as a beginning would be an event in time. Origin as the logical principle of the mathematically formulated principle of motion has to accompany every progression of the motion anew, otherwise the progression could not endure mathematically. In the same way, Being as God as the logical requirement of Becoming has to accompany every moment of Becoming in order to render it logically conceivable. It is for this reason that Cohen says that creation is not a material relation; Becoming does not issue from Being, it does not emanate from it, it is not contained in it in a material sense. God has only logical significance for Becoming.

Even in his interpretation of messianic history we find the religious formulation of Cohen's definition of time only from the *Logik*. We had occasion to refer to his concept of time earlier. Let us consider it once more. Time according to the *Logik* is anticipation of the future. Says he: "The future contains and reveals the character of time. The past is strung and graded to the anticipated future. It did not come first. First came the future. . . ." Or in another context: "The proper activity of time is future-oriented, which it anticipates." [87] In much the same vein does he speak of the age of the fulfillment of the messianic ideal toward which all history is moving. History is no mere repetition of the past as with the heathens, no mere "travelogue," but movement toward a goal—thus time becomes the future.[88] This future is the thread on which all past is "strung" and thus receives its position.

The question arises: what is the religious value of pouring principles of logical thinking into containers marked with religious labels? This God, this creation, this revelation, this correlation, this messianic future, are they anything else but methodological requirements of logical thinking? Of course, if one fully embraces the idealistic point of view and identifies thought and reality, something might be gained from it all for religion. However, if such identification is not accepted, Cohen's religion of reason remains a cold and soulless construct without the life-blood of reality.

2.

Cohen is so deeply wedded to his pure ethical past that one wonders whether he fully gained the objectives that he planned for when he was moving from his *Ethik* to his "religion of reason." One of his objectives was to find a place for the individuum, the I, the person, standing by himself. It would seem to us that he established the individual human being qua individual only to lose him again to the old ethical concept of the individual as mankind. This happens in the tortuous interpretation of the idea of immortality that Cohen receives from religion.

In his analysis of this idea, Cohen uses some traditional language on the subject. He speaks of the spirit that God gives and that returns to God after death. But God being unique, how can soul return to God? And would not man lose his self-identity by such return? What then is return after death? Says Cohen: ". . . nothing but the regaining and the affirming of the origin which was given to the spirit of man." [89] But what does this mean? The return to the historic existence of the spirit that has God as its origin. In other words, only by returning to Becoming does the individual soul return to God, for only within Becoming does it regain and affirm God as Being, the origin of the spirit of man. The meaning of this may be put as follows: The task of the soul is self-sanctification by way of ethical realization. The task, however, is eternal. It can therefore, not end with death. But how does it continue after death? Every step in the endeavor of self-sanctification is a moment of the upswing of the spirit. At every such moment the soul is separated from its empirical being. Thus, the union with the body is transitory. The development of the soul is an infinite process because the task is infinite. The development is, therefore, not tied to the body. It is rather related to the infinite development of matter, guaranteed by messianism, as the negative condition for the infinite task of sanctification. Messianism, guaranteeing the infinite development of the human race in history, provides the "eternal" connection of the soul with matter. Such a connection is the necessary condition for the development of the soul's potentialities (*Seelenanlagen*) by way of heredity. Because of messianic development man is freed from the limitation to the biological or even historical individual being.

Thus, Cohen can write: "In the endless development of the human race towards its ideal spirit of holiness alone may the individual soul achieve its immortality. It [the soul] is always only the upswing, always only the totality of the upswings that are gathered together in the endless development."[90] What, now, is immortality? The eternal preservation of each individual "upswing" within the infinity of messianic development in history. For this reason Cohen would interpret the biblical phrase of "coming to one's fathers and being gathered to one's people" as immortality, which has the meaning of the continued historical existence of the human being in the continuity of its people.[91]

Since the individual soul is identical with the sum total of the "upswings" in the eternal process of messianic development as it is reached at any moment in history, Cohen calls the ethical individual the *Allheitsindividuum,* the "universal individual." In this manner the individual does not disappear, but accomplishes its perfection in the historical development as indicated by messianism. Without such development of the human race the ethical concept of man would not be realizable.[92] In other words, immortality is the preservation of every soul, of every upswing in the process of endless self-sanctification, in the sum total of all the upswings of the human race in the course of its messianic history.

All this, of course, is extremely close, and in essence identical, with the concept of man as given in the *Ethik*. Once again man has been separated from his empirical, biophysical existence and has become a sample of mankind in the process of its realization. If the function of religion is to redeem the individual soul from its failings and thus establish the I, the person, this rather forced idea of immortality has lost the person again and returned man into the womb of mankind be it even by way of the *Allheitsindividuum,* the "universal individual." At all costs Cohen is holding on to the religious idea of immortality, but empties it of all religious contents.

No less tortuous and artificial is his analysis of love, for the sake of which he invoked religion to broaden the field of ethics. As we saw, ethics could not fully approve of it. From Cohen's ethical point of view, love was not an ideal, since it was not universal. It was always relative to a smaller group than the totality (*Allheit*) of mankind. But how was one to deal with the poor and the disadvantaged in society? Ethics could only offer honor and respect, which however could not relieve the sufferings of the poor. With the help of religion Cohen validated pity and sympathy as the proper response to human suffering, affects which were eventually sublimated into love. Is this really the love that is meant by the biblical command, "Thou shalt love Thy neighbor as thyself?" Is this really love? Does one really get to love by the roundabout way of pity and sympathy? Is love only a sociopolitical ideal, to become reality in response to the plight of the poor in society? [93] Cohen's concept of immortality and love shows that to the end he was attempting to tie religion to the apron strings of ethics and thus determine the meaning of religious ideas.

3.

The truth is that, there is quite a bit more in "the religion of reason" than what may claim admission on the grounds that it represents "reason's share" in religion. There are a number of concepts of a purely religious character which forced their way into Cohen's religious philosophy, which "reason's share" in religion can hardly legitimize. We have discussed earlier how the religious idea of God differs for Cohen from the God-idea which he introduced into his *Ethik*. There God was a postulate that was required as the logical basis for the continuity of nature which is needed for ethical realization. Ethics cannot go beyond the postulate. Religion, however, through its trust in God, provides the reliance on the messianic realization of the ethical God-idea.

Now, what he says about religion is quite correct. It does know of the trust in God and, therefore, it has confidence in the messianic future. But can Cohen's idea of God, as it appears in the religion of reason justify such trust and confidence? We do not think so. What is given to us is Becoming. This Becoming demands for its explanation the logical ground of Being, which is identified as God. To expect of this God to guarantee the eternity of Becoming is a logical fallacy. Being can only be used insofar as Becoming requires an origin in rest. It can, however, add nothing to the nature and character of Becoming. It is from Becoming that Being is concluded and it is not from Being that Becoming derives. If Becoming does not on its own reveal its quality of eternal duration, the Being concluded from it cannot show it either. One is reminded of Kant's argument against the cosmological proof for the existence of God. Since it is from the cosmos of man's finite experience that one concludes the existence of God, there is no reason to assume that God of a finite world is infinite.

On a number of occasions Cohen speaks of trust in God. This, of course, is a familiar religious concept; but it implies faith in a personal God. But Being as the logical ground of Becoming cannot serve as a personal God. Cohen himself warns often enough against such interpretation. The correlation is logical and not personal. There is no legitimate reason for trust in God and reliance on him in Cohen's religion of reason, yet it was given an important function within it. It is vital for the idea of forgiveness. We have seen how important it was for Cohen to find a solution to the problem of man's ethical failure. Ethics could not help the man who was alone with his sin. Man enters on the path of "return" by self-sanctification whose goal is God. As we saw, it was the God of the paradigm, the *Urbild,* of action.

Cohen is right in saying that man alone could not bring about his liberation from sin. It is essential for our understanding of God to know that God alone is the redeemer. This indeed, is the meaning of God in Judaism. What we are unable to see is how one may trust in God's forgiveness if God is the ground of Becoming, the logically required origin of nature as well as the logically required origin of the human spirit that conceives him as the ideal norm for human action? How does a paradigm forgive, how does it redeem? A God who is not in some "personal" way involved in history cannot do it. Cohen quotes the biblical "And God said, I have forgiven according to your words." But the God of the Bible is a personal God; he stands in a personal relation to man. He "speaks," whatever the non-anthropomorphic meaning of the phrase may be. He communicates and "says": I have forgiven! But the God of Cohen's religion of reason does not act, does not communicate. He is the silent ground of the All. Forgiveness is an event that happens between God and man. But where God is only the "goal" of human endeavor, nothing is happening between the two. In vain does Cohen comment that in forgiveness God as the Good One has to perform a "personlike" deed of goodness.[94] The God of his religion of reason cannot do it. It is more like man, conceiving of goodness as an act worthy of the ideal of goodness, forgiving himself.

It would seem to us that having locked the front door against a personal God, Cohen unwittingly let him enter through the back door. He even quotes the Hebrew terms of *ḥesed,* lovingkindness, and *raḥamim,* mercy, and declares that God's love is not intellectual. It has to be an effect, since it has to correspond to sympathy.[95] This, of course, is in agreement with everything he has said about the love of God for man from the point of view of "reason's share" in religion. Accordingly, we know of God's love for man through the pity which he awakens in our heart by his laws of social justice, which are revealed to us through our reason.[96] Surely, this kind of a logically derived knowledge of God's "love" from what man discovers in his own mind should not be called an affect. It has nothing in common with the biblical *ḥesed* and *raḥamim.* "Affects" are the prerogatives of a personal God, but should not be ascribed to Being, the ground and the paradigm. Cohen even admits the idea of God as the ruler and judge of the universe. He acknowledges the majesty of the thought as it found its expression in the liturgy of *Rosh Hashanah,* the New Year, which is the Day of God's World Judgment.[97] The idea was precious to Cohen. Yet, on the basis of the "share of reason" in religion as he understood it, there is no place for it in his religion of reason.

4.

Perhaps the greatest inconsistency in Cohen's religious philosophy may be discerned in the various ways he sees the relation between God and man. In the development of the theme of revelation he finds it necessary to make the point that since God is spirit, man too must be spirit. This is supposed to be the result of the correlation. This is, of course, a *non sequitur*. If the conclusion were valid, we would have to say that nature is spirit too, on account of the correlation between God and nature. However, apart from that, it is surprising to hear him say that while, of course, there could be no identity between the spirit of God and that of man, they would have to be comparable to each other. Even in this connection Cohen emphasizes the uniqueness of God, which is inviolable, yet he allows the spirit of man to be similar to God, who is all spirit.[98] We recall what he said about the uniqueness of God. God alone has Being, everything else is Non-being. The world has existence (*Dasein*) but not Being. This, of course, means that Being and Becoming are not comparable. One would have to conclude that if God as Being is spirit, man as having his place within Becoming would have to be non-spirit. The very language that Cohen uses here, saying that

God gave man his spirit, is personalistic. Quite clearly, Cohen was attempting to preserve the biblical idea of man's having been created in the image of God.

Actually, if we follow Cohen further, we have to assume a form of identity between the spirit of man and that of God. Religion does speak of the laws of God. This seems to contradict a fundamental principle of the ethics of pure will, hallowed by the authority of Kant himself, that of the autonomy of the will. Does not the recognition of divine laws contradict the ethical autonomy of the will? Cohen explains: "The fact that religion speaks of the laws does not contradict the principle of the autonomy of the will, since it is the will of reason that the religion of reason considers to be the law of God." [99]

The idea is repeated in a number of passages. God's commandment is the religious expression that parallels the fundamental principle of autonomy in ethics. The moral law, which is the law of God, is also the law of moral reason. The moral law, declares Cohen in good Kantian tradition, is the autonomous law of my reason. [100] This would indicate that the law of my reason is identical with the law of divine reason. There is only one reason and that is divine. We have now to assume that the spirit of God and that of man are identical. It is an idealistic position that goes even beyond the traditionally religious interpretation of the idea of man's creation in the image of God.

Surprisingly moving is Cohen's final description of the God-man relation in the closing section of *Die Religion der Vernunft*. There he discusses the meaning of prayer. He sees in prayer a "dialogical monologue," most authentically expressed in the Psalms. What is a dialogical monologue and how is prayer such a monologue and yet a dialogue? Cohen explains: "The lyrical confession has to sing the monologue as a dialogue. The soul unites both persons of the dialogue; for the soul is really God-given, therefore it is not exclusively human soul (*Menschenseele*). Thus, it may seek God and talk with him." [101] This is Cohen's final confession and it is a turning away from the God of his "religion of reason" and yet not a complete turning to the God of his fathers, the God of his youth for whom his soul was longing.

Only a few pages earlier Cohen was speaking of prayer as the longing for God who can never be reached. "Prayer is longing. The desire of the prayer for God is a search for God and remains forever only a search. One can never find the reality only the "nearness" of God. The approach to God alone is the goal." [102] As such, prayer could only be a monologue. And yet, Cohen could not give up the idea of the dialogue completely. It is the sign of the inner struggle between the intellect of the Neo-Kantian sage and the heart of the *baal t'shubah,* the old Jew returning to the house of his fathers. Thus, he conceives of prayer as the dialogical monologue. He is still not facing God in a dialogical situation. His Neo-Kantian past does not let him. Man is alone and God is only the "goal." Yet, he does not give up the dialogical meeting with the God of his fathers completely. God is really so near. This soul of mine is not completely mine, it is God's too. Thus it can bring together the two *persons* of the dialogue. It can not only search God; it can also speak to him. Finally he dared say—God, a person, but said it as if by a slip of the pen.

Herman Cohen the *baal t'shuba* was in essence a tragic personality of the all-too-short golden age of German Jewry. After complete estrangement from the God of his people, having given the fruits of the great powers of his genius to the enhancement of Germany's philosophical glory, rebuffed by anti-Semitism that came to new life even in the highest seats of German culture, he returned proudly to his people. And yet, he could not make the return complete. Intellectually, the system put the breaks on the heart's desire; emotionally, the loyalty of his stiff-necked Jewishness even to a Germany that kept no faith with him, blinded him to the vision of the historic Israel. Did he ever find peace? My teacher told us once about a visit with Hermann Cohen in the last days of Cohen's life. The old man led him to a room in which stood a bookcase full with old rabbinical works of classical Judaism. Pointing to the shelves, Cohen said with tears in his eyes: "The *s'forim* [books] of my father."

CHAPTER 2

Franz Rosenzweig's Philosophy of Judaism
(1886–1929)

Franz Rosenzweig was the child of a completely assimilated Jewish family, in which the only somewhat nostalgic reminder of Judaism was an old uncle. Otherwise, Judaism meant chiefly anti-Semitism. Having the means from an affluent home to support him, he was able to rove over many areas of knowledge. His was a brilliant mind that mastered the entire realm of Western thought and was comfortably at home in all the manifestations of Western civilization.

Rosenzweig was a man of absolute intellectual honesty and of a most sensitive conscience. During his intellectual odyssey he reached a point at the age of twenty-seven, when he decided to convert to Christianity. However, before actually carrying out his decision, he attended services on the Day of Atonement in Berlin in a *shteebl,* a small Orthodox synagogue. He went in as a completely alienated Jew ready for Christianity; he came out a radically transformed person, his soul aflame with unquestioning commitment to Judaism. From then on his entire life belonged to God and Judaism. He wrote, he taught, he translated, and interpreted. Original ideas continually emanated from him, he toiled tirelessly for the renewal of Judaism in the midst of a more or less assimilated German Jewry. He was the great *baal t'shuba,* the man of return, if not the greatest, during the final phase in the history of German Jewry, among the purest of *zadikim* (the world is untranslatable) of his generation. His life showed the way for many and has remained an inspiration to this day. If we subject his philosophy of Judaism as expressed in his *magnum opus, Der Stern der Erlösung* (The Star of Redemption) to criticism, it is done with the full realization that in the case of Rosenzweig, as is often the case in the history of the

37

philosophies of Judaism, the man's intellectual validation of his position does not do justice to his existential commitment and to the truth of his life. The philosophy is a rationalization, and often a poor one. Not even with Maimonides was it any different.

I.   THE PHILOSOPHY

1.   *Eternity, Holiness, and Redemption*

Rosenzweig's thoughts on Judaism center around three main ideas, eternity, holiness, and redemption. Eternal life was planted in the midst of the people of Israel in the revelation at Sinai.[1] The meaning of eternity in this context is not continuous duration in time, rather it is a "Now" that stands between a solidified past and an unchanging future. How is this to be understood? Change is the essence of vitality in the life of nations. Vitality consists in pushing each day into the past to make room for another day, and so on ad infinitum. Nations are alive in such change which finds its expression in custom and law. Custom arises from the past, whereas the law is formulated in the present for the sake of the future. "Nations live in revolutions, in which the law continually sloughs off its old skin. . . ."[2] Not so, with Israel. The Torah, which is teaching and law in one, is holy, it is eternal. One may leave it, give it up. One cannot change it. What with other nations is custom and law, responsible for the division of time into past and future, with the Jewish people is the eternal Torah, which solidifies past and future. Time thus becomes "an unchangeable present." The Jew lives in an everlasting present, in an eternal Now.

The historical memory of the Jew does not refer to a definite point in the past. Every year of the past is equally near to the present. It is for this reason that at the festive *Seder* meal the Jew affirms that "in every generation one has to look upon oneself as if one too had shared in the exodus from Egypt."[3] What is said about the exodus applies also to every other event in Jewish history. They are all equally close to the lived moment. This establishes a form of contemporaneity between the generations. All generations of Jews are, in a sense, contemporaneous. Living together in the unchangeable Now is the bond between the generations. "Through this bond, the people become the eternal people. For as grandson and grandfather behold each other, in the same moment they also behold in each other the latest offspring and the first forebear."[4]

The eternal law eternalizes the present moment. But as the Now becomes "eternal," it is removed from the stream of time. The Torah lifts
Israel out of time and history. God withdrew the Jewish people from
the dimension of history in which the nations live by giving Israel his
law, which like a bridge arches over the flow of time, "that rushes under-
neath it powerless in all eternity."[5] This is the essence of the sanctification of the life of the Jew, to live above time, outside of time, in the
eternal Now. Such timelessness is holiness. And Rosenzweig has to add
the melancholy thought that "as life is being sanctified, it is no longer
alive."[6] We gain then an eternal life which is not alive in historic time.
In the midst of the time of the nations and history, the people of God
enjoy a "lifeless" life of holy eternity.[7]

All this, however, means that the people of God is already at the end,
it is at the goal.[8] It is beyond time, because it is complete and fulfilled.
It lives in a state of redemption. The redemption, which is awaited by
the world at the end of time, is anticipated by the Jew. Especially on
the Sabbath and on the *yamim noraim,* the Days of Awe, of *Rosh
Hashanah* and *Yom Kippur,* the Jew feels that he is already redeemed.
It should, however, be noted that there are passages in the *Stern* where
Rosenzweig seems to indicate that the "lifeless" life of holy eternity in
which the Jew exists thanks to the Torah is the life of redemption. It
is not only on the Sabbath or the Holy Days that he feels already redeemed. It is the life outside and above time which is the state of redemption. The Jew is at the goal means that he has reached redemption.
Thus, Rosenzweig speaks of the community's kneeling before God on
Yom Kippur, not while confessing its sins, but in a supreme act of
worship free of all personal desire and requests, as the celebration of
redemption. To which he adds: "for only we live a life in redemption
and are, therefore, able to celebrate it."[9] In an unredeemed world, the
Jew lives at the end of time and history, the "lifeless" life of holiness in
a state of redemption.

Consistent with his basic position is Rosenzweig's interpretation of the
reconciliation between God and man which is the precious fruit of the
Day of Atonement. Clothed in the *kittel,* the white gown in which the
Jew is buried, he stands in prayer before God on the Days of Awe,
facing him as if on the day of final judgment ". . . thus he stands before
the eye of the Judge in complete solitude, a corpse in the midst of life,
and a member of an assembled humanity who all—like himself—in the

midst of life have already placed themselves beyond the grave. Everything already lies behind him." [10] In a sense this is only an intensification of the "daily life" of the Jew in the eternal Now. Since the Jew is already at the end, living in the *eschatom,* the "lifeless" life of eternity, he is daily placing himself "beyond the grave" in the midst of life. He is at the goal, therefore always—and not only on *Yom Kippur*—everything is already behind him. Eternity is bought at the price of the temporal life.

Manifold consequences follow from this understanding. If the eternal people is outside of time, what then is temporality to it, to which its body is after all still attached? It cannot mean growth and development as with other nations. Growth and development would be an indication that Israel has not yet reached its completion in time, that it was not at the goal and did not exist in the state of redemption. Any change in time would be a denial of eternity.[11] Thus it can only wait and wander. It takes no part in the temporal processes of history. It can, therefore not share "fully and creatively" in the historical life of the nations of the world. "The eternal people must forget the growth of the world. For itself, the world, its own world, must be accepted as complete." [12] At times, Rosenzweig formulates Israel's nonparticipation in the historical life of the nations differently. Not only can a completed people of God not participate in the historical processes which carry the nations towards the goal which Israel has already reached, it is as if the holiness of the people prevents it from spending its energies on an unredeemed world. "The consecration which is spread over it as a kingdom of priests, renders its life barren. Its holiness prevents it from giving its soul to the as yet unsanctified world of the nations, however much its body may be fastened to that world." [13]

Perhaps the most far-reaching consequence of Rosenzweig's philosophy of Judaism is his radical rejection of the state as a structure within which to order the life of the eternal people. "For the state is the continually changing form, under which time moves, step by step, toward eternity. In the people of God, however, eternity is already there in the midst of time." [14] The nations live in pure temporality. The state for them is the forever repeated attempt to secure eternity in the midst of time. In such attempts the state becomes "the imitator and rival" of the people that carries its eternity within itself. If the state could succeed in achieving its desire for eternity, Israel would have no right to its own specific form of timelessness.[15]

2. *Survival*

The eternity that we have thus far analyzed is of a metaphysical, spiritual nature. It was achieved in the immediacy of the encounter with God in the act of revelation and through the eternal law that has lifted Israel out of the stream of history. However, one has also to find yet another foundation for the eternity of the eternal people. While the people of God may well be spiritually complete and at the goal, living the "lifeless" life of redemption, its body lives in time and is attached to the life of the world. Existing outside of time in its soul, how does it maintain its physical eternity in time? Here Rosenzweig surprises us with his most daring idea. Israel possesses the guarantee of its eternity in "the community of the blood" that binds the generations to each other. Only the blood can vouch, already in the present, for the realization of the hope for a future. With hardly believable boldness Rosenzweig declares: "Only the blood community feels the guarantee of its eternity already today pushing through its veins . . . it need not trouble the spirit. It has the guarantee of its eternity in the natural procreation of its body." [16]

Because of this "self-created eternity," that Israel carries in its own blood, it is independent of all those elements to which the nations attempt to attach their eternity, land, language, and the changing customs and laws. Since the nations tie their lives to the land, they spill their blood for it. They love the land more than their life. But when the land is lost, life is lost too; for he who owns the land also owns the people. "Thus, the land betrays the people that entrusts its survival unto it. Indeed, it endures; but the people on it perish." [17] Not so the eternal people. It alone trusted its blood and left the land. Rosenzweig presents us with the fantastic statement, "Thus we (meaning the Jews) saved the precious life juice which offered us the guarantee of our own eternity." [18]

From here Rosenzweig develops the roots of a kind of a philosophy of Jewish history. Unlike other nations, the history of Israel does not start with an autochthonous people which lives in its own land. The patriarch Abraham is a stranger in the land of Canaan, and Israel first becomes a nation in the Egyptian exile and experiences its national rebirth "in the bright light of history" in exile in Babylon. Even its own land is never fully in its possession. Even there, it is a stranger and sojourner, "for the land is mine" says God to the Jew. The exile from its own land was, therefore, neither a mere accident of history, as one might think, nor punishment "because of our sins," as tradition would have it. It was the logic of the "self-created" eternity from "the dark wells of the blood" that this people was not allowed to age and fade away by dwelling "at home." For the Jew, the lost homeland becomes "in the deepest sense the land of his longing as—holy land." The longing, however, cannot be a longing for return. According to Rosenzweig's idea of the "blood community," exile from the land was not so much a loss as a meaningful liberation from a dangerous bond. For, as Rosenzweig also says: "the will to peoplehood must not cling to any dead means [i.e., land]. It may only be realized through the people itself. The people is a people only through the people."

What then is the aim of this longing? It would seem to us that within the context of Rosenzweig's thought the longing for the holy land can only have a negative function. It is not a longing for return, for repossession of the land. As he himself seems to indicate, its sole purpose is not to allow the eternal people to find a real home in any other land.[19] This is an essential requirement for the preservation of the eternal people. Israel must not be allowed to live in unison with time and world history. It would lose its eternity. The Jew finds his place in the world within himself. His own kind, that came to him in his birth, he carries around like an "internal homeland: . . . like a magic circle, from which he is as likely to escape as from the circle of his blood, just because he carries it around—like his own blood—wherever he may go, wherever he may stand."[20] This people has its roots within itself. One might then say, following the inherent logic of Rosenzweig's position, that "the holy land" is the landless land, just as "the holy life" is the lifeless life. The longing for it guarantees Israel's homelessness for the sake of the preservation of its timeless existence.

The "holy language" of the Jew also has a function similar to that of the "holy land." The holy language is the language of prayer. The Jew speaks in this tongue only to God, according to Rosenzweig. Thus, it diverts the Jew from the immediacy of his contact with daily life. The holiness of his language does not allow the life of the Jew to take root in the soil of a language of his own. As the "holy land" prevents him from finding home in any other land, so the holy language does not let him become one with the language that he happens to speak. Even where the Jew does speak the language of his host country, according to

Rosenzweig, he uses it in a manner specifically Jewish, which reveals that the language is not really his own. This, too, means that nowhere can the Jew settle down for good. Nor should he. He has his home within himself.

We have seen earlier how the eternal law removes the Jew from time and establishes the timeless perfection of Israel. Other nations which had the anchor of their life in land and language, customs and laws, are dead. For us, however, land, language, and law have long since left the circle of the living and have been raised out of life into holiness. We are eternal, for our life is not dependent on anything external. "We took root in ourselves; without roots in the earth and therefore eternal wanderers, yet deeply rooted within ourselves, in our own body and blood. And this rootedness in ourselves, and only in ourselves, vouchsafes us our eternity." [21]

In summation we might say that the result of Rosenzweig's position is a concept of the Jewish people that at the goal of all history lives the "lifeless" life of holiness outside of time and history, whose eternity is safeguarded in the blood community that binds all the generations.

3.   *Judaism and Christianity*

Rosenzweig's view of Judaism and the Jew is inseparable from his understanding of Christianity and the Christian. It is not our intention to analyze his interpretation of Christianity. However, a few words need be said about the relationship between the two religions. Whereas in Judaism man knows God directly, in Christianity he can only come to him by the mediation of the Son. The Christian can approach only the Son with same intimacy and trust with which the Jew comes before God himself. This is, indeed, so natural for the Jew that he cannot grasp why the same immediacy should be impossible for anyone else. Only at the hand of the Son dare the Christian come near the Father, because the Christian cannot imagine that the Holy God would lower himself to him as he desires it, unless he became himself Man. Thus, if the Son were not Man he would be useless for the Christian. In the need for a Man-God, Rosenzweig sees "a bit of paganism" present in every Christian which cannot be eliminated. For the heathen desires to be surrounded by "human gods." It is not enough for him that he himself is man, God too must be Man.[22] This, however, means that the Christian is by nature and birth a heathen.

Christianity comes to the Christian from without and gives direction to his life. As Rosenzweig puts it in Latin: *Christianus fit, non nascitur.* Judasim is direction from within. The Christian has to leave his condition at birth and has to be reborn as a Christian. The Jew, on the other hand, had his "rebirth" long before his natural birth, when his people was reborn in the divine covenant of the revelation. Therefore, he is born a Jew. But just because of that the Christian is always at the beginning, always young, whereas the Jew is always already at the goal.[23] In other words, Christianity is within time, between rebirth and the Second Coming, in history, just as Judaism and Israel are beyond it. Christianity, young and full of vitality, is on the way with the task of spreading out and filling out time and history. The Jew has the eternal life; the Christian, the eternal way which is illuminated by the rays from the self-contained fire at the heart of the eternal life. "Eternal life and eternal way—they are as different as the infinity of a point and that of a line. The infinity of a point may consist only in that it (i.e., the point) cannot be erased; thus (the point) maintains itself in the self-preservation of the procreating blood. The infinity of a line, however, ceases when it is no longer possible to elongate it." [24]

Christianity as the eternal way has to expand continually. Simply to preserve itself would be the renunciation of its eternity and with it, death. Christianity has to be missionary, no less than the eternal people has to preserve itself by closing "the pure wells of the blood" against all foreign admixture. Christianity is eminently suitable for its eternal way through the world. At the hand of its Man-God it marches on, unlike the Jew, full of conquering strength. ". . . for flesh and blood will submit only to that which is, like itself, of flesh and blood. And just that element of "heathenism" enables the Christian to convert the heathens." [25]

To formulate again and again the distinction between Judaism and Christianity, between the Jew and the Christian, seems to be an obsession with Rosenzweig. He forever defines his Judaism in juxtaposition to Christianity. "To be rooted in deepest self was the secret of the eternal people. To spread through everything outside itself is the secret of the eternal way." [26] Because the Jew has his eternity within, anchored in his essential nature, as he descends into his innermost self, he ascends to the highest. Therein lies the deepest difference between the Jew and the Christian. Whereas the Jew is Jew from home and certainly from birth, the Christian is a heathen at least from birth. Thus the way of the Christian must be a way of alienation from himself. He must forever move away from himself. He must give up his natural self in order to become a Christian. Whereas the Christian life "denationalizes" the Christian, Jewish life leads the Jew more closely to the "Jewish kind" of his inborn nature.[27] This rootedness of the Jew within himself, this self-sufficiency, as it were, Rosenzweig compares to a self-sustaining fire (as referred to earlier). This fire is the symbol of the eternal life of the Jew. Therefore, speaking metaphorically, Rosenzweig would also say that because of this self-sustaining fire the Jew is in no need of the sword to go out into the forests of the world to get what it needs to feed the flame.[28]

As the eternal life of the Jew is the fire, so is the eternal way of the Christian the rays, the rays from the fire, which shining into the world, illuminate the way. Judaism and Christianity are thus linked to each other in the philosophy of Rosenzweig. The same light, in different forms, determines them both; the fire at the center—the eternal life of the Jew, the illumination of the rays—the eternal way of the Christian. Rosenzweig maintains therefore that "both Jew and Christian, are workers on the same task before God. He can spare neither of them." [29] Neither of them is capable of accomplishing the task by himself. "We [speaking for the Jews] behold in our hearts the faithful image of the truth; however, because of it, we turn away from the temporal life and the temporal life turns from us. They, on the other hand, are running after the stream of time, but have the truth behind them." [30]

With the help of these ideas Rosenzweig is able to offer us an original interpretation of the Christian hatred of the Jew. The way of Christianity through the world has been most successful. It has triumphed over the gods of the peoples, their myths, their heroes, and their entire cosmos. Christianity has been uniquely triumphant. Who would dare to challenge it! Yet, the Jew does it; not in words but by his mere existence. "This existence of the Jew forces the thought upon Christianity at all times that it is not reaching the goal, that it is not coming to the truth, but remains forever on the way. This is the deepest reason for the Christian Jew hatred which, ultimately, is only self-hatred, transferred onto the objectionable, silent reproacher, who yet reproaches only by his existence—hatred against one's own imperfection, against one's own not-yet." [31]

Nevertheless, Rosenzweig does look forward to ultimate reconciliation; he sees it in the metaphor of Yehuda Halevi, the poet and philosopher of Judaism in the eleventh century. God has a secret plan with the Jew, which may be compared to a plan with a seed that falls to the ground. In the earth it appears to change into soil, water, and dirt. Nothing seems to be left to be recognized by the eye. Yet, it is itself which transforms the soil and the water into its own substance and, degree by degree, breaks down their elements and, reforming them, incorporates them into its own being. The tree then grows, it yields the fruit, a fruit like the one from which its own seed came. Similarly, the Torah of Moses transforms all those who follow after it to its own truthfulness, though they appear to reject it. These nations, followers of other religions, are the preparation for the expected Messiah, who is the fruit. They will all become his fruits as they recognize him. The tree then will become one. They will then honor and praise the root, which they had despised.[32] In that hour, when the fruits will be ripe and recognize the seed from which they sprang, the nations will have arrived at the goal towards which they were moving all through history, at the goal where Israel stands waiting for them. "The way is at an end when the home is reached. The way may be eternal, since its end is eternity; yet, it comes to an end, for eternity is its end. Where everything is aflame, there are no rays any more. There everything is one light." [33]

In the meantime, the Jew may wait. He may be oblivious to the rays. He who has the flame is in no need of its rays. The flame burns silently and forever. The seed of eternal life has been planted; it can wait now till it will spring up. Of the tree which grows from it the seed knows nothing, though it cast its shadow over the world. One day, however, a seed will come from the fruits of the tree that will be like its original. Blessed be the One who has planted eternal life in our midst.[34] In the light of all this, one may be justified in saying that Rosenzweig makes room for Christianity by removing Judaism from history, but the Christian will find eternal life by returning to Judaism. In time, Christianity is triumphant; in eternity, it is Judaism. The Christian is needed, for there is a job in the unredeemed world which the Jew, already living the "lifeless" life of redemption, cannot perform.

II. Criticism

1. *History*

With all due respect to the saintly genius of Franz Rosenzweig, it would seem to us that it is impossible to accept any of his categories as fitting either the essence of Judaism, the nature of the Jew, or the history of the Jewish people.

It is true that the history of the Jewish people commenced in exile, that Israel became a people in exile. Yet, it was history in the time of the world and not outside of it. The holy land was the land of their longing, but not as Rosenzweig interprets the term as a device by which the Jews were prevented from finding a home anyplace in the world. On the contrary, it was the land of the divine promise, a very real land in time and space, where they were to find a home, a place of rest. For centuries the holy language was the everyday language of the people in which the Jew communicated not only with his God, but also with his fellowmen, it was the language in which he prayed, in which he spoke to his beloved, and cursed his neighbor, in which he spoke the truth and told a lie. The state, far from being alien to Judaism was envisaged by the Torah, and had—at least in theory—a Torah constitution; it was to be organized by the laws of the Torah. Yet, according to Rosenzweig all this could not have been. For with the covenant of the revelation God planted eternal life in the midst of the people. With it Israel was completed; it reached the goal; it was taken out of history. When did that happen? In 70 C.E. at the destruction of the Second Commonwealth? Surely, not. He could only mean the revelation at Sinai. Was, then, everything that followed already outside of history? Was it not Jewish history in time and worldly space? Or was there some kind of development of the Jewish people to the genuine Judaism of the "lifeless" life of holiness at the goal? At least in one place Rosenzweig does refer to Jewish history as having become petrified.[35] But when did that happen and why? What was it and what Judaism, prior to the petrification? Did it acquire eternity through petrification and not through revelation? Is it possible to read the Bible without realizing that its main theme is the story of an eminently historical people?

The God of the Bible is the God of history. The prophets are the earliest people for whom history is not a mere repetition of the past but a flow toward a goal whose progress is determined by the ethical interaction between God and man and by man's conduct in the sight of God. Whatever happens is of importance because it occurs in the space-time dimension of daily human existence.

Judaism and the Jew are vitally involved in the history of all mankind. The very significance of both lies in the fact that the viability of a specific way of life is demonstrated in the same historical time in which all mankind lives. The goal, far from having been reached, is always in the future. Much more than the history of any other people, Jewish history is future-oriented. Its very essence is not the eternal "now" of Rosenzweig, but the everlasting "not-yet." It is the history of a promise that God and man made to each other, the world history of the struggle for the realization of that promise. Its entire value and meaning lies in the fact that it is battling for its realization along the path that is trodden by all mankind. The eternal life of Israel has universal relevance because it leads through the time of the world, because it is woven into the fabric of world history. Unfortunately, Rosenzweig's categories blind him to the historic reality of Judaism as well as of the Jew.

2.   *Holiness and the Law*

One of the keys to Rosenzweig's inability to recognize the historical reality of Israel can be found in a short sentence to which we had occasion to refer earlier in our presentation of his ideas: "As life becomes sanctified it is no longer alive." [36] We can hardly think of a statement less characteristic of Judaism than these words of Rosenzweig. According to him the sanctification is effected by the eternal law. A number of statements are made about the law in the third part of *Der Stern,* but only one aspect of the law is actually discussed and interpreted: its ritual aspect in the limited sense in which it found expression in the holy days of the Jewish year and in its liturgical formulation. But it is not in this extremely narrow sense that one can grasp the essential nature of the law. In fact, there is no safer way of missing the essential quality and purpose of the law than by trying to explain them within such a very limited and artificial frame. The law is all-embracing. It comprehends every aspect of the life of the individual as well as that of the entire Jewish people. It regulates all interhuman relationships; it lays down the principles of an economic and social order; it provides the constitution of a state—its judicial system, its civil and criminal laws. Its significance lies in the fact that it deals with the temporal life of the Jew and of the Jewish people. Its whole purpose is to give meaning and direction to the daily life of the Jew. It aims at life, this life, in time and history. Can one doubt it, for instance, in the light of the words in Deuteronomy? [37] "I have set before thee life and death, the blessing and the curse; therefore choose life, that thou mayest live, thou and thy seed; to love the Lord thy God, to hearken to His voice, and to cleave unto Him; for that is thy life, and the length of thy days; that thou mayest dwell in the land which the Lord swore unto thy fathers, to Abraham, to Isaac, and to Jacob, to give them." The emphasis is forever on life on this earth in the world's time. "Mine ordinances shall ye do, and my statutes shall ye keep to walk therein: I am the Lord your God. Ye shall therefore keep My statutes, and Mine ordinances, which if a man do, he shall live by them. . . ." [38] The rabbis comment on it: ". . . that he shall live by them and not that he shall die by them." [39]

The law does sanctify life, but sanctification does not remove the Jew from history; on the contrary, its very significance lies in the fact that it is the sanctification of life in time and history. The biblical chapter that begins with the words: "Ye shall be holy, for I the Lord your God are holy" [40] deals mainly with the sanctification of the daily intercourse with one's fellow men. Let only a very few of the laws of sanctification stand here to illustrate the point.

> Ye shall not steal; neither shall ye deal falsely, nor lie one to another. And ye shall not swear by My name falsely. . . . Thou shalt not oppress thy neighbor, nor rob him; the wages of a hired servant shall not abide with thee all night until the morning . . . and if a stranger sojourn with thee in your land, ye shall not do him wrong. The stranger that sojourneth with you shall be unto you as the home-born among you, and thou shalt love him as thyself. . . . Ye shall do no unrighteousness in judgment, in meteyard, in weight, or in measure.

The whole of the Torah is dedicated to life, for life, the everyday life of man, has to be dedicated. "The living, the living, he shall praise Thee, as I do this day" [41] exclaims the prophet; it is the living in time and the praise from history that really matter. Sanctification is not to remove man from time, but to bring holiness into time. Rosenzweig's interpretation of the Day of Atonement is movingly beautiful, yet it is not the *Yom Kippur* of the Jew through the ages. It is a misinterpretation because it is a perfect application of his category of holiness as "lifelessness." We have heard him describe it as the day in which the Jew, clothed in his burial garments, faces God from beyond the grave, having already everything behind him. It is hardly conceivable how anyone familiar with the liturgy of that holiest of days, as surely Rosenzweig must have been, could have made such a statement. Practically every page of the *Maḥzor,* the festival prayer book, is concerned with life, the life lived daily by the Jew and by all peoples of the earth. It is a day for the sake of life, for the right and better life of tomorrow. The confession of sins and the prayer for forgiveness is felt to be a necessity as a first step toward a new day. A basic element in the act of *t'shuba,* of return to God, is the resolution for the life one is determined to lead in the future. Everything is directed at the renewal of man for the year that is ahead. Everything is prayer for the spiritual and material blessing in the days ahead. Far from having everything behind him on *Yom Kippur,* he has everything before him: his past life as a subject of examination; the future, for which to prepare. A recurring prayer of the day is: "Bring us back unto thee, O God, and we shall return; renew our days as of old. . . . O cast us not away from thy presence, nor take thy holy spirit from us. O cast us not off in old age, forsake us not when our strength fails." Are these the words of people who have everything already behind them and have retained the "lifeless" life of eternity? Or is it the prayer that the dominion of wickedness may disappear from the earth, that God may grant honor to his people, hope and praise to all those who fear him, seek him, and want him, joy to his land of Israel and to his city of Zion, speedily in our days? Is this spoken from beyond history, in a state beyond all wishes, desires and needs? How is it possible to maintain that the great *Abinu Malkenu* prayer, recited at least three times during the day, is prayed from beyond the grave and not from the very midst of man's temporal life!

> Our Father, our King, we have sinned before thee.
> Our Father, our King, renew a good year for us.
> Our Father, our King, annul the plans of our enemies.
> Our Father, our King, remove pestilence, sword, famine, captivity, destruction, iniquity, and persecution from thy people of the covenant.
> Our Father, our King, forgive and pardon all our sins.

Our Father, our King, bring us back in perfect repentance to Thee.
Our Father, our King, inscribe us in the book of maintenance and
sustenance.

The prayer characterizes the mood of the entire day. Though withdrawn completely from all normal daily activities, on *Yom Kippur*
the Jew faces God from the very heart of his personal existence as well
as from the very core of the historical existence of his people, for the
sake of that life from which he so completely withdraws on that day.
Like all Jewish history, the Day of Atonement too is future-directed.
It is a day in the midst of life, a day of sanctification of living in time
far beyond the limits of that one day. Never is the Jew more concerned
about his life on earth, in the world, and with the world, than on the
Day of Atonement. It is the day, from which he derives his main
strength to remain in time, to face the trials and tribulation, to give it
meaning and direction, to sanctify it.

A holiness of eternity, one which is—to use a phrase of Rosenzweig's
—"bought at the price of man's temporal life" is no concern of Judaism.
Eternity needs no holiness; it is man's desires and wishes, his needful
temporal life that alone requires sanctification. Thus "the holy land" is
not the never-never land of the Jew's longing that is to separate him
from all these worldly attachment to any land, as Rosenzweig sees it; but
the land that because it is the land of the Jews is the most conducive
place on earth for the sanctification of the life of an entire people. The
holy language is not holy because it is not used for communication between Jew and Jew, but because in it the Jew was called to the life of
Judaism on this earth, because in it the "Torah of life," the Torah for
this earthly life, was planted in his midst. Rosenzweig sees the holy law
of the Torah as taking hold of the this-worldly and transforming it into
the contents of the future world, the world beyond.[42] We know nothing
of that. The law does not change the this-worldly into the other-worldly,
but transforms the profanity of the this-worldly into the sanctified this-
worldly. The Jew sees in the transformation not only his goal, but that
of all history. Just because of that neither Israel, nor the world have as
yet arrived at the goal; just because of that the place of the Jew and of
Judaism is in time and history. Eternity is in no need of holiness; the
Torah was not given to angels, say the rabbis.[43] Not even the Torah is
eternal according to Jewish tradition. As one of the great teachers of
the Talmud said: "The commandments of God were given in order to

purify man." [44] Once the goal is achieved, the Law will no longer be necessary. Only in the imperfection of the temporal world does the law serve a purpose.

3.   Exile and Redemption

Rosenzweig's categories cannot recognize the historic reality of Israel's exile. The word does occur two or three times in *Der Stern,* but its only significance for him lies in the fact that Israel became a people in exile; beyond that there is no place for it in the thought of Rosenzweig. Whereas through the centuries Jews have been declaring that "because of our sins we have been exiled from our land," Rosenzweig says that trusting their blood community they left the land.[45] According to him, one would have to say that exile was not so much a loss as a desired liberation from a dangerous attachment. We referred earlier to his statement that the Jewish people could not tie their life to anything dead, like a land. It would have jeopardized their eternity which must not depend on anything outside itself. One would also have to assume that according to his views in *Der Stern,* the prayers of the Jews through the ages for a return to Zion and Jerusalem were pointless. The Jews were at the goal; they had arrived; there was nowhere for them to return to. They were only waiting beyond the river of time for the nations to arrive at eternity, which was their condition. If anything, homelessness was an achievement; the right condition of a people that was complete in itself. Exile would then mean being bodily attached to the not-yet-redeemed world of the nations. Rosenzweig does say that to be "the Beloved of God" is only the beginning and that man remains unredeemed as long as only this beginning is realized. But it is not his opinion that the Jew is at the beginning. For the Jew there is no road; he is at the *eschaton.* And thus Rosenzweig adds in the same context: "As against Israel the eternal Beloved of God, the ever faithful, the forever complete, stands the eternally coming, eternally waiting, eternally wandering, eternally growing—stands the Messiah." [46] From this and other similar passages[47] it would seem that the logic of Rosenzweig's position indicates that the Messiah comes to the gentiles only, bringing them redemption. The Jewish people received eternal life in the revelation and changes no more.

Needless to say, this metaphysical neglect of Israel's exile and this concept of its relationship to the holy land is contrary to the entire

Jewish tradition. It is contradicted by the rich prophetic pronouncements on the subject. When the prophets spoke of exile they meant the homelessness of the Jew expelled from his land; and when they spoke of the promise of return, they meant return home to Zion and Jerusalem, in its literal sense. What follows from Rosenzweig's ideas is a rejection of every word of prophecy on the subject. Rosenzweig does not see how necessary the connection is between the spiritual and the material; that homelessness affects not only the body, but also the spirit of the Jewish people. The law, because it is not just synagogue and home ritual and liturgy, but all-embracing, is not realizable in the political, economic, social unfreedom of the homelessness of the Jewish people. The "lifeless life" of holiness is life stunted, life denied. Holiness must have its base in life, must build on its this-worldly secular reality. Rosenzweig does not see that in the homelessness of the Jewish people the law too is in exile; he is not aware of what Judaism has called the *galut hashkhina,* the exile of the divine Presence. He also disregards completely the material condition of the Jewish people in exile. There is not the slightest attempt made to come to grips with the martyrology of Jewish homelessness, as if the life of the Jews were nothing more than a metaphysical enterprise.

The *galut,* the exile of the Jewish people that features prominently in the Jewish consciousness and has overwhelming significance for the understanding of the place of Judaism and that of the Jew in world history, has to be ignored by Rosenzweig beacuse of his understanding of the "lifeless" life of eternity. Towards the end of *Der Stern* he writes, for instance: "To live in time means to live between Beginning and End. He who would live outside of time—which the one must do who desires to live, not in the temporal but the eternal life—he who wants that must deny the in-between." [48] This, of course, is said of the life of the Jew. He denies the "in-between," but the "in-between" is the *galut.* Since the Jew is already at the end, there is really no *galut.* Exile is really a misnomer. The Jew might think he is in exile; in truth his is eternal life; he has reached redemption already, the end toward which the history of the world is moving. At this point, the vast difference between the categories of Rosenzweig and those of Judaism becomes once more clear. Redemption, for Rosenzweig, is the condition of wishless fulfillment; it is the overcoming of all temporal existence. It is timelessness. When it is complete, all life ends. Not only man and the world are redeemed, but, most directly, it is the redemption of God, who is freed from what is not himself, freed of the world as well as from the concern for the soul. The three elements of Rosenzweig's philosophical structure, God, man, and the world, everything, will be as it was originally prior to creation. The All will become reality. God will be Alone and He will be the All. Now in Judaism redemption is within time and history. God is the redeemer of Israel because he redeemed his people from Egypt, from Babylon. He is the Redeemer from exile. He is the Redeemer of man because he saves him from the hand of his enemies, from oppression and persecution, at times even from the grasp of death. Redemption in Judaism is altogether this-worldly and not other-wordly.

4.   *The Blood Community*

Nothing is more surprising in Rosenzweig's thoughts on Judaism than his idea that the survival of the Jewish people through the world time of the unredeemed world is due to the community of blood, on which alone the Jew relies. The Jew has his anchor within himself and is thus independent of anything outside himself. His independence is the guarantee of his immortality. Rosenzweig makes some astounding statements in this connection. According to him, the leaving of the land and trusting the blood guaranteed survival. For, whereas other nations, tied to a land, let the blood of their sons be spilled for the land and over it, the Jews alone, having been freed from the burden of the land, "were able to save the precious life juice, which guaranteed them their own eternity." [50]

It is hardly believable to what extent metaphysical preoccupation could blind a brilliant mind to facts. What Rosenzweig is saying is that the state of homelessness in time and place, enabled the Jews to preserve their life blood, which alone secured their survival. One sees here how radically he denied the "in-between" of the *galut*. Has exile through the centuries indeed been "a saving of the precious life juice"? Is there any nation on earth that has spilled as much of its blood over its land as the Jewish people have lost in their homelessness? What guarantee is there in the blood of a people that has been materially as powerless as the Jewish people has been in its exile? When Rosenzweig maintains that there was no need to trouble the spirit in order to survive, because survival was safeguarded automatically in "the natural procreation of the body" [51] he, without realizing it, desecrates the self-sacrificial martyrology of the *galut*. The Christian world saw to it that to be a Jew had always to be a response to an ever renewed challenge. The gates for desertion were wide open. The pressure and the temptation to give up Judaism and to join the Christian masters of the earth were ever present. To be a Jew was a continuous decision to remain a Jew. The privilege of remaining a Jew had to be purchased daily anew with sweat and blood. Jewish survival through the hell of world history may indeed be one of the great mysteries in all human experience. It is, however, certain that it could never have been accomplished without the supreme spiritual commitment of the Jew to the truth as he saw it. The blood was helpless; it was the spirit that sustained it.

Indeed, there is a Jewish blood community. The Jews are a people; Judaism is not a church, it is not even the synagogue. However, in Rosenzweig's thoughts the blood community appears as something naturally given. The idea sounds almost racist when he says that in order to preserve itself the eternal people had "to seal off the pure wells of its blood against all alien admixture." [52] It shows how little Rosenzweig understood the basis and the nature of the blood community of the Jews. The truth is that there is nothing in Judaism that aims at preserving "the pure wells of the blood," but there is a great deal to preserve the pure wells of the spirit that are the lifestream of Judaism and of the Jewish people. It is true, Judaism is against mixed marriage, but only when the non-Jewish partner does not convert to Judaism at all or converts without inner conviction. Mixed marriage is frowned upon not because of the mixing of the blood, but because of the mixing of the faiths. As the rabbis say, the doors are always open and anyone who wishes to enter may enter.[53] What is required is sincere acceptance of Judaism. In the course of the centuries many have indeed entered. They have been considered the children of Abraham, who himself was a "convert." There are no "pure wells" of Jewish blood.

It is true, Judaism is not a missionizing faith. This, however, has nothing to do with the protection of the purity of the blood, as Rosenzweig believes. He misses the vital distinction here between Judaism and Christianity. Christianity must missionize, but not because of Rosenzweig's fanciful construction of the eternal way that must expand into eternity. It must missionize because of its basic dogma. According to that dogma God gave his only begotten son to all men; he died in order to bring salvation to the entire human race. If so, the "good news" must be brought to the notice of all mankind. Christianity cannot help missionizing; without it, it could not be Christian. Not so with Judaism. It does not maintain that Judaism is the way of salvation for all men. The Torah was given only to the Jews. From the Christian position, it is obligatory upon every human being to acknowledge Jesus; from the Jewish point of view, it is not obligatory upon non-Jews to accept the Torah. Judaism is obligatory only for the Jews just because it does not believe that it is the only way to the salvation of man. The prophet Micah speaking of "the end of days," when the nations will "flow to the mountain of the Lord, to the house of the God of Jacob," also says: "For let all the peoples walk each one in the name of its God, but we will walk in the name of the Lord our God for ever and ever." [54] Since it is the time when the nations will desire to learn from the God of Jacob, their God must be the God of the universe, just as "the Lord our God" is the God of all creation. By "its God" of the text is then meant each nation's specific way, its specific approach to the God of All.

The prophetic teaching has been intensified by a rich rabbinic tradition. We shall quote only a few examples. In the *Tanna debe'Eliyahu Rabba* the following words are put in the mouth of the prophet Elijah: "I call to witness heaven and earth that be one a Jew or a gentile, man or woman, male or female slave, the holy spirits rests upon a person in accordance with his deeds." [55] Another characteristic midrashic passage is attached to a verse in Psalms in the form of a commentary. The verse maintains: "No good thing will He withhold from them that walk uprightly (literally: in wholeheartedness). [56] The explanation of the rabbis runs as follows:

> He that walks "in wholeheartedness" is Abraham. To him were the words addressed: "Walk before Me and be wholehearted." But if the verse meant only Abraham, why the plural form, *"Them* that walk in wholeheartedness"? This teaches us that as in the case of Abraham, who, because he walked in wholeheartedness before the Holy One blessed be He, God became his shield, so it happens to everyone who walks before Him in wholeheartedness, God becomes his shield. And how does the text continue? Abraham is not mentioned here, but "man"; it applies to any man.[57]

It was the opinion of the rabbis that one did not need to be a Jew in order to walk before God "in wholeheartedness." Thus they could also declare: "The righteous of all the nations have a share in the world to come." [58] Judaism is the Jewish way; others may have different ways. Ultimately decisive is not the creed, but the deed. This is the essence of Jewish universalism. [59] Not so with Christianity. It maintains that no one may get to the Father except by way of the Son. It has to say it, since otherwise the sacrifice was unnecessary. It has to say it because on account of original sin no human being can be saved unless by the supernatural intervention of the divine sacrifice. Judaism, on the other hand, rejects the idea of the corruption of human nature. Man is responsible for his actions; though he needs divine assistance, he has to seek the way himself and may find it, any man. The rabbis believed that because of this to impose Judaism on a non-Jew would be the imposition of an unnecessary burden. The universalism of Christianity is totalitarian, that of Judaism democratic. Christianity has to conquer the world; Judaism is available to all.

In a certain sense it is possible to say that Judaism is a community of blood, but not to the exclusion of any alien blood. Because of the nature of the faith, any new blood that enters is absorbed into the community of the people. This is due to the specific nature of Judaism. Judaism is not a religion in the normally accepted sense of the term; it is the life of a people lived in the awareness that all life is forever lived in the sight of God. What is more, it is not the people that conceived Judaism, but Judaism that formed the people. Because the Torah comprehends the entire life of man, because the law deals with every aspect of human existence, it is people-founding. The structuring of the whole of life, personal and communal, economic, civic, social and political, that the Torah prescribes, the all-comprehensive deed which is required, can ideally be achieved only by a community that is in control of its daily life. Such a community in history thus far has to be not a church or a synagogue, but a nation. Even the mere striving by men for the realization of life in accordance with the Torah would lead to their becoming a biological entity, a blood community, a blood community formed by the spirit of man. Saadia Gaon expressed it saying: Our people is a people only because of the Torah. [60]

Only because of this is it true when Rosenzweig asserts that the more the Jew identifies himself with the natural inheritance of his birth, the more Jewish he becomes. This, however, is not due to "the blood community," but to the fact that the blood community has its foundation in the spirit community of Judaism. It is rather different with Christianity. Its main concern is not with man's all-comprehensive deed, but with the right creed, the creed that saves. Christianity is essentially individualistic. The creed is a personal affair between the individual soul and its God. What really matters is the salvation of the individual. Thus, the community formed by the faith is of a necessity a church, a collection of individual souls. Christianity never created a nation. Notwithstanding the rhetoric to the contrary, in all history there has never been a Christian nation. Apart from the Jews no other nation—as a nation—ever concluded a covenant with God, which is the true meaning of the chosen people. The Jewish people is not a blood-community, but—as my teacher the late Rabbi Yeḥiel Yaacob Weinberg called it in an essay—a faith nation. The juxtaposition between Judaism and Christianity is not valid. Christianity is a religion, Judaism is not. The juxtaposition should be between the secular nations and the faith nation.

III.   THE CORRESPONDENCE ON JUDAISM AND CHRISTIANITY

1.   *"Enemies in Space"*

As indicated earlier, Rosenzweig's views on Judaism in *Der Stern* are developed in continuous contradistinction from Christianity. Thus, his philosophy of Judaism is intrinsically linked to his understanding of Christianity. The two faiths complement each other. One might also say that Rosenzweig's philosophy of Judaism as developed in *Der Stern* is the final form of his answer to his cousin, Eugen Rosenstock, a convert to Christianity, with whom he had been engaged in an intense dialogical correspondence on the subject in 1916.[61] In a sense, in *Der Stern* Rosenzweig was still answering Rosenstock.

Rosenstock was hitting Rosenzweig with all the tactless zeal with which Jews have been familiar through the centuries and that has remained to this day so typical of the renegade Jew. The trouble with the Jews is that they won't listen to the truth. Thus, the Christians alone know the truth and, of course, nothing proves it better than the fact that they say so themselves. The Jews are stubborn and proud. They are a tribal blood union, who do not care for the growth of men to a united universe under the scepter of Christianity and, as a chosen people, know nothing of a final union of all the children of the Father. They do have some faith that one day all the peoples will assemble in God's house in Jerusalem and yet they crucify *daily* the one who comes to make good this promise. In truth the Jews are the image of Lucifer on earth. The Jews don't die for any country, for any cause. They really have nothing, that is why they are so proud of what they had. They can only participate in the life of others. They live on credit, always borrowing from others everything that makes life worth living.[62] There is nothing missing here of the threadbare arguments from the medieval armory of the Christian "theological" contempt and hatred of the Jew.

Rosenstock did add something rather original to the medieval equipment. He compares the sacrifice of Abraham to that of Jesus. Abraham sacrifices only what he has, only his son; but Jesus, what he is. One wonders how crude a renegade Jew may become once he embraces the truth of Christianity. He treats a child as a piece of property. Abraham gave up something that he owned, but not his own life. As a Jew one cannot help wondering what kind of a perversion must it be that allows a human being to maintain that it is easier for a man to kill his only child with his own hand than to surrender his own life! Ultimately, the argument reveals an ethical insensitivity that is, from the point of view of Judaism, typically heathen, i.e., that it is easier to kill someone else then to die oneself.

A Jew once came before the Talmudic teacher Raba: "Rabbi! The ruler of the city has commanded me to kill someone. If not, I shall be killed. What shall I do?" He was given the answer: "Who told you that your blood is redder than his!"[63] According to Judaism, the saving of a life supersedes all the other commandments of the Torah, except that one must rather die than save oneself by taking another life. To maintain that it was easier for Abraham to sacrifice another human being—even if it were not his only son—than to give his own life, is akin to the arguments of the Nazi murderers of Jews who defended themselves by saying that had they not killed, they would have been killed. And who can say that there was no causal nexus between the Germanic Christianity of a Rosenstock and the way some of the more decent Nazi murderers evaluated their own lives as compared with the lives of others?

Not unrelated to Rosenstock's evaluation of Abraham's sacrifice is the statement that the Jew lives by "a ghostly reflection of all real life, which is unthinkable without sacrificial death and nearness of the abyss."[64] One wonders what sacrificial death and nearness of abyss he was

speaking about? When was the last time that Christians had to bear witness—and did bear witness—to their faith with their lives and what did
they know as Christians of the nearness of the abyss! How largely looms
the figure of the author of the "Attack upon Christendom" besides the
sickness of the renegade Jew! How glorious a Kierkegaard's struggle to
penetrate the drama of faith revealed in the sacrifice of Isaac as compared with the vulgarity of a Rosenstock! But to say to Jews that they
live by a ghostly reflection of real life because they live "without sacrificial death" and because they don't know of "the nearness of the abyss"
is no longer vulgarity; it is obscene.

Rosenstock's attack on the Jews is a convincing illustration of how
near the theological enmity of Christianity is to the most vicious forms
of anti-Semitism. Stripped of its theological trappings Rosenstock's
letters to Rosenzweig contain all the familiar accusations: the selfish
Jew, who is only concerned with his possessions; the Jew, the devil; the
Jew, the deicide; the Jew, the parasite; the Jew, the coward; the Jew,
without beauty, without creative ability, without idealism; the Jew, an
uncanny ghostly creature. There is only one short step from Rosenstock's theology in the letters to discrimination, pogroms, massacres.
Indeed, however innocent Rosenstock might be in this respect, for the
less sophisticated, the ultimate logic of his theology leads to the
crematoria.

2.   The Christianizing of Judaism

Our concern is not with Rosenstock. He was neither the first, nor
will he be the last in the line of theological Jew haters. One must, however, listen well in order to understand fully Rosenzweig's own position.
In his essay, *Das Neue Denken,* Rosenzweig writes that the greatest
single influence in writing *Der Stern* was Rosenstock.[65] It would seem
to us that it is especially visible in Rosenzweig's own philosophy of
Judaism. Actually, the vulgarity of Rosenstock's attack on the Jews, so
familiar to the Jew, deserved no answer. Yet, Rosenzweig had to meet
it, because in a sense it was written from the same position that was
reached by Rosenzweig himself in that nightlong discussion in the sum-
mer of 1913 between Rosenstock, Rosenzweig, and another cousin and
convert to Christianity, Rudolf Ehrenberg. It was as the result of that
discussion that Rosenzweig decided to convert to Christianity. In a
letter to Ehrenberg, in which he announced that conversion was no longer

possible for him, he explains that at the close of the discussion he realized that there was no room for Judaism in this world.[66] On the other hand, the gist of Rosenstock's attack on the Jews was that they did not realize that, indeed, there was no room left for them on earth. He was, in other words, calling Rosenzweig back to the position of July 1913.

It would seem to us that to the end Rosenzweig never overcame the position that there was no place for the Jew in the world. He really accepted most of the assumptions of Rosenstock, but he gave them a different significance. It is true that the Jews have no place in this world, that real life belongs to the Christian nations, but that has its valid reason. The Jew leads a life of holiness, and holiness is lifelessness; holiness is not of this world. The Jew lives in eternity, in redemption, and pays for it by forgoing all temporal life. The Jew is beyond time, outside of history. The Jew has nothing? Indeed, it is so; but because he is already beyond everything; everything is "behind him." He is at the goal. The temporal life of the Jew is indeed "a mere ghostly reflection of real life"; the Jew has given up historical reality. He does not die for any country, any cause? That is so. His "holy land" is merely the "land of his longing," to prevent him from finding home anywhere in space and time where he does not belong. Yes, he does not know of "sacrificial death and the threatening abyss"; and rightly so. Being at the goal, his deathlessness must be secured. Therefore, he does not make his survival dependent on anything outside himself. He carries his immortality in his blood. The "precious life juice" must not be wasted on such things as "country and cause." Neither can the blood community go out into the world and toil for the universal reconciliation of all the nations, their union as children of the one Father. It cannot do it for two reasons: It cannot spend the energies of its redeemed soul on an unredeemed world; having reached God without a divine mediator incarnate, it could not bring the "message" to the heathens. Christianity had to be called in. The Christian is born a heathen and a "piece" of the heathen remains with him forever; thus, it alone is equipped to bring God to the heathens. As to Abraham's sacrifice, Rosenstock is almost right. That is to say, he is not wrong, because for an Abraham it would have been much easier to give his own life than to sacrifice the life of another human being, and especially his own child. He is wrong, because Abraham sacrificed not only what he was, but everything he could have become through his son.[67] In other words, Abraham's sacrifice was very much like that of

Jesus, only more so. In *Der Stern* this became the contemporaneous existence of all the generations of the Jews, as the result of which, when a grandson and a grandfather look at each other, they behold the first ancestor and the last offspring, which is the secret of the "eternal now," of true immortality.

In *Der Stern* he moves even more strictly within the framework of Rosenstock's categories than in the *Correspondence.* The blood community of the Jews is really an old Christian concept, repeated by Rosenstock. In the letters, Rosenzweig responds to it by saying that the law "must keep open the possibility of proselytism, because of the messianic character of Judaism. According to this the blood relationship is maintained only on account of its symbolic meaning." [68] In *Der Stern* the blood community is not a bit symbolic, just as it was not symbolic for Rosenstock. It is a closed community that protects itself against any admixture of alien blood from without. The "pure wells of the blood" have to be safeguarded. In the *Correspondence,* Rosenzweig declares that Judaism cannot make common cause with the world-conquering fiction of Christian dogma, "because it is a fiction." [69] In *Der Stern,* Christianity is a truth. Rosenstock is right again, Jews don't acknowledge the truth of Christianity, but one cannot really say that that is the trouble with the Jews. There are two truths, the Jewish truth, valid at the goal, in the *eschaton,* in which Jews already live, and a Christian truth in time and history, which is the place of Christianity. Or as one might also say: There is only one truth—with a Jewish half and a Christian half. Keeping the blood community open now for the proselyte? The idea has to be abandoned now. There is a strict division of labor now, time and the work in time belongs to Christianity; Judaism, at the goal, is just waiting for the harvest of history to be garnered into eternity. Judaism is no longer messianic, as it still was in the *Correspondence.* It is already at the goal. Only Christianity is messianic, for it is the nations of history that are in need of redemption.

The two agree with each other even in their attitude to Zionism, though for Rosenzweig Zionism has a different significance. According to Rosenstock Zionism is the end of the "Wandering Jew." But the eternal Jew's return to Zion is not the fulfillment of a messianic promise. How could it be? If it were, it would mean the refutation of everything he believed in and stood for. It is the end, in the literal sense; the end, not as a goal, but the end, the finish; the finish of the people of the

Bible—in other words, the end of the Jew and Judaism.[70] Zionism as an element in the continuity of Jewish history is inconceivable to Rosenstock. And rightly so from his point of view. In essence, it is also Rosenzweig's evaluation of it. He could not see it as a moment within the history of the Jewish people. Where there is no history, there can be no continuity either. A people redeemed is in no need of a return to Zion. The true Jew is, indeed, the wandering Jew, just as Rosenstock also believed. Only Rosenstock could not understand the true significance of that fact. He believed that Jew had to be an eternal wanderer because he was rejected; Rosenzweig maintained that the Jew had to wait and wander along "the banks of the flow of world time" because he was elected. For both of them Zionism was not for real. In the letters, the martyrdom of Israel in a Christian-dominated world still has some significance, but in *Der Stern* "the lifeless life" of eternity has taken such possession of Rosenzweig that only once or twice is there a fleeting reference to the "body of the Jew" which was rather embarrassingly attached to a temporal reality, where there was really no place for it. Rosenzweig never understood what exile meant. Had he understood it, his entire philosophy of Judaism and of Christianity would have been altogether different. It would have allowed him a genuine breakthrough from the prison of his intellectual preconditioning into a more authentic interpretation of Judaism.

The entire philosophy of Judaism in *Der Stern* is anticipated in the letters in three pithy sentences in Latin: *fiat veritas, pereat realitas*—let there be truth and let reality perish; *fiat regnum Dei, pereat mundus*—let there be the kingdom of God and let the world be destroyed; *fiat nomen Dei Unius, pereat homo*—let the name of God be One and let man pass away. This is the essence of what is taught in *Der Stern*. The Jew beholds the truth within himself by turning away from outside reality. That the Kingdom of God is the kingdom of priests, and a holy people is outside of time and history implies a rejection of the world. And the name of God becomes One when He becomes All in All and man and nature return into the divine bosom as it all was before creation.

I dare say that nothing of this is found anywhere either in the sources of Judaism or in Jewish tradition. It all sounds much too Christian. That the Kingdom of God is not of this world is classical Christian dogma. The truth that requires a turning away from reality makes good sense within an outlook that sees all reality as fallen and corrupt because of original sin. And finally, the name of God, One without man and the world, is reached in Christian dogma when Jesus brings mankind back to God and he surrenders his lordship—God thus becoming All in All. This is completely alien to Judaism. The goal of the Jew is to be realized on earth in working for the establishment of the world as God's Kingdom. Truth is meaningful for man only insofar as it finds its place in reality. It is man's responsibility to make room for it in reality. Jeremiah calls God the God of Truth and that is for him the parallel to *Elohim Hayim,*[71] the God of Life; the true God is the living God. And the living God is the God who is present, however mysteriously, in the life of man and the history of the nations. Where the psalmist exclaims: "Thou has redeemed me O Eternal, Thou God of Truth,"[72] he does not mean: redeemed from all this-worldly desires which enable him to exist, as the Jew on *Yom Kippur* does according to Rosenzweig, as if beyond the grave. What he means is clearly indicated in the context: God is his "rock and fortress"; God "leads and guides" him and brings him out of "the net that they have hidden" for him. In the Bible of the Jew, "God is true" means that man may rely on him, trust in him in time and history.[73]

The Psalmist also says: "Truth springeth out of the earth." [74] The rabbis declared truth to be one of the three pillars of the world maintaining it together with justice and peace.[75] All three must be real in time. A truth which is not to be realized in this world is no concern of man. A Jew will give his life for the truth of God so that it may grow from the earth. Finally, in Jewish tradition, when God's name will be one, he will not be All in All. Man will be man; nations will be nations; and nature will be nature—as God intended them to be. On that day, when God will be One and His name one, he "shall be On that day, when God will be One and His name one, he "shall be King over all the earth." There will be earth, and there will be man; and "all the land shall be turned as the Arabah . . . and man shall dwell therein, and there shall be no more extermination, but Jerusalem shall dwell safely." [76] The purpose of God with man and the world has to be fulfilled in time and history. Let there be truth so that reality may not be absurd; let there be the Kingdom of God on earth "speedily in our days"; let God be One and His name one, so that—to quote from the great prayer of *Rosh Hashanah* and *Yom Kippur*—"men may become one brotherhood to do thy will with a perfect heart."

3. The Failure of Success

Rosenzweig's other-worldly categories fit Christianity far better than Judaism. At least, in its basic dogmas Christianity is other-worldly. Accordingly, the Kingdom of God is not of this world. This other-worldly Kingdom was "at hand" and it was to be revealed in the Second Coming, which, according to the faith, was to have been immediate. In its original intention Christianity was a move out of history, against history. More recent Christian theologians put it succinctly. Mircea Eliade formulated it as follows:

. . . it must not be lost sight of that Christianity entered history in order to abolish it: the greatest hope of the Christian is the second coming of Christ, which is to put an end to all history.[77]

Rudolf Bultmann, quoting another author, writes:

To the Christian the advent of Christ was not an event in that temporal process which we mean by history today. It was an event in the history of salvation, in the realm of eternity, an eschatological moment in which rather this profane history of the world came to an end. And in an analogous way, history comes to an end in the religious experience of any Christian who is in Christ.[78]

Within Christianity, the Kingdom and history are antithetical. All history is Fall and all cultures fall into history. At the very heart of Christianity there is a split between civilization and faith, between culture and redemption, between the city of man and the city of God.[79]

How then did Christianity enter history? The problem arose from what is known as the "delayed *perousia*". Jesus came and went, but the promise of an other-worldly redemption remained unrealized. This was rather embarrassing. Some compromise had to be reached between the utopian other-worldly Kingdom and the actual condition of human existence. Christianity entered history with a vengeance. The compromise has been continuous, an ongoing surrender of the original other-worldliness in order to gain the world. Christianity became the Church, and the Church, a conqueror. Thus, the world was given Christian culture, Christian civilization, and Christian history. Thanks to the sword of Constantine, Christianity became a this-worldly power of the first magnitude. According to the rhetoric, it was the Word turned Flesh that was victorious. It would indeed have been important to see what the Word could have accomplished in history without the sword. Christianity became extremely successful in this world; and the more it compromised its original conscience the more successful it became. On the scene of world history, Christianity became the rhetoric of humility, mercy, love, universal brotherhood, redemption; in fact, it was intolerance, violence, persecution, massacre, war—the most distinguishing features of Western civilization. The Jew was not impressed; nor was he fooled. No one knew better than he, how unredeemed the world was. Redemption, indeed!

Is the Jew outside of history? Yes, outside the history of success. The Jew preferred faithfulness to success. There are really two histories: power history and faith history. The Church, which has been triumphant with the sword of Constantine, decided to move into power history; the Jew lives in faith history. For the superficial eye, it is far less glorious there, far less majestic. But it is surely cleaner. The Jew will not accept Rosenzweig's neat division of labor between Judaism and Christianity. As long as the world is not at the goal, the Jew is not at the goal either. The Jew toils in history, works in history, no less than the Christian. But the Jew works in the faith dimension of history; Christianity, in its power dimension. The methods are different and one also judges failure and success differently. In the letter to Rudolph Ehrenberg, to which we have referred earlier, Rosenzweig wrote that when he agreed to convert to Christianity he realized the staff of Judaism was a broken one. He envied Christianity its ruler staff. The two staves are of course nothing but a self-flattering Christian fairy tale. The staff of Judaism is not broken, simply because Judaism never held the ruler staff in its hand. In the realm of faith history there are no rulers. Judaism never had the ambition to conquer. Judging history by Germanic-Christian standards Rosenzweig believed that there was no place for the Jew in *the* world. He was right and yet not right. There is indeed no place for the Jew in *that* world. Yet, he lives in the world. The true significance of his life is that he makes a stand in time and history and is still there without might and without power, the only proponent of the feasibility of life in the faith dimension of history, which may be the mysterious point that God wishes to make through the Jew at this juncture of man's pilgrimage on earth.

Rosenzweig relates Judaism and Christianity to each other. The truth is that while Christianity cannot do without relating itself to Judaism and without defining itself in contradistinction from Judaism, Judaism as such has no relationship to Christianity. Unlike Rosenzweig, who, because of specific circumstances, was returning from the very edge of Christianity, a Jew does not have to affirm his identity by continuous discussion with Christianity. Christianity is irrelevant for being a Jew. Just as Rosenzweig was deeply influenced by Rosenstock in his interpretation of Judaism, so, it would appear, was Rosenstock influenced by Rosenzweig in his final view of Christianity. This one gathers convincingly from the essay on the *Correspondence* by Alexander Altmann.[80] Rosenstock, as if summing up Rosenzweig's point of view, came to see the Gentiles as "God's alpha," the Jews as "God's omega"—"the end of human history before its actual end," Christianity "the yoke that joins alpha and omega." Or, using Rosenzweig's terminology—the rays sent out from the central fire (i.e., Judaism). In a poem Rosenstock said of the mutuality of this relationship: "Enemies in space, brethren in time." This, of course, is the Christian view. It has the added advantage that it makes the inhumanity and barbarism inflicted by Christianity on Judaism quasi reasonable and justifiable. A Jew will not accept it. Just because the Jew does not have to define himself in contradistinction to Christianity, he has no enmity either towards Christianity or Christians. If he hates, he will hate oppressors, persecutors, and murderers, because they oppress, persecute, and murder, but not because they are Christians. "Brethren in time" true, and not only in time, whatever that may mean, but in time as well as in space; and not only Jews and Christians, but all men, brethren in the sight of God, brethren in truth—but alas! not yet in history.

Franz Rosenzweig: we can only think of him with love and stand before his memory in awe—the great Jewish soul who found home to brighten the sky over German Jewry as the lights were about to go out. And yet, intellectually he was unable to liberate himself from the net of an arrogant civilization that claimed to be the world.

What was started in 333 C.E. with the sword of Constantine the Great was completed in the concentration camps and crematoria. At Auschwitz, Christian history and civilization as we have known them came to an end—long before omega, long before the *eschaton*. And in Zion and Jerusalem a new dawn is mysteriously breaking for the land, the language, and the law, that were lifelessly holy for Rosenzweig.

CHAPTER 3

Martin Buber's Religion of the Dialogue

1.

I.   THE TEACHING OF BUBER

I and Thou

It is mainly due to the writings of Martin Buber that the term, I-and-Thou, has become a household phrase in modern philosophical and religious thought. It may prove profitable to develop the important ideas implied in this term by starting with Buber's description of two aspects of the human ego, which he calls its two poles. The ego may appear as individual being (*Eigenwesen*) and as person. It all depends on how a man relates to the rest of the world. As individual being, man insists on his specific identity as something apart from the world. In this position he looks upon all reality outside himself as a thing to be mastered, to be owned and used. Man becomes a person when he is aware of a personal presence in the world, when he discovers the personal aspect of reality, when he goes out and "meets a meeter" and enters into a relation of reciprocity with him.[1]

The distinction is, of course, most obvious in the manner in which a man relates to his fellow. As individual being, he will treat other people as "things" to be used and controlled. As a person, he will know them as persons, enter into mutuality with them, and dwell and live in the relation. However, the two attitudes may be adopted to all being. One may, for example, encounter even a tree as one encounters a person and, for a short and quickly passing instant, one may look into the eyes of a house cat as one meets the eyes of an old friend. And so it is with the world of intelligible beings too. The artist does not *have* an idea which he attempts to realize; he is confronted by a presence that "speaks" to

68

him and to whom he must give answer in his work. All reality has its
personal essence which may be met in the immediacy of mutual intercourse.[2]

The two poles of human existence correspond to two aspects of all
reality. The one may be called its thinghood, the other, its personal essence. As individual being, one experiences the world as a thing, as It;
as a person, one encounters all reality as Thou. The two attitudes Buber
designates by the two concepts, I-It and I-Thou. He calls these concepts,
primary words (*Grundworte*), because whenever one says I, one uses it
either as individual being or as a person. The I is always related, either
to an It or to a Thou.[3] It follows, therefore, that the I that a human
being uses does not always mean the same. In its relatedness to an It,
the I stands for a functional manifestation of the ego, as it affirms itself,
observing, experiencing, using, and possessing. On the other hand, the I
of the I-Thou, dwelling as it does in the relation with the personal essence, stands for the wholeness of the human personality. The immediacy
of the encounter engages the human being in its entirety. One says Thou
in the fullness of one's humanity; one never relates to an It in such a
manner. Yet, the partial engagement of the ego in the I-It context may
appear more active than the totality of human engagement in the encounter with a Thou. The elimination of all specific and partial functions
that occurs in the spontaneity of the meeting between person and person
may appear as a form of inactivity. In truth, however, in the I-Thou
relation man becomes effective in the wholeness of his being. Thus, the
I of I-It is much less real than the I in I-Thou.

One might also say that as individual being man uses the world, he
manipulates it. Reality submits to him. However, as a manipulator, he
is outside, he cannot participate. Only as a person is he present; only so
does he meet and associate. As the I of I-Thou, he participates. The non-
participating I is unreal. Reality in its essence must be encountered. It
reveals its true nature in participation. To be real means to participate.
To say all this means also that the world confronted as It is the world
of separation and estrangement. Only when encountered as personal
presence may the universe become cosmos and home for man.[4]

A significant difference between the two manifestations of being is to
be seen in the fact that only as a thing does the world have solidity and
tangible durability. Only as It can the world be circumscribed by the
coordinates of time and space. Being, however, as a personal presence,

as Thou that meets us, does not endure in time, nor can it be placed in space beside another presence. The relation between I and Thou is only possible in the spontaneity of a timeless *now*. A meeting remembered is no longer the living relation. In memory, one's former Thou has already become an It. In each encounter one meets only one presence at a time. The moment the I becomes aware of a new presence, one has brought an encounter to a close and entered into a new relation. The former Thou has now sunk down into the world of thinghood as a past experience. All presence exists for me in the actuality of my encounter with it. Without such actuality all reality turns for me into thinghood. All relations with one's Thou are exclusive. The It borders on other Its; the Thou does not border. However, being that cannot be caught in the net of the time-space coordinates lacks solidity. Thus, the I-Thou aspect of reality is fleeting. One encounters one's Thou unexpectedly and loses it again without warning. A Thou may reveal himself to one in a flash and will fade away again with equal speed. It is man's melancholy lot that every Thou must turn for him into an It most of the time of his life.

Only the It-world, because of its solidity, may become the ordered world. As such, it can be the object of common discourse between people. Concerning the ordered world of the It, they may reach any measure of agreement. The world of the Thou, with its sudden appearances and equally unexpected withdrawal, can never become an object of agreement or disagreement between people. One is always alone with one's Thou. Yet, only in the encounter with a presence is it possible for man to catch a glimpse of a world order. Of course, one cannot live in the relation with the Thou; one must endure in the world of the It. But he who knows not of the encounter with the Thou, cannot be the I as a person either; he cannot be truly human. No man is only individual being; no man is only person. The question, however, is, which is the dominant element in a man. According to the dominance of each of the poles, some people will be persons, as other will be individual beings.[5]

Pure Relation

The most intensive form of the I-Thou is established when man succeeds in encountering being in its full independence, the absolute as a person. It is the authentic realm of religion. The absolute in its personal manifestations is the only possible knowledge of God. One cannot derive God from something else whose existence is explained by the assumption of a first cause, which is then called God. One cannot deduce him from nature as its originator or from history as its ruler. God is the nearest to us. He is the one who confronts us most immediately as eternal Presence.[6] The living contact with the absolute as the eternal Presence is called the pure relation. All other meetings with a Thou are only "portals" by which one is led to the presence of the eternal Thou. It is not possible to enter into the pure relation except by way of the portals. One cannot treat all the world as It, subject to the egocentricity of the whims and wishes of the individual being, and at the same time know God as a person knows his Thou. All the I-Thou relations are so many "stations" on the road to the ultimate encounter.[7]

In order to understand the specific nature of the pure relation, we must bear in mind the distinction between it and all other I-Thou situations. As we saw earlier in our analysis, the I-Thou relation is not subject to the time-space coordinates. A Thou does not border; one is alone with one's Thou. This entails that I-Thou is exclusive. Buber hastens to add that this does not mean that all else is disregarded, but that it appears in the light of the actuality of the relation. Everything outside the relation derives its significance for the I from inside it. Ultimately, however, especially—as it always happens—when my Thou has turned into an It for me, the exclusiveness of the relation becomes an injustice done to the world. The exclusiveness, so vital for the relation, degenerates into the exclusion of all. It is not so, however, in the case of the pure relation. Like all I-Thou encounters, it, too, is exclusive. He who enters into the absolute relation is no longer concerned with singulars, either as things or as persons. But his Thou is "the essense of all essences," the Presence in all presences, that which constitutes the Thou in every individual Thou. Encountering him, one encounters the All Presence. All relations are comprehended in the pure relation. In it, exclusiveness and inclusiveness are one. "For the step into pure relation is not to disregard everything, but to see everything in the Thou, not to renounce the world, but to establish it on its true basis. To look away from the world, or to stare at it, does not help man to reach God; but he who sees the world in Him stands in His presence . . . to eliminate or leave behind nothing at all, to include the whole world in the Thou, to give the world its due and its truth, to include nothing beside God but everything in Him—this is full and complete relation."[8]

Another specific feature of the pure relation is to be seen in the fact that the all-inclusive Presence of the eternal Thou provides the continuity of the personal quality of all reality. At first, we found solidity only in the connectedness of the It-world in time and space. The I-Thou encounters between finite beings could not properly be considered forming a cosmos. They were separated from each other by the massive dimensions of the It-world into which to dissolve was the fate of every Thou. The pure relation, however, becomes the center of a universe of relation, in which all relations meet and from which they expand. Because of it, there is a continuum in the world of Thou too. Thanks to it, the isolated instances of the encounters link up to form the universal reality of association and participation. Without the pure relation, the power of the It might be overwhelming and man would be doomed to estrangement and to the loss of reality, for he would lose the ability to encounter and to participate.[9]

Dialogue and Revelation

It is, of course, necessary to probe further into the nature of the pure relation. Who is man's partner in the relation? We have seen that Buber calls him the eternal Thou, the Being of all beings, the Presence in all presences, the "soul of my soul," or God. What, then, does he mean by God? One cannot call him the Absolute. This would be describing him in terms of an idea, as an It. Nor can the absolute be defined in intelligible terms. Is he then, person? But person is exclusive and God is all-inclusive. The truth can be expressed only paradoxically by calling him, the absolute Person. This is no description or definition; the paradox renders the term unintelligible. One knows him from the relation. In the encounter, the all-embracing Presence addresses man; in the relation, man may address him as Thou. "It is . . . impossible to point out the true absolute as 'the absolute' in itself, i.e., in intelligible terms. The true absolute can be pointed out only as God; i.e., though to our thinking it is the absolute, it is so only in term of a personality, or, paradoxically expressed in terms of the absolute personality who addresses us . . ."[10] And we may add, who addresses us and whom we may reach by addressing him. God is the Unknowable, the eternal mystery, and yet our "true vis-à-vis," who makes his Presence known to us by his address.

There is, however, one more question still to be asked: how does He address man? How does He reveal his presence to man? How does the relation come about? Buber does not consider the address by which the absolute Person makes himself known to man a supernatural event. Nothing really happens beside, or in addition to, the normal course of man's everyday life. God appears to man "in infinite manifestations in the infinite variety of things and events." They speak for God. Man recognizes the world, his own existence, the "concrete situation" into which he is placed, as something given to him, something to which he has been appointed. Thus, in the "concrete situation" of his own life, he encounters the Giver. Through everything that he experiences he hears the voice of the Giver calling him to his responsibility and to his appointed task. All the world is God's sign language addressed to man. This is the theme that, in innumerable variations, runs through all the writings of Buber. It all begins with the "fear of God," which Buber defines in the following terms: "It comes when our existence between birth and death becomes incomprehensible and uncanny, when all security is shattered through the mystery. . . . It is the essential mystery, the inscrutableness of which belongs to its very nature; it is the unknowable. Through this dark gate . . . the believing man steps forth into the everyday which is henceforth hallowed as the place in which he has to live with the mystery. He steps forth directed and assigned to the concrete, contextual situations of his existence. That he henceforth accepts the situation as given him by the Giver is what Biblical religion calls the 'fear of God.' " Such is the fear of God, the beginning. The encounter with God takes place "in God's very giving and in his, man's, receiving of the concrete situation." This is possible because out of the concrete situation man hears himself addressed. "The forms in which the mystery approaches us are nothing but our personal experiences." It approaches us by means of the voice that speaks to us "in the guise of everything that happens, in the guise of all world events. . . ." These thoughts are most markedly summarized in a passage that one finds in the essay *The Faith of Judaism,* where Buber says: "The world is given to the human beings who perceive it, and the life of man is itself a giving and a receiving. The events that occur to human beings are the great and small, untranslatable but unmistakable signs of their being addressed; what they do and fail to do can be an answer or a failure to answer. . . ."[11]

The interpretation of the encounter with "the Lord of the one voice" establishes the relation as a dialogical situation. The whole of human life and all human history is thus seen as a dialogue between God and man, "a dialogue in which man is a true, legitimate partner, who is entitled and empowered to speak his own independent word out of his own being." The dialogue, of course, is not one of words, but of action. God speaks to man through everything that befalls his creature and man answers by everything he does or fails to do in response. Expressing it in Buber's own words: "In this dialogue God speaks to every man through the life which he gives him again and again. Therefore man can only answer God with the whole of life—with the way in which he lives this given life." [12] The encounter is a dialogical one; the encounter and the dialogue are one.

We can know God only because he addresses man; the relation is his revelation. Needless to say, the relation does not make the mystery intelligible. As we have heard, the Unknown is the essentially unknowable. Revelation consists in what is revealed by the Voice, in what is made known in the address. Revelation and the relation thus become identical and are indeed described in identical terms. Revelation begins when God gives man his "appointed work," which is of course the concrete situation revealed to man as the one in which he has to prove himself. Thus Buber may say that "revelation is nothing else than the relationship between giving and receiving." Receiving, however, implies acknowledging the concrete situation as "the appointed work," acknowledging the giver and responding to his address. Once again we find ourselves in the dialogical situation. The relation and the dialogue are also the revelation. A number of significant insights follow from this position. Since revelation itself is dialogical, it is only started by God and must be completed by man. "Revelation lasts until the turning creature answers and his answer is accepted by God's redeeming grace." What is revealed to man is thus not God—Buber does not know of God's self-revelation—but man's "appointed work," his responsibility, his freedom and ability to answer. "Revelation does not deal with the mystery of God, but with the life of man. . . ." [13] In revelation God reveals man unto himself. The meaning of revelation emerges from man's response to the divine address "through the engagement of one's own person." Thus, man becomes God's partner even in the unfolding of revelation. [14]

Every encounter is a minor revelation, but essentially it is the same as the major revelations that are claimed to be at the origin of the great religions. [15] Buber, therefore, calls revelation, "the eternal, primal phenomenon, present here and now." He lists its essential features. Most important among them is that the human being does not come out of the supreme encounter the same that he was when he entered it. Something happens to him. He notes an increase in being, something added to him, of whose existence he did not know before and of whose origin he is unable to render a proper account. It should, however, be understood that what is received is not "a content," but a Presence that joins one as a Power and makes itself known, as it were, with a threefold significance. First, there is a sense of complete mutuality and reciprocity of being accepted and standing in relation. Secondly, one gains an assurance of meaningfulness. From now on, nothing can ever be meaningless. The meaning, however, cannot be formulated conceptually. We learn that there is a meaning for us, that the Presence wants something of us, and we have to choose and decide in the spontaneity of every new moment and go and do it. What we then do is what He desires of us. This is the third element in the revelation. The meaning, however, is for me and for me alone in my situation at this moment. It cannot be transmitted as theology or religion, or as generally valid wisdom, to others; nor can the living of the meaning by me be transcribed unto tablets of law, "to be raised above all men's heads. . . . We cannot approach others with what we have received and say 'You must know this, you must do this.' We can only go, and confirm its truth. And this, too, is no 'ought,' but we can, we must." [16]

Freedom and Destiny

The dialogue, the human responsibility to respond to the Voice presupposes freedom. Without freedom man could render no answer; without freedom there can be no relation. How is, then, freedom possible in the midst of a world that is held together by the principle of causation? In solving the problem, Buber elaborates further a distinction between the It-world and the Thou-world. The It-world alone exists within the coordinates of time and space. It alone has the continuum within which the principle of causation may function. The world of the It is indeed one of unfreedom. The man who lives only in it is completely subject to fate. The human being who has encountered the Thou knows of freedom. I and Thou confront each other in freedom. The relation is untinged by causal determinism. The category of the personal is the category of spontaneity. The freedom of one's own being, as well as that of Being, is vouchsafed in the spontaneous reciprocity of the relation. Only he who knows relation and is aware of the presence of the Thou is capable of deciding and responding. Of course, no one can ever live in the I-Thou situation for any length of time. Again and again, he must leave the presence and enter into the It-world. But he who knows about the freedom in the relation is not oppressed by the causality of the It-world. He understands that human life is "a swinging between Thou and It." He realizes that it is the very meaning of human existence to leave the world of Thou again and again and to prove oneself in the realm of It. There, on the threshold of the sanctuary, "the response, the spirit is kindled ever anew; here in the unholy and needy land, the spark has to prove itself." [17]

Obviously, the determinism of the It realm does not cease to be effective even for the man who returns to it with the spark from the encounter with the Thou. However, it becomes transformed. Understanding how this happens leads us to another one of the key thoughts in Buber's philosophy. The man who stood in the presence of the Thou may well forget all causality. He is confronted with innumerable possibilities of action and he knows he has to decide. At the same time, he is circumscribed by the situation in which he finds himself and which is given. He cannot really do as he pleases. Somewhere in his condition there is a deed waiting for him in order to be done by him. Unless he chooses the deed that "means" him, he will not fulfill the meaning of his life. The deed is destined for him, but it will not be done unless he discovers it in responsible choice. When this happens, fate is transformed into human destiny. Man is free to choose what has been destined for him. He may use his freedom in order to learn what it is that the Voice, addressing him in the concrete situation, desires of him. Even if the dominion of causality should not allow him to perform "his deed" as he envisaged it, even in such resistance he will recognize his destiny which does not limit his freedom but completes it. Freedom and destiny embrace each other in order to reveal to man the meaning of his life.

On the strength of this, Buber is critical of the exclusively scientific attitude which attempts to interpret all reality in terms of cause and effect. It finds everywhere lawfulness, the law of life, of history, of society, of culture; everywhere it sees only a gradual process that follows well-established rules. One must either submit to the rules or be eliminated. It is the strictest belief in inescapable fate. Buber calls it "the dogma of the gradual process" and sees in it "man's abdication before the teeming It-world." [18] At the same time, he rejects, for instance, the Kantian solution of the antinomy of freedom and necessity. Only in thought may one relegate necessity to the realm of appearances and freedom to the world of transcendental being. However, the man who stands before God in the reality of his concrete situation knows that, while it is true that he is what he is of necessity it is also true that "it all depends on him." He must live with the paradox; he must accept both truths. In the one life they become one.[19] Thus, blind necessity is transformed into meaningful human destiny. Buber may, therefore, in another context say of human existence that it "means being sent and being commissioned." [20] .

However, has not the essence of religion been described as a sense of complete dependence on God? Is not such absolute dependence, too, a situation of unfreedom? Buber does not agree that either Schleiermacher or Rudolf Otto fully describe the contents of the I-Thou relation with God. This relation is bipolar. Both I and Thou are most real in it. It may well happen that as the result of one's own religious attitude the significance of the I-pole may escape the attention of the reflective memory, yet in truth the experience represents a *"coincidentia-oppositorum."* As Buber says: "Yes; in pure relation you have felt yourself to be simply dependent, as you are able to feel in no other relation— and simply free, too, as in no other time or place: you have felt yourself to be both creaturely and creative." [21] We have to see in this the deepest significance of the dialogue. Man needs God more than anything else, but—says Buber—God, too, needs man for the fulfillment of the very meaning of human existence. Creation happens to us, but we also participate in it, meeting the Creator, lending ourselves to him, helpers and partners. If we understand the pure relation merely as dependence, we eliminate one of its poles. Thus, the relation itself loses its reality.[22]

As is well known, the feeling of absolute dependence often leads to the complete submerging of individuality in the mystical union with the All. As Buber corrects Schleiermacher's definition of the essence of religion, so does he also correct the mystic's description of the essence of the mystical experience. The mystic is mistaken, maintains Buber. The union with the All never really occurs; the two never become one. At times, however, it may happen that the ecstatic experience of the relation is so overwhelming that its two poles almost fade away and the I as well as the Thou may be forgotten. "What the ecstatic man calls union is the enrapturing dynamic of the relation, not a unity arisen in this moment . . . that dissolves the I and the Thou, but the dynamic of relation itself, which can put itself before the bearers as they steadily confront one another, and cover each from the feeling of the other enraptured one." [23] Finally, mysticism in its various forms is rejected by the strength of the sense of selfhood that man carries within himself and that of 'the sense of being," which cannot be included in man's idea of the world. Man knows himself as being present in the world but not identical with it. Man and the world are ultimate entities and cannot be reduced any further. And here Buber adds the significant sentence: "I know nothing of a 'world' and a 'life in the world' that might separate a man from God." What is often thought of as an alienation from God due to involvement with the world is in reality "life with an alienated world of It which experiences and uses. He who truly goes out to meet the world goes out also to God." To go out "truly" to meet the world is of course to live in the dialogical situation, acting on the world in response to the address that reaches a man from the midst of his given situation. [24]

Criticism of Historic Religions

There seems to be no subject under the heavens that, according to Buber, is not amenable to illumination by his magic formula of I-Thou. In his earliest writings he had already applied it to a criticism of historic religions.

Buber is prepared to acknowledge that all religion is revelational. Yet, as is well known, religions do promulgate knowledge and prescribe action and behavior. Revelation in historical religion has content; it knows of Thou-shalt and Thou-shalt-not. This, of course, is not in keeping with Buber's interpretation of revelation. How do the Presence and the Power originally encountered in revelation become contents to be formulated as creed and as religious rites? At first, he answers the question from the point of view of the human psyche. We noted that the encounter with God does not occur in the time-space continuum. The encounters are few and far between and they pass quickly. They have no duration in time; then, man must go out again in the loneliness of his selfhood to meet God. I-Thou has no expansion in space. But man longs for solidity. He hungers for continuity. He wishes to have his God and desires to expand the basis of his meeting with him from I to

We. And so it happens that man's desire for duration in time transforms the living reality of Thou into an object of faith. Instead of going out to the absolute Person ever anew, man rests in his faith in a God-thing. God himself is now turned into It, which one owns, enjoys, and uses for one's security and wellbeing. Similarly, man's need for spatial presentation of his religion reduces God to a mere object of cult and rites, which one may share with a community of believers. Man imagines that thus he may overcome his solitude and stand in relation with the eternal Thou as part of a community.

Both these attitudes are mistakes. The continuity of the relation in time may only be assured by incorporating relation into the whole of man's life in the world. The pure relation is realized as man meets the whole of being with the Thou on his lips, by making every day his contribution to the revelation of the Thou in everything that exists. This way, the reality of participation, the only reality Buber recognizes, gains steadfastness and continuity. "Thus the time of human life is shaped into a fullness of reality, and even though human life neither can nor ought to overcome the connection with It, it is so penetrated with relation that relation wins in it a shining, streaming constancy; the moments of supreme meeting are then no flashes in darkness but the rising moon in a clear, starlit night." [25] In a previous part of our analysis, we heard Buber say that the pure relation restores to the Thou-world the privilege of continuity which originally belongs to the It-world alone. We understand now more clearly how this was meant. It is a continuity that does not really exist, but has to be established by man in partnership with God.

So too, man's longing for constancy in space can be satisfied only by means of the life in the relation itself. A community exists when the radii, which run from every individual I to the eternal Thou in the center, form a circle. The origin of the community is not due to the continuity of the periphery; not the periphery comes first, but the radii, the relation that binds every individual to the living center. Buber applies here his definition of the community which he expresses in another context. According to it, the existence of a community depends on two conditions: that all its members stand in living mutual relation to a living center; that they are associated with each other in living relations of mutuality. The second condition depends on the fulfillment of the first. The community is established by the living mutual relation of all its members; the master builder, however, is the living and effective center.[27] We note that in describing the nature of the specifically religious community no mention is made of the second condition. In every other case, Buber can say that the second condition has its source in the first, but it is not necessarily given with the first.[28] However, when the living center is the eternal Thou, then of course the relation of every I to it is all-inclusive. As we have heard, one cannot treat the world as It and stand in the I-Thou relation to God. Therefore, in the specifically religious community, if every member is related to the living center, he will also be united to every other member in the mutuality of a living and effective relation.

Buber does not leave it at that. There is yet another reason for the transformation of "the Presence and the Power" of revelation into "contents" of historic religion. It is connected with what he calls "the primordial phenomenon of religion" as it becomes manifest in history. There are times when the human spirit matures, be it even suppressed and, as it were, underground, with readiness for the touch by the eternal Presence. When, then, revelation occurs, it takes hold of the whole shining element of the spirit of man in all its expectation and, melting it down, impresses on it an image, a new image of God in the world. This is not due to human strength alone, nor is it simply God's passage through the human substance. It is a mixture of the divine and the human. "He who is sent out in the strength of revelation takes with him . . . an image of God." [29] Yet, not even this image is a contents communicated. It comes about as a result of the dialogical situation. The spirit responds through a beholding which is "formative." Beholding the Presence, we shape the image of God. The image is also called an admixture of Thou and It. As image it is an object of thought, and it may serve as basis of belief and cult. Yet, it is not altogether object; the essence of relation lives on in it. Thus, the image itself may ever again become a presence.

Often, however, man removes the image from God. The image then becomes a mere It, rendering the saying of Thou impossible. When this happens, the Word, born in the original encounter, has disintegrated.[30] Man must ready himself for the new encounter. "The images topple, but the voice is never silenced . . . the voice speaks in the guise of everything that happens, in the guise of all world events; it speaks to the men of all generations, makes demands upon them, and summons them to accept their responsibility. . . ." [31] We cannot hide our feeling that especially here would it have been most advantageous if beauty of language were matched by power of clear thinking. We must confess that this concept of the image of God took us completely by surprise. We were unprepared for it on the basis of the rest of Buber's philosophy. We assume what he means is something like this: At the moment of revelation, man hears himself addressed by the Voice which reaches him from the concrete situation. As he responds to the call, revelation is completed and meaning is revealed in man's engagement to do and to live. Man knows: this, then, is what God wants of me. In the light of this knowledge, he forms the image of God. God, the Unknown and Unknowable, must be loving, since he desires me to act with lovingkindness. He must be just, since he wishes me to be just. Thus the image comes into being. Such an interpretation of the idea will be borne out by what Buber says in another connection: "Our own life is, therefore, the only sphere in which we can point him out, and then only through this life of ours." [32]

Philosophy, Ethics, and the Eclipse of God

The understanding of the full implication of the primary word I-Thou yields for Buber the distinction between philosophy and religion. Philosophy often assumes that religion too is founded on an act of intellectual cognition, which, however, is not as clear as philosophical thinking. This is a mistaken notion. Intellectual cognition treats the divine and the absolute as objects of thought. This is, indeed, typical of philosophy. "Religion, on the other hand, insofar as it speaks of knowledge at all, does not understand it as a noetic relation of a thinking subject to a neutral object of thought, but rather as mutual contact, as the genuinely reciprocal meeting in the fullness of life between one active existence and another." [33] Unlike philosophy, religion does not deal with an object comprehended, but knows only the presence of the Present One. In religious reality one meets God; in philosophy one objectifies him in thought. The man who is incapable of meeting with the divine can only inquire whether God's existence may be proved by derivation; but where there is no actual relation with the eternal Thou, no indirect proof is of much avail.

Objectification in thought means, of course, that philosophy abstracts from the particular and concrete and sees the absolute in universal concepts or ideas. Religion, however, is essentially involvement in the concrete situation, in which man, the particular, meets God, the Absolute. The covenant between the particular and the Absolute, as it is revealed in the relation, is at the core of the meaning of religion. In this I-Thou covenant the whole of the human being is engaged, whereas in philosophy only the faculty of thinking is at work. The objectifying thought knows the world itself as object, whereas in the reality of religion man confronts Being in its personal essence. "I-Thou finds its highest intensity and transfiguration in religious reality, in which unlimited Being becomes, as absolute person, my partner. I-It finds its highest concentration and illumination in philosophical knowledge." [34] Furthermore, the philosophical process of objectification establishes a continuum of intellectual discourse in which all thinking beings may share. The reality of relation with absolute Being, however, cannot be demonstrated. One may only testify to one's own experience and point toward "the hidden realm of existence." [35]

Closely related to a proper evaluation of philosophy is, according to Buber, the question of ethics. The connection is well illustrated by Kant's struggle with the problems, "What is God?" and "Is there a God?" as it is reflected in his unfinished posthumous work. What Kant was after was a God who could establish the absolute quality of the categorical imperative, a God to serve as "the source of all moral obligation." Kant did not succeed because he did not know of the relation to the Absolute. The absolutes of philosophy, objects of human thought, may at best yield us a concept of God as "a moral condition within us" or derive the authority of ethical obligation from the existence of society. Either way, one places the validity of the distinction between good and evil in man. "And yet," says Buber, "I am constitutionally incapable of conceiving of myself as the ultimate source of moral approval or disapproval of myself, as surety for the absoluteness that I, to be sure, do not possess, but nevertheless imply with respect to this yes or no." [36]

What then is required? Buber believes that his concept of I-Thou provides the answer. Only the Absolute may be the source of absolute obligation. But we know the Absolute only in the encounter as "the absolute Person." It follows, then, that the quality of absolute obligation which attends the ethical values depends entirely on man's encounter with the eternal Thou. The man who seeks for an ultimate basis for the distinction between good and evil, as well as for the ethical commitment, cannot derive it from his own soul. "Only out of a personal relation with the Absolute can the absoluteness of the ethical coordinates arise . . . it is the religious which bestows, the ethical which receives." [37]

Buber adds to this thought an interesting reflection on the distinction between Christianity and Judaism. The significance of Israel he discerns in the fact that it stood in "a fundamental relationship" to God as "the people of a covenant." Christianity, on the other hand, replaced the concept of the people by that of the individual. The idea of the "holy people" was given up for that of personal holiness. In Christian individualism the relationship between the ethical and the religious is thus impaired. In Judaism ethics is an inherent function of religion. And since religion is based on the covenant of God with the people, the entire area of public and national life becomes a matter of spiritual concern and ethical engagement. This is the powerful motivation of prophecy in Israel. Behind the prophets of Israel stood the injunction. "You shall become a holy people unto me." Therein lies "the true binding of the ethical to the Absolute." However, when sanctification is not required of a people as a people, "then the peoples accept the new faith not as peoples but as collections of individuals. Even where mass conversions take place, the people as a people remains unbaptized; it does not enter as a people into the new covenant that has been proclaimed." [38] Where the norm, grounded in the encounter with the absolute Person, loses its centrality for the public life, it is made easy for "the secular norm" to gain more and more recognition at the other's expense.[39]

In modern times, the absolute quality of ethical values has come under considerable criticism. Understandably, such criticism is not to be separated from the modern crisis of religion—a crisis due to a philosophical movement that has abolished the Absolute as a personal reality confronting man. One may see the prelude to the present phase in the thoughts of Hobbes; its beginning, in Feuerbach; by way of Marx and Nietzsche the movement has reached our own days. Its present protagonists are Heidegger and Sartre, on the one hand, and the psychologist, Jung, on the other. What they have in common is that each, in his own way, has shifted the concept of God from the realm of objective being to "the immanence of subjectivity." [40] Thus, "the silence of God" means the relativity of all ethical obligation and the resurrection of the old adage of Protagoras that man is the measure of all things. It may mean, as Heidegger puts it, the "elimination of the self-subsisting supersensual world by man";[40] or, as Sartre believes, that God is "the Other," who just looks on but does not communicate and thus becomes a matter of indifference to man. A similar approach is adopted by Jung in the realm of psychology. According to Buber, the result is "a religion of pure psychic immanence." [41] In all these modern attempts at ontological and psychological interpretation there is a turning away from "the God believed in by the religious, who is to be sure present to the soul, who reveals Himself to it, communicates with it, but remains transcendent to it in His being." [41] The crisis in religion and ethics is due to the fact that man is determined "to interpret encounters with Him as self-encounters." As a result, "man's very structure is destroyed. This is the portent of the present hour." [42]

What of the future, what of tomorrow? Nietzsche was wrong in speaking of the "death" of God. The eternal Thou lives on "behind the wall of darkness." It is modern man who is no longer able to attain to an I-Thou relation with Him. For this reason, Buber speaks of "the eclipse of God as the character of the historic hour through which the world is passing." [43] By this metaphor, he expresses the belief that man may indeed "glance" at God, as it were, as he may glance at the sun; and as between the human eye and the sun, so too between the human being and God something may intervene and shut out the vision. This something is recognized in the tremendous increase in the dominion of the I-It relation in our times. "The I of this relation, an I that possesses all, makes all, succeeds with all, this I that is unable to say Thou, unable to meet a being essentially, is the lord of the hour. This selfhood that has become omnipotent, with all the It around it, can naturally acknowledge neither God nor any genuine absolute which manifests itself to men as of non-human origin. It steps in between and shuts off from us the light of heaven." [44] Yet, Buber remains optimistic. The I-Thou relation has been forced underground. Who can tell but that already tomorrow it may break forth with renewed power, relegating the I-It to its rightful place of assisting and serving! Buber is aware of something that "is taking place in the depths . . . tomorrow even it may happen that it will be beckoned to from the heights, across the heads of the earthly archons. The eclipse of the light of God is no extinction; even tomorrow that which has stepped in between may give way." [45]

2.

II.   BUBER'S TESTIMONY

Having concluded the presentation of the main trends in Buber's thought, we cannot but agree with him completely when he says that the validity of his teaching cannot be demonstrated or proven. It is of the very essence of what he tells us about that he can only testify to what he himself has encountered and to what he himself has committed himself. Nevertheless, as he mentions on various occasions, the witness does not speak about himself alone, about a purely subjective experience. He speaks about reality; he testifies to the objective nature of reality, to what being truly is. As we have heard him say, the witness points toward "the hidden realm of existence." Only because of that is his testimony more than a moving private confession. The testimony obviously desires to be teaching for all of us. Buber does not only bear witness, but, as he says, he "calls to witness him to whom he speaks." [46] It is up to us to encounter what he encounters, to meet whom he meets. The question is, therefore, inescapable: Can the testimony be accepted on the strength of its own internal evidence? We believe that on a number of important points the answer will be in the negative. What is at stake is the objective significance of the testimony in its various ramifications, its value for all those to whom Buber wishes to speak.

Subjectivity of Experience

Anyone who wishes to penetrate the nature of pure relation cannot suppress the question: If the I can reach that far, why not continue in the course and bring it to a culmination by submerging the I in the Thou in a mystical union? We have heard Buber answer the question. In essence, he maintained that there was no such thing as mystical union. The mystic misinterprets his experience. The I and the world, the I and the Thou, are final entities, which cannot be reduced any further. The two may never become one. We do not mean to question the objective validity of the answer. What we should like to understand is how Buber can bear witness to it. The mystics of all ages also testify. According to their testimony, I and Thou are further reducible to the undifferentiated All. They experience the union no less convincingly than Buber experiences the relation. When Buber says that the mystical union never really occurs, may it not just be that it never occurred to him? One might perhaps argue that since in the encounter I and Thou are revealed to each other as real and their relation as the essence of reality, they can never again lose their identity. To argue in this manner would be begging the question.

The point may be illustrated by taking another glance at the I-It and the I-Thou relations in the teaching of Buber. Needless to say, Buber never suggested that the It-world did not exist. He never demanded that I-It relations should be dispensed with. On the contrary, he fully realizes that they have their places in the scheme of living, that, indeed, life without them would be impossible. What he maintains is that they must not be the dominant relations; they must subserve the realm of I-Thou, where alone meaning can be found. Obviously, he to whom, for whatever reason, the access to the realm of I-Thou is closed, evaluates the significance of I-It differently. The status of the It-world is validly established for Buber in the light of his acquaintance with the world of Thou. The It does not cease to exist when man encounters the Thou, but the nature of its existence and its significance are now understood differently. May it not be the same as regards I-Thou, should there be a further realm of complete union in the All? No one need doubt the reality of the encounter. Yet, seen through the eyes of one who knows of the mystical union, Buber's evaluation of the encounter may be no less distorted than is, from Buber's point of view, the evaluation of I-It by the man who knows nothing of the pure relation. The problem is all the more serious, since Buber acknowledges that God is unknowable, that his definition of the absolute Person should be understood more like an attribute of personal being among the infinite number of divine attributes.[47] May it not indeed be conceivable that in the encounter with "the absolute Person" one has not yet reached the Ultimate? When he affirms that I and Thou are ultimates, and the relation the very essence of reality, is he still testifying?

Subjectivity of Response and Meaning

However, what of the meaning which unfolds itself dialogically in the relation and is present in the encounter? Is it not ground enough to testify that the relation is indeed not still further reducible? The question only puts the finger on another weak spot in the testimony. It is of the very essence of the dialogue that God calls man and that man answers in freedom. He has to give his own answer. The revelation, which takes place in the encounter, we have heard Buber say, has no contents. It reveals a Presence that assures meaning. The meaning, however, is not to be formulated in intelligible terms. It is unraveled by man when he responds to the call in the freedom of his choice and decision. It emerges from the course of action to which man commits himself in response to the divine call. We assume that the very nature of the dialogue excludes the possibility of the communication of a contents, a law and a command, in the revelation. Such a contents would destroy the mutuality of the relation, the dialogical situation itself. But if so, one should like to know, how does one ascertain that one's response to the Voice which speaks from the concrete situation is the valid response; that the meaning which has unfolded itself as a result of man's own participation in the revelation is the authentic one accepted by God? How can one know that one's own participation has not distorted the meaning?

The question touches also on the important issue that we discussed in the preceding section under the heading Freedom and Destiny. There is this deed, hidden somewhere in the concrete situation, waiting to be done by me, meaning me and destined for me. Yet it is up to me to choose it from among the unlimited number of possibilities. I choose, I act and discover meaning. How do I know that I have chosen correctly? We are quite willing to accept Buber's assurance that the meaning "is not 'subjective' in the sense that it originates in my emotion or cerebration, and then is transferred to objective happenings. Rather, it is the meaning I perceive, experience, and hear in reality. The meaning . . . is not an idea which I can formulate independent of my personal life. It is only with my personal life that I am able to catch the meaning . . . for it is a dialogical meaning." [48] But just because it is a dialogical meaning its authenticity is subject to questioning. There is subjective participation in its revelation. True, man's response is invited and demanded; but when it is forthcoming, how is it validated? All that is left, is our own experience of the meaningfulness of the course of life in which we are engaged. Is that sufficient? There may indeed be something objectively present as meaning; but what we finally perceive and experience in the creative freedom of the dialogue, could it not be distorted by our own subjective limitations? Buber does occasionally use such phrases as, man's answer "is accepted by God's redeeming grace." [49] Does he suggest that every time man responds correctly to the challenge, he is applauded by the Lord of the One Voice, speaking to him from his own deed? If only he wrote less movingly and with greater clarity of thought! [50]

Occasionally, one has the feeling that Buber would like to provide more solid foundations to assure the objectivity of the testimony. While he does not admit any contents or definitive teaching in the encounter and revelation, yet he does seem to acknowledge divine commandments addressed to man. Of the Decalogue, for instance, he affirms that "they were uttered by an I and addressed to a Thou. They begin with the I and every one of them addresses the Thou in person. An I 'commands' and a Thou—every Thou who hears this Thou—'is commanded.' " [51] In itself, this sounds like good Orthodox teaching. The phrase, however, *every Thou who hears this Thou,* indicates that the dialogical situation is not given up. As he explains later, like everything else, the Decalogue too is revealed to man dialogically. The human being "in the midst of a personal experience hears and feels himself addressed by the word 'Thou.' 'Thou shalt not take the name of the Lord thy God in vain,' and 'Thou shalt not bear false witness against thy neighbor.' " [52]

We must not overlook the phrase, *in the midst of a personal experience.* It is our old familiar friend, the concrete situation. Buber is still standing on his own ground that there are no contents or commands communicated in revelation. There are divine commandments which emerge dialogically from personal experience. The elucidation of his meaning may be derived from a passage where he declares: ". . . God wants man to fulfill his commands as a human being and with the quality peculiar to human beings. The law is not thrust upon man; it rests deep within him, to waken when the call comes. The word which thundered down from Sinai was echoed by the word that is 'in thy mouth and in thy heart.' Again and again, man tries to evade the two notes that are one chord; he denies his heart and rejects the call." [53] We are given here an interpretation of the revelation at Sinai in terms of the dialogical freedom that has to choose but chooses rightly only if it decides for the deed which is waiting for man. Man is called, but he is called to perceive the law that is implanted within his own heart. He does not *have* to hear and thus the decision is his very own; yet he chooses the law of God, which "means" him. In this way, one might surmise, man's response—and the dialogically emerging meaning—receive validation. The call and the response are two notes of the one chord: The law given is the same as the law chosen. However, does the concept of the divine law, resting deep within man, remove the quandary in which Buber's testimony got entangled? How does man in the dialogue know that this something, deep down within him, is indeed a divine law? How can he know that there is such a thing at all as a divine law embedded in human nature?

Again, we emphasize, we do not question the correctness of the statement as such. That God created man in his image is good Orthodox teaching. We question Buber's testimony. How can he make the statement on the basis of his understanding of the I-Thou relation? Hearing himself addressed, man knows of a Presence. He has to respond. Groping for an answer, he perceives the law within himself. Is he compelled to obey it? This would be the end of the dialogue. Is he free to accept it, as one of the innumerable possibilities open to him? Who is then to say which is the divine law within him and which is not divine? Does he, on the other hand, receive explicit divine confirmation that in his response he has embraced the law of God? That would be a new revelation with a contents and a law unilaterally communicated; it, too, would abolish the dialogical situation. We would have a form of revelation which according to Buber's testimony is not possible. Try as we may, the problem of the authenticity of the response and the meaning remains unresolved.

Absolute Obligation

The question of the validity of the meaning "revealed" bears of course heavily on the question of the relationship between religion and ethics. We have heard Buber maintain that all ethics instituted by men is of necessity relativistic. This, of course, is commonplace. But he went on and, in his search for the ethical absolute, tied ethics to religion. Absolute obligation may originate only in the absolute Person. "Only out of a personal relationship with the Absolute can the absoluteness of the ethical coordinates arise, . . ." Buber proclaimed. Let us now take a closer look at the idea. How can the absoluteness of the ethical coordinates arise out of the dialogical relation? Needless to say, Buber cannot mean that the absoluteness of the obligation is explicitly transmitted. This would introduce contents into the relation; it would mean the end of the dialogue. He makes this clear himself when he protests against the assumption that he was upholding "so-called moral heteronomy or external moral laws in opposition to so-called moral autonomy or self-imposed moral laws." [54] Only when man attempts to derive the quality of moral obligation from his own soul may we speak of autonomy; and only when laws are imposed upon man from without can we speak of heteronomy. In the relation, however, heteronomy, or theonomy, and autonomy are one.

Let us see how Buber explains this. Says he: "Where the Absolute speaks in the reciprocal relationship, there are no longer such alternatives. The whole meaning of reciprocity, indeed, lies in just this, that it does not wish to impose itself but to be freely apprehended. It gives us something to apprehend, but it does not give us the apprehension." Clearly, this is once again "the two notes that are one chord." Should anyone have any doubts about it, let him read on: "Our act must be entirely our own for that which is to be disclosed to us to be disclosed, even that which must disclose each individual to himself. In the theonomy the divine law seeks for your own, and true revelation reveals to you yourself." [55] It is only now that Buber's idea of revelation may be completed. The divine law, as we have heard him say, "rests deep within man." Thus, it is identical with man's true self. This is the meaning of man having been created in the image of God. [56] When man apprehends this, he apprehends himself; at the same time he has also embraced the law of God. But how are we to understand that reciprocity "gives us something to apprehend?" Once again, it does not give us teaching or commandment. It gives us the opportunity to apprehend, if we are willing to apprehend. In the reciprocity the Voice calls us to responsibility. It is then up to us to "waken" the law implanted within us. It is then we who must apprehend the law within us as divine and it is we who decide that what we have "wakened" is indeed what has been implanted there originally by God.

Can this be the source of the absoluteness in the moral obligation? How mistaken Buber is, one may see clearly in the most succinct formula in which, consistently with all his other opinions on the subject he defines his concept of revelation by saying: ". . . it must be mentioned here for the sake of full clarity that my own belief in revelation, which is not mixed up with any 'Orthodoxy,' does not mean that I believe that finished statements about God were handed down from heaven to earth. Rather it means that human substance is melted by the spiritual fire which visits it, and there now breaks forth from it a word, a statement, which is human in its meaning and form, human conception and human speech, and yet witnesses to Him who stimulated it and His will. We are revealed to ourselves—and cannot express it otherwise than as something revealed." [57] In this clarification by Buber the point we have been arguing becomes manifest. A revelation that reveals dialogically can indeed reveal only man unto himself. The meaning revealed must be human meaning, the speech, human speech; and for the same reason, the obligation perceived in the meaning, human obligation. Dialogical revelation cannot provide the quality of absoluteness in ethical values and moral obligations.

Responsibility

The question into which we have been probing reaches deeper still. It poses not only the problem of absolute obligation, but that of obligation in general. By everything that a man experiences he is being addressed. We know, however, that the address is only a challenge. Beyond that, it contains no guidance, no teaching; it provides no direction. All this is left to human choice and decision. The question that arises is: Assuming that man is so addressed, what is the source of the obligation to answer? Why does he *have* to answer? We cannot maintain that while the address has no contents of teaching, it does carry within itself the command of respond. This would violate man's freedom and partnership in the dialogue. What is more, once the obligation to respond becomes the contents of a revelation, why not some other obligation as well? Whence, then, does Buber derive the responsibility to respond to the challenge? It is true, man may be able to answer, to participate in a dialogue. But how may such an ability of human nature be turned into an obligation? How may one speak here about an *Erzgebot?*[58] Is this original command anything but the voice of human conscience, a sense of responsibility that man discovers within himself? Buber does hint at this possibility in a few places.[59] But for him conscience is not what most people understand by the word. It is something deep down in human nature. It is Meister Eckhart's "spark." Be that as it may, either the obligation to respond comes from the Presence that confronts man, in which case we have contents, command, and teaching in revelation; or the obligation has its source in man's obligating himself in freedom to respond. Since the first alternative is excluded, we are left with an essentially relativistic ethics which Buber otherwise is most anxious to reject.

Nor is Buber's "philosophical anthropology" of much help here. He may rightly affirm that human nature is only revealed in the fulness of human relation with all the world and that without the "dialogical life" man is lacking reality.[60] We shall not get obligation this way. Man may indeed be unreal, if he does not enter into the dialogue with his whole being. But supposing, he—very foolishly, perhaps, and rather unrealistically—prefers being a mere ghost, how can it be shown that he is ethically wrong? That the human being has a certain nature is a statement of fact; by itself, it does not imply the obligation to be human.

Whereas in the main body of Buber's work the concept of man's obligation to respond is taken for granted, there is at least one passage where the author allows himself to draw the conclusions clearly from the logical implications of his position. In *Zwiesprache* Buber says to his "dear opponent": ". . . I beg you to notice that I do not demand. I have no call to that and no authority for it. I try only to say that there is something and to indicate how it is made: I simply record. And how could the life of dialogue be demanded? There is no ordering of dialogue. It is not that you *are* to answer, but that you are *able*." [62] Exactly so! This is the decisive point. Buber cannot show that man is obligated to enter into the dialogical situation. He may well say: Woe unto him if he does not. He will fail to realize himself. He will "carry away a wound that is not to be forgotten." [63] It may be excellent mental hygiene to follow the advice of the doctor, but it does not yield ethical obligation.

Inseparable from these investigations of the validity of the dialogically revealed meaning and truth is the ultimate issue that has its place here, i.e., the question, who is it that addresses man in the dialogue which constitutes the pure relation. It is the question that Buber asks himself in the *Zwiesprache*.[64] Everything that happens to us is a sign by which we are addressed. "Who speaks?" asks Buber. Before giving the answer, he warns us that we must not reply with the traditionally handed down word, "God." We must reply existentially, "out of that decisive hour of personal existence when we had to forget everything we imagined we knew of God, when we dared to keep nothing handed down or learned or self-contrived, no shred of knowledge, and were plunged into the night." How do we know, then, who is the giver of the sign, who it is who addresses us through the daily experiences of our lives? Obviously, from Buber's point of view we can know him only from the experience itself, "from time to time from the signs themselves." The speaker is always the speaker in a single experience, addressing man in a unique, never-again recurring situation. Buber concludes, therefore, correctly that "if we name the speaker of this speech God, then it is always the God of a moment, a moment God." But we did hear Buber speak of the Lord of the One Voice. How does one get from the innumerable moment gods to the One God? In order to explain this, Buber uses what he calls a "gauche" comparison. Because of the importance of the matter, we shall let him speak for himself.

Says he: "When we really understand a poem, all we know of the poet is what we know of him in the poem—no biographical wisdom is of value for the pure understanding of what is to be understood: The I which approaches us is the subject of the single poem. But when we read other poems by the poet in the same true way their subjects combine in all their multiplicity, completing and confirming one another, to form the one polyphony of the person's existence. In such a way, out of the givers of the signs, the speakers of the words in lived life, out of the moment Gods arises for us with a single identity the Lord of the voice, the One." We remain so unconvinced by this interpretation that the only part of it we are able to accept is that the comparison is a very "gauche" one indeed. The many assumptions of the example itself are, from the point of view of literary appreciation, highly questionable. Our concern, however, is mainly with the application to our immediate problem. The assumptions granted, the basic difference betwen the "true and real" understanding of a poem and the signs that reach us through our daily experiences is that a poem does have content, it does reveal a meaning, a teaching, a truth, that it desires to communicate. The "signs," however, only challenge us. They are question marks addressed to us. They reveal no contents, they must give no indication as to what kind of a response is expected of man. The answer must be altogether man's own. How can one identify the speaker in such circumstances? The question, what now little man? may be addressed to us by a devil no less than by a god. How to know, how to distinguish? If there is no indication in the address what the response ought to be, who can tell who the speaker is, whether there is one speaker or whether there are many speakers?

It is quite interesting to note that as Buber sees life as "a sign language" addressed to man by the absolute Person, Karl Jaspers similarly recognizes a code of Transcendence which is incorporated in Existence and which requires deciphering. However, Jaspers is careful to point out that the code of the devil may not be less visible than that of the deity. Buber is, of course, right in saying that such a remark shows how different his position is from the position of Jaspers. What he does not prove is that he makes more sense than Jaspers does. He argues with Jaspers very eloquently, exclaiming: With all due respect to the devil, surely one should not concede him so much power as to enable him not only to disarray but also to distort the code writing of God. Continuing the argument, he also reasons in the following manner: "If the 'code' is to have a uniform meaning, one must predicate an authority that instituted it, and that, desiring that I decipher that part of the code destined for my life, though rendering the task difficult enables me to do so." [65] This is bravely proclaimed, but, unfortunately, rather poorly reasoned. Buber is right, *if* the code is to have a uniform meaning and *if* the one who instituted it does desire that I decipher it. But Buber does not speak hypothetically; he is rhetorically affirming, and thus he begs the question of questions, i.e., "Who speaks?" In that "decisive hour of personal existence," when, according to Buber, man has to forget everything he ever imagined he knew about God, all he is confronted with is a sign and an unknown speaker, a moment god. He perceives a code, but it is entirely up to him to break its secret. He may add moment gods to moment gods, he will still have nothing but moment codes. How will he know whether the codes do have one uniform meaning, whether it is indeed the kind of god speaking whose signals could not be interpreted by assuming a less respectable presence than a deity! In spite of all Buber's eloquence, the question remains unanswered.

The Problem of the Community

The question of the objective significance of the I-Thou relation with God has to be raised in yet another sense. The man who goes out to meet the Presence is a lonely soul. We also know that all I-Thou relations with finite beings are of necessity exclusive. How does the complete absorption of the individual in the pure relation affect his relationships with other people and with the world? Is this another case of the "alone flying to the Alone?" This, as we have seen, is not Buber's view. In our presentation we noted that being exclusive as well as inclusive was one of the specific features of the pure relation. In utter loneliness man turns towards God only to find that his relation to the eternal Thou includes all the other I-Thou relations which he ever entertained, because He is the Presence in all the presences.

This is, of course, a difficult concept. It is yet a new variation on the theme of "the two notes that are one chord." How important the thought is for Buber's teaching, one may judge by the fact that it forms the theme of one of his major tomes, the one entitled: *Die Frage an den Einzelnen*. It is mainly a discussion of the case of Kierkegaard, who dissolved his engagement to Regina Olsen because she was the "object" that stood between him and his love for God. For Kierkegaard, the I-Thou relation to God is exclusive. It is so exclusive that one has to choose between God and the world. Turning to God, one must be "the Single One." One must give up Regina, or whatever else takes her place in one's life; indeed, one must give up the world. Kierkegaard sums up his position in the sentence: "Every one should be chary about having to do with 'the others,' and should essentially speak only with God. . . ." The tragic greatness of Kierkegaard's life found expression in his ceaseless striving to become "the Single One" who speaks essentially only to God. Kierkegaard's course runs counter to Buber's affirmation that the pure relation is exclusive and inclusive in one. As against this Buber maintains that God desires that we come to him "by means of the Reginas he has created and not by renunciation of them." One does not come to God by renouncing creation but by embracing it. He reaffirms the position he has evolved in his *Ich und Du* by maintaining that the "exclusive love is to God, *because he is God,* inclusive love ready to accept and to include all love." The true nature of his argument we discern in the exclamation: ". . . who could suppose in decisive insight that God wants Thou to be truly said only to him, and to all others only an unessential and fundamentally invalid word— that God demands of us to choose between him and his creation?" [66] For once, one is inclined to remind Buber that no less a man than Kierkegaard supposed just that. It is reasonable to assume that he did so "in decisive insight," since he did give up Regina and the world and did choose in fact between God and his creation.

It would seem to us that in this case it is Kierkegaard who testifies and Buber who "theologizes." The whole life of Kierkegaard is testimony that for this great soul the relation to God was exclusive and not inclusive. Buber meets the testimony with arguments, with theories, and with philosophy. Surely, God the creator could not have created the world and yet demanded of man that he renounce it. This, and his other arguments, may or may not be good theology; they do not show how, in fact, an intensively exclusive relation to God may in reality include and preserve man's all other I-Thou relations. Buber believes he can refute Kierkegaard by quoting the latter's saying that "the only means by which God communicates with man is the ethical." To this Buber adds: "But the ethical in its plain truth means to help God by loving his creation in his creatures, by loving it toward him." Assuming this to be correct, he has still failed to show how in the act of loving God's creation in one or the other of his creatures, one may actually remain in the I-Thou relation to God himself at the same time. No doubt, Kierkegaard could not do it.[67]   Neither does Buber succeed anywhere in showing that it can be done.

The concept of an exclusive-inclusive relation is so difficult to grasp that Buber deemed it necessary to elaborate it further in a postscript to his *I and Thou*. How can exclusiveness be one with inclusiveness? In his answer he treats us to a short dissertation about God. He asserts that to the two attributes named by Spinoza we have to add a third one, that of personal being. We have direct knowledge of this from the pure relation. However, God is absolute; therefore, we have to describe him paradoxically as "the absolute Person." With all this we are, of course, familiar from Buber's other writings. Having explained his notion of the absolute Person, he believes he is now in a position to clear up the difficulty of the inclusivness in the pure relation. He continues: "But no limitation can come upon him as the absolute Person, either from us or from our relations with one another; in fact we can dedicate to him not merely our persons but also our relations to one another. The man who turns to him therefore need not turn away from any other I-Thou relation but he properly brings them to him, and lets them be fulfilled 'in the face of God.' "[68]

Let us disregard all hazy rhetoric and see whether what he says makes sense. That the absolute Person cannot be limited is obvious. Therefore, he includes all personal existence. He is "the Being of beings," of trees encountered as "persons," of people met as Thou, of intelligible being confronted as a presence. But are we not now at the brink of tumbling into mystical union with the All? Buber parried this danger in the text to which he supplied the postscript by declaring: "God comprises, but is not the universe. So, too, God comprises, but is not my Self. In view of the inadequacy of any language about this fact, I can say *Thou* in my language as each man can in his, in view of this, *I* and *Thou* live, and dialogue and language, . . . and the Word in eternity." [69]   In other words, God as eternal

Person embraces all personal existence, yet selfhood remains inviolate. This, of course, cannot be proved; but it is so. We know it, says Buber, because of the experience of the encounter with the absolute Person. But does it follow from this that "man who turns to him therefore need not turn away from any other I-Thou relation?" His interpretation of the absolute Person means that within God exclusiveness of personal being and inclusiveness of all personal existence are one. However, it certainly cannot mean that, because God is absolute and personal, therefore, the finite I can encounter every other personal presence in the pure relation with the eternal Thou. It is believable to testify that in the relation with the eternal Thou one has the experience of having encountered "the Being of beings"—and this in itself will have its profound implications for all one's future encounters with finite beings; but it makes little sense to maintain, as Buber does, that confronting the "Being of beings" one also confronts all finite beings in actual I-Thou relations. If these finite beings retain their personal identity without which they cannot enter into I-Thou relations, and, in the integrity of selfhood are so mysteriously comprised in the absolute Person, then the inclusiveness of the pure relation would require, on the part of the I, entering into innumerable I-Thou relations at the same time. In order to accomplish such a feat, the capacity of the finite self for the encounter would have to be akin to the capacity of the absolute Person. If, on the other hand, the selfhood of the finite beings does not remain inviolate but merges into that of the absolute Person, then, while the pure relation may well be described as all-inclusive, it will not "include all other I-Thou relations of this man"; it will absorb and dissolve them.

Related to this problem is the question of the community. How is one to establish a community on the basis of the I-Thou relation? Community between an individual I and an individual Thou, yes! but a community of people, a society of men, how? Buber is well aware of the seriousness of the problem. We have noted that he is of the opinion that the element of exclusiveness in all I-Thou relations may even become an injustice to the rest of the world. We reach such an intimacy between I and Thou that it threatens to undermine all community in the broader sense of the word. Buber tackles the dilemma by declaring that the very essence of community is to be found in the spirit that unites men with each other. The spirit for him is of course not spirituality. "The spirit in its human manifestation is a response of man to his Thou." [70] Community exists only where "the spirit that says Thou" is dominant. [71] But is not this a contradiction? Does not the spirit that says Thou exclude community with all those who are not included in the Thou? Buber meets the problem by laying down two conditions which must prevail in order that "true community" may come into being. We discussed those conditions in our presentation of Buber's criticism of historic religions in the first section of this study. We shall list them here once again. Community arises where people stand in living reciprocal relation to a living center and also stand in such living relation of mutuality to each other. [72] Even though the community thus defined seems to reflect the Hasidic fellowship around the living center of the *tsadik,* we believe that if Buber's conditions are indeed the requirements, then a "true community" never existed on this earth. The second condition is obviously never to be fulfilled. People can never stand together in living mutual relation with one another. It is always in the isolation of I-Thou that they can so stand. One and the same person is, of course, capable of a varied number of such relations. He may be a father, a husband, a son, a disciple. But he can stand only in one living relation of reciprocity at a time. In moments when I-Thou relation is realized between husband and wife, all other I-Thou relations may only be latent. They may be called into actuality, each one by itself and in its own time. But whenever this happens, the newly actualized relation forces the preceding one back into latency. Even if one should admit the latent relations into the category of the living mutual ones, how limited is the human capacity for the I-Thou encounter! Shall we say that the boundaries of the true community are identical with man's subjective capacity for entering into I-Thou situations?

But perhaps the "living center" might help us here. Buber calls it "the architect" of the community. Let us examine whether the architect may help us. If "the living center" is a finite Thou, then it cannot be a living center. No finite Thou can enter into relation with more than one Thou at a time. If the center is a finite person, there can be no "radii" of I-Thou emanating from it to form a periphery. The "common quality of relation to the center" will be missing. We have then to conceive of the living Center as the eternal Thou. This would, of course, limit the true community to the specifically religious community. However, we are thus back to our previous problem of the inclusiveness in the pure relation. While it is true that innumerable "radii" may join innumerable beings to the absolute Person in reciprocal relations, it is not conceivable that the individual being, standing in the pure relation, should at the same time be able to stand in living mutual relations with all other beings. What is more, even if we accepted the possibility of inclusiveness in the pure relation, the true community would last only as long as the pure relation lasts. It would be a momentary incident, without historic reality and without living constancy.

We must consider Buber's attempt to base community on the interplay of living, mutual relations a failure. His inability to deal with the problem comes to full expression in his discussion of economics and of the state. Those are obviously areas of the It-world. Their very existence depends on the effective functioning of the principle of utility. Both have to use and organize people according to their ability to produce and to serve in the context of the innumerable needs of society. It is as He and not as Thou that people must be treated by the state as well as by the economic system. But, says Buber, look where this has led man! Is man still the master of his fate, does he still control, intelligently, the economic order of society! Is it not rather that we have been overwhelmed by the tyranny of the It and delude ourselves imagining that we are the masters?

It is very easy to agree with Buber's social criticism. We are also prepared to follow him when he declares that "the communal life of man can no more than man himself dispense with the world of It" and that, therefore, his will to profit and to be powerful has its proper place and function in life, "as long as they are linked with, and upheld by, his will to enter into relation." However, into how many relations may each of us have to enter, in order to bring the state under "the supremacy of the spirit that says Thou?" [73] That economics and the state "share in life as long as they share in the spirit," that if "they abjure spirit they abjure life" is nobly said. But what next? Let us not forget that by spirit Buber means man's "response to his Thou." How, then, are economics and the state to be expected to respond to their Thou, especially if we bear in mind all the intricacies of the dialogical nature of the response! Buber insists that they can "share in the spirit" if they stand "in living relation with the center." What he has in mind must be the true community, and whatever we have said in criticism of that idea applies here too. On the basis of Buber's teaching, just as the true community is inconceivable, so must also the state and society forever remain unredeemed from the thraldom of the tyranny of the It.

The Problem of Israel

What we have called the problem of the community cannot but have its most serious implications for our understanding of the place that must be rightly alloted to the Jewish people and to Judaism in the context of Buber's teachings. Buber has said a great many fine things about both Israel and the nature of Judaism. In an essay on *Hebrew Humanism,* for instance, he declares: "Israel is not a nation like other nations, no matter how much its representatives have wished it during certain eras. Israel is a people like no other, for it is the only people in the world which, from its earliest beginnings, has been both a nation and a religious community. In this historical hour in which its tribes grew together to form the people, it became the carrier of a revelation. The covenant which the tribes made with one another and through which they became 'Israel' takes the form of a common covenant with the God of Israel." [74] This is said in the best of Orthodox Jewish tradition. Many are the passages in Buber's writings and speeches that manifest the same attitude. The uniqueness of the Jewish people Buber, in common with good Orthodox teaching, sees in the fact that whereas in all history creed and nationhood are separated from each other, in the one instance of Israel they coincide. "Israel receives its decisive religious experience as a people . . ." At the very outset of its history, Israel experienced the Divine as a people. [75]

Let one more quotation show with what passionate fervor Buber believes in the universal significance of the uniqueness of Israel. In the essay, *The Spirit of Israel and the World of Today,* he says: "We men are charged to perfect our own portion of the universe—the human world. There is one nation which once upon a time heard this charge so loudly and clearly that the charge penetrated to the very depth of its soul. That nation accepted the charge, not as an inchoate mass of individuals but as a nation. As a nation it accepted the truth which calls for its fulfillment by the human nation, the human race as a whole. And that is its spirit, the spirit of Israel. The charge is not addressed to isolated individuals but to a nation. For only an entire nation, which comprehends peoples of all kinds, can demonstrate a life of unity and peace, of righteousness and justice to the human race, as a sort of example and beginning. A true humanity, that is, a nation composed of many nations, can only commence with a certain definite and true nation. The hearkening nation was charged to become a true nation." [76]

We are rather inclined to agree with him on all this. At the same time, we cannot forget that Buber often uses the traditional terminology of Judaism but invests it with his own meaning. We confess to a sense of mental discomfort, caused by his use of the term, "a true nation." It reminds us too much of "the true community," which we had occasion to discuss earlier. And when he speaks of the Jewish people as "the carrier of revelation," we felt sure that the phrase should be understood in the light of what Buber means by revelation. So interpreted, what he has in mind will turn out to be quite different from what most of his readers may think he wishes to say. If anyone should think that by "the charge" addressed to the people and accepted by the people, Buber refers to traditional concepts of *Mattan Torah* and *Kabbalat haTorah,* let him turn, for instance, to the *Two Foci of the Jewish Soul*. The God who appears to Israel is encountered in the same manner as in the I-Thou relation. He appears "in infinite manifestations in the infinite variety of things and events." The people is "the carrier of revelation" in the same sense in which the individual person was described to be one. Buber maintains that "the community of Israel experiences history and revelation as one phenomenon, history as revelation and revelation as history." [77] This is, of course, nothing but "the concrete situation," out of which one hears the Voice speak 'in the guise of everything that happens, in the guise of all world events." Only this time, it is the concrete situation of a people. It is not an I that hears, but a We. This then is what Buber means by "the hearkening nation" that was "charged to become a true nation." It was charged in the same way in which the individual is charged in the I-Thou relation to become a true human being, i.e., charged dialogically. The revelation of which the people is a carrier comes about in the same manner in which the I is able to receive revelation. History, which is one and the same phenomenon as revelation, is also called "a dialogue in which man, in which the people, is spoken to." [78] As man, by responding, discovers meaning and "the divine law within him," so too the people becomes "the carrier of revelation" by participating in the revelation in the act of responding.

How then does Buber explain the biblical story of the revelation at Sinai? He cannot accept it as the report of a supernatural event, but as "the verbal trace of a natural event." It is the record of "an event that took place in the world of the senses common to all men and fitted into connections that the senses can perceive. But the assemblage that experienced this event experienced it as revelation vouchsafed to them by God. . . . Experience undergone in this way is not self-delusion on the part of the assemblage; it is what they see, what they recognize and perceive with their reason, for natural events are the carriers of revelation, and revelation occurs when he who witnesses the event and sustains it experiences the revelation it contains. This means that he listens to that which the voice, sounding forth from this event, wishes to communicate to him, its witness, to his constitution, to his life, to his sense of duty." [79]

If one reads this important passage carefully, bearing in mind some of the basic concepts of Buber's teaching, one need not be confused by its Buberian opacity. What is told here is the, by now for us, familiar story of the encounter, the dialogue, and the dialogical revelation. However, the rather surprising aspect of this interpretation of the revelation at Sinai is that what was originally maintained as regards the I-Thou relation is now asserted of a We-Thou relation. The people encountered the eternal Thou in a concrete situation. This happened when at some juncture in their history they, as a people, accepted 'the concrete situation as given to them by a Giver" and thus were able to hear a voice addressing them. The voice was not uttering any explicit statement, or pronouncing any divine truth. It was a wordless Voice, challenging the people to choose and to decide to respond to the demand inherent in the natural event, which in its givenness was carrying a message to them. The message, however, was in code and could only be deciphered dialogically. They "sustained" the event, which, in Buber's terminology means that they endured the challenge of the situation and responded to it. Through their response they broke the code of the sign communication and experienced revelation. In order to complete Buber's idea, we ought to add that in the dialogical response they found "the divine law resting deep within them." And indeed we hear Buber say that "the true spirit of Israel is the divine demand implanted in our hearts." [80]

Let us now consider whether this makes sense within the context of Buber's own testimony about the encounter, the dialogue, and revelation. The Jewish people became Israel as a result of their becoming the carrier of a revelation. The revelation was completed in the dialogue, when they responded to the challenge of the concrete situation. At that moment, we assume they were a true community. They stood in living mutual relation to a living Center and also stood in living mutual relations to each other. Prior to the great event of the founding of Israel, however, they were a nation like any other nation. In other words, from the point of view of a possible encounter with the eternal Thou, they were "an inchoate mass of individuals," who as a people and as a society lived essentially in the It-world. What we should like to know is how such an inchoate mass of individual souls could encounter the Divine as a people. How is it conceivable that millions of human beings should as a people be able to encounter the Presence in the givenness of the concrete situation, in the natural events of their everyday experience? It is difficult enough to imagine that they would all hear the same wordless challenge reaching them from the event as one people; but it is certainly beyond all comprehension that, standing in the full freedom of the dialogical situation, they could as one people render the one response that alone established "the supremacy of the spirit that says Thou." This would seem to us so fantastic that, compared with it, the simple soul's most naive acceptance of supernatural revelation would have to be considered a triumph of sheer rationalism.[81]

Buber is unable to appreciate the fact that the I-Thou relation, as he describes it, is a relation of isolation. It is so charged with subjective insights and commitments, be they however existential, that they cannot serve as a basis of community or constitute "a holy people." Buber is right when he insists that, as far as he is concerned, "just as the meaning itself does not permit itself to be transmitted and made into knowledge generally current and admissible, so confirmation of it cannot be transmitted as a valid Ought; it is not prescribed, it is not specified on any tablet, to be raised above all men's heads. The meaning that has been received can be proved true by each man only in the singleness of his being and the singleness of his life."[82] All this follows indeed, logically from the I-Thou, as Buber understands it. It is of the very essence of Buber's concept of meaning that what is revealed dialogically refers to the single person that encounters the Thou, to his specific situation at a given moment, to be proved true by his personal commitment to a definite course of realization. If this were to apply to a people, then the people would have to be in existence as a single entity already prior to the encounter, in the same way as the I is. As one entity it would have to establish the relation with the Thou, as one entity it would have to respond. In other words, it would have to be a true community already prior to the encounter and the revelation in order to consummate both relation and revelation as the result of which alone—according to Buber—it may *become* a true community. This, of course, is completely fallacious.

On the basis of Buber's premises only individual souls can enter into relation and only individual souls may come out of it with individual meanings for their individual lives. Even if a multitude should encounter the eternal Thou at the same time, each one of them would be alone with *his* Thou at the moment of the encounter. Even if they all should come out of the encounter with meanings commiting each one to the same course of action, each one of them would still stand alone with *his* meaning and *his* life. The "charge" would still be addressed to each one of them individually and not to all of them as to one people. There is no bridge from Buber's I-Thou to a We; nor is there a possibility for a We-Thou, as a result of his interpretation of the encounter.[83]

In our presentation of Buber's teaching, in the paragraph *Philosophy, Ethics and the Eclipse of God,* we referred to Buber's remark on the distinction between Judaism and Christianity. In Christianity, individual piety replaced the concept of the holy people of Judaism. As a result, the public life of the people was withdrawn from direct commitment to faith as well as from its ethical implications. The people as a people remained "unbaptized." Unfortunately, Buber fails to show how a people "as a people" can enter into a covenant with God. While it is correct to say that the concept of the holy people is fundamental to Judaism, Buber's interpretation of the encounter does not allow such a people to arise. It is, perhaps, the most bizarre aspect of Buber's work that although he has been teaching, preaching, and interpreting Judaism through a long and rich life, the basic principles of his teaching renders Judaism inexplicable.

We may now summarize the result of our examination of Buber's testimony. We have found that on the basis of his testimony

a. the relation between I and Thou need not be considered the ultimate form of reality—the possibility of a further reduction through the mystical merging of the I in the All is left open;

b. the meaning, received in dialogical revelation, may have existential significance for the I; it lacks objective validity;

c. the concept of absolute obligation is mistakenly derived from the relation with the absolute Person; nor is there any basis for the concept of obligation in general;

d. there is no way from I-Thou to We or to We-Thou, no bridge between mutuality of relation and the community or society;

e. the singularity of the I-Thou relation may serve as a basis for the personal religion of the individual soul; it cannot account for Judaism and the concept inseparable from it, that of the holy people.

3.

III. THE BIBLICAL ENCOUNTER

Our final conclusion is indeed surprising. From Buber's writings one might easily gain the impression that he is interpreting basic biblical ideas. Is it not the case that biblical religion is not grounded on conceptual meditations on the nature of God, but on the actual confrontation between man and God? Every page of the Bible seems to tell the same story: God addresses man and man answers God. Is this not the relation of mutuality and the dialogical situation?

Creature and Creator

There can be little doubt that the foundation of biblical religion is indeed the encounter between God and man. The God whom Adam and Eve knew was the one who spoke to them in the Garden of Eden. The history of the patriarchs begins with God's call to Abraham. The revelation at Sinai is the manifestation of an actual relation between God and the people. The Prophets' message to Israel normally commences with the words, Thus says the Lord. All of this is true, but is it the I-Thou relation of Buber? In order to understand the nature of the biblical encounter, it is not enough to read the story of the confrontation. One of the encounters in the Bible that comes closest to Buber's I-Thou is Abraham's struggle with God for the preservation of Sodom and Gemorrha. There is meeting there; the Present One is present and so is Abraham, and between the two a genuine dialogue seems to be conducted. There is, however, nothing in the record to inform us of the

How of the encounter. We are not told how the relation comes about and thus we cannot judge the nature of the dialogue. To say, as Buber would have to, that out of some natural event of his everyday experience Abraham heard a voice addressing him and realized that he was challenged to plead the cause of justice and mercy with the Presence seems extremely far-fetched. Moreover, whether such an interpretation was justified or not could hardly be decided on the basis of the record of the story itself.

In order to catch a glimpse of the nature of the biblical encounter, we have to see how the confrontation is described by those who actually experienced it. When God reveals himself at Sinai, the people are overwhelmed with terror and trembling. This need not be attributed to the phenomena of the thunder and the lightning. It is the experience of the actual encounter itself that threatens to crush them. Only part of the revelation is addressed to them directly; the people cannot endure the full power of the divine word. Buber occasionally indicates that the encounter has to be endured. However, what he means by it is something quite different from the biblical significance of the idea. Buber maintains that "to endure the revelation is to endure this moment full of possible decisions, to respond and to be responsible for every moment." [84] Undoubtedly, an entirely different kind of a test is implied in a biblical revelation whose quality is reflected, for instance, in these words of Deuteronomy: "Behold, the Lord our God hath shown us His glory and His greatness, and we have heard His voice out of the midst of the fire; we have seen this day that God doth speak with man, and he liveth. Now, therefore, why should we die? for this great fire will consume us; if we hear the voice of the Lord our God any more, we shall die. . . ." [85] There is no reciprocity here, no mutuality. On the contrary, the Thou is so overwhelming that it threatens to extinguish the reality of the I completely. All other biblical testimonies as to the nature of the experience are of a similar kind. About his encounters with the Divine, Ezekiel reports: "I fell upon my face, and I heard a voice of one that spoke." [86] The context shows that this falling upon the face is due to human weakness. The force of the vision saps the strength of the prophet. He cannot stand up and confront the Divine. Most impressively is the nature of the experience described by Daniel when he says: "So I was left alone and saw this great vision, and there remained no strength in me; for my comeliness was turned in me into corruption, and I retained no strength. Yet I heard the voice of his words; and when I heard the voice of his words, then I was fallen into a deep sleep on my face, with my face toward the ground." [87] Far from entering into a relation of mutuality in the encounter with the Divine, man becomes aware of his utter helplessness in the presence of God.

It is true, the I is nevertheless not extinguished. It is sustained, but by the mercy of God alone. When the Voice orders the prostrate Ezekiel to stand up and listen, he is still unable to move. He has to be brought back into life, as it were. "And spirit entered into me," reports Ezekiel, "when He spoke unto me, and set me upon my feet; and I heard Him that spoke unto me." [88] How movingly is the same experience described by Daniel! After relating the condition of utter helplessness from which he passed into a deep sleep, he continues: "And, behold, a hand touched me, which set me tottering upon my knees and upon the palms of my hands, And he said unto me. . . ." [89] Even as he is upheld by the kindness of God, his condition of creaturely powerlessness has not left him completely. He is still shaky, resting on his knees and, in the position of an animal, supporting himself on the palms of his hands.

The rabbis in the Talmud and Midrash had the right appreciation of the nature of the biblical encounter. We read, for instance, in the Talmud that Rabbi Joshua, the son of Levi, explained: "At the impact of each word at Sinai, their souls left the Israelites. For so we read, 'My soul failed me when he spoke.' [90] But if their souls departed at the first Word, how could they receive the next one?—God brought down on them the dew with which he will quicken the dead and thus revived them. For so does the psalmist declare, 'A bounteous rain didst Thou pour down, O God; when Thine inheritance was weary, Thou didst confirm it.' " [91] According to the Bible, and to biblical tradition, man can indeed not endure the encounter with God. It is true, as Buber says, that in revelation man is revealed to himself; but in exactly the opposite sense in which Buber understands it. It is man's nothingness that is first of all revealed to him in the presence of God. He cannot but realize that, in his own right, he is indeed but "dust and ashes." He is not annihilated, but he is at the brink of nothingness. He is brought back into existence by the love of God. His I is returned to him as a gift of God.

We saw how Buber, in opposition to Schleiermacher, affirmed that in the pure relation one experiences freedom as well as dependence and knows oneself as creature as well as creator. He cannot be speaking of the immediacy of the biblical relation. There is no trace of freedom or creatorship for man in the biblical encounter. The essential experience there is human worthlessness and powerlessness that, nevertheless, is redeemed by the love of God. Man may stand upright in the encounter because he is held up; he may hear because the spirit from God sustains him; he can speak because the dew from God revives him. The situation is not a dialogical one. Man is not a partner of God in the actuality of the I-Thou. He is altogether a creature, if ever there was one. As long as the actuality of the revelation lasts, man has no freedom. He cannot deny his Thou, he cannot disobey him. Only when the encounter has passed, is he dismissed into a measure of selfhood and independence; only then can he deny and disobey.

There are two opposing ways of misunderstanding the nature of the biblical encounter. The one is reflected in Rudolph Otto's work, *Das Heilige;* the other is the one pursued by Buber. Otto, because of his Christological bias, could only perceive the "mysterium tremendum" in the encounter of the Hebrew Bible and stubbornly closed his eyes to the redeeming presence of God that in the same encounter raises man from "dust and ashes" to creaturely dignity. Buber, on the other hand, overemphasizes the reality of the I in the relation, establishing man as a partner of the Thou who responds to God's address in the freedom of selfhood. Contrary to Buber, the biblical encounter is not a dialogical I-Thou relation. It is God's relation to his creature who is established by God and sustained by him. The I in the relation is altogether God's possession. He lives with life lent to him by his Creator; he stands with His strength; he listens and answers sustained by His love. Man is never as unfree as he is in the actuality of the biblical encounter. However, confronted with the nothingness that he is in his own right and experiencing his selfhood as wholly granted, he stands in the light of God and knows no desire for freedom. Contrary to Otto, the encounter is an encounter; it is a relation. God's creature is not just "dust and ashes." In spite of the "mysterium tremendum," he hears the words that Daniel heard, "O Daniel, thou man greatly beloved," and lives. He stands in the relation because he is called into the relation by God.

Rather characteristically Buber remarks: "You know always in your heart that you need God more than anything; but do you know too that God needs you—in the fullness of His eternity needs you? How would man be, how would you be if God did not need him, did not need you? You need God, in order to be—and God needs you, for the very meaning of your life." [92] In other places Buber has softened his proud "God needs you" to "God wants to need man." This is the culminating significance of his statement that man is God's partner, that in the relation man knows himself not only as creature but also as creator. Notwithstanding Buber's repeated assurance that he only testifies but does not demonstrate—the nature of his truth being undemonstrable— this is obviously no testimony. It is the result of speculation. It is reasonable to say that if God did not want man to be, he would not exist. Ergo, God wants man. But to go on from there and conclude, since God wants man He needs him or wants to need him, is poor theology. One thing is certain: that God needs man can never be a religious experience. Man may know in his heart that he "needs God more than anything." He may believe in his mind, as apparently Buber does, that God needs him. But he can never know in his heart that God needs him. The need in the biblical encounter is all man's. It is of the very essence of that encounter that man experiences his entire being as one great need that can only be satisfied by the One who is infinitely needless. The idea that in the pure relation man experiences himself as a creaturely creator needed by God is so foreign to the biblical encounter that it starts one wondering whether Buber's I-Thou is indeed a genuine confrontation between man and his Creator.

Revelation and its Contents

This leads us to the consideration of the important question of the contents of revelation. Buber, as we saw, does not allow any contents in revelation. This of course follows from his interpretation of the relation as reciprocal. Of necessity, in the dialogical freedom of the encounter, meaning and contents can emerge only dialogically as the result of the human response. The revelation of a contents, in the form of teaching or command, would violate the nature of the dialogical situation. A teaching or a law revealed by God would be an imposition from without and an interference with human freedom and responsibility. As a result, we saw how Buber was obliged to solve the problem of ethical heteronomy versus autonomy by the tortuous mental construction of a free human response that reveals man's true nature unto himself as being in conformity with the divine law "resting deep within him." Since the biblical encounter is the very opposite of the dialogical situation, the reasoning of Buber as to the contents of revelation does not apply to it. As we saw earlier, in the biblical pure relation the question of freedom does not arise. It is not that man is denied freedom, but everything he is, he owes. In this knowledge he is wishless, for in it he finds his greatest affirmation. To assert that in this situation the explicit revelation of a divine law would interfere with man's responsibility to choose and to decide in freedom would be as meaningless as it would be dogmatic. In the biblical encounter all meaning is due to divine interference. In it, man left to himself could only discover his nothingness. Within the context of biblical tradition, there is certainly no necessity for excluding the possibility of a contents in revelation. Indeed, the plain meaning of the tradition affirms that God explicitly reveals his Torah and his law. Buber's dialogical revelation is altogether foreign to the spirit of the Bible.

However, beyond the possibility of revelational content, it is not difficult to show that there is a religious need for such a content. Nothing may illustrate the point better than Buber's own predilections. We have found that Buber's I-Thou cannot serve either as the basis of a true community nor as the foundation of a holy people. Buber's dialogical encounter is only conceivable between an individual person and his Thou; and the meaning which is revealed in the individual response is valid only in the single life of the single responding soul. We could find no way from there to a religious community or a holy people. An entirely different picture presents itself to us if we investigate the possibility of a true community from the point of view of the biblical encounter. It is not correct to say of this encounter that "the forms in which the mystery approaches us are nothing but our personal experiences," that God reveals his presence to man "in the variety of things and events" of our everyday experience. It would be presumptuous on our part to attempt to describe how the encounter comes about. One thing, however, seems to be certain: It is not in the natural events that man meets God in the Bible. The biblical encounter is always a supernatural occurrence, "something happening alongside or above the everyday." [94] He who rejects the supernatural no longer stands on biblical grounds. Because biblical revelation is much more than the "Voice addressing man from the midst of his concrete situation," it does not have to be limited to the individual alone. Because it is not "the verbal trace of a natural event," but manifestly and overwhelmingly a super-natural approach of the divine Presence, can it be directed not only to individual souls but also to the full assemblage of an entire people; only because of that may it be a public event and not a mere individual experience. Only an individual may testify to Buber's pure relation; it is a whole people to whom God says, "Ye are my witnesses."

If, as we pointed out, the nature of the biblical encounter does not exclude the possibility of content in revelation, when the encounter occurs between God and a people, all possibility for a dialogically revealed meaning is indeed excluded. It is not conceivable that a people should ever respond in unison as one people in dialogical freedom and should then, as a result of its response, conclude the revelation with one meaning for the entire people. In the encounter with an entire people, meaning must be revealed explicitly, it must be communicated in the act of revelation. If, after the conclusion of the encounter, the meaning should remain with the people as significant for their existence as a people, then they must come out of the encounter with a meaning that has objective validity, that can be formulated as teaching, that can be transmitted or engraved on tablets "to be held above their heads." The encounter itself may indeed be complete without any contents revealed. The assurance of the divine Presence and the ex-perience of God's sustaining mercy, are abundantly satisfying in them-selves. No man may hope for more; no man needs more.

But alas, the actual encounters with the Divine are few and of ex-tremely short duration. What would happen to a people that after the supreme moment of the confrontation with God, would leave the pure relation with only the memory of their awareness of the Presence once experienced? What would happen to it in the dry wastelands of history during the long stretches of divine silence? Not even the memory of the experience could be a national one. After the encounter, in the actual concreteness of the historic situation, the people would no longer stand in any relation to God as a people. Whatever the individuals would do with the memory, it would have only individual significance. At best, we might get an "inchoate mass" of believing individuals, but not a people who, as a people, would be committed to living in the presence of God. Only the objective contents of the revelation, ex-plicitly revealed to the people in the encounter, preserves them as God's people after the encounter. The teaching and the law with which they come out of the encounter is the bond that unites them as a holy people of history. The joint commitment to the law of God alone makes of a people the people of God. Without the teaching and the law, communicated in the encounter, the religious community cannot arise. Buber is right in saying that the individualism of Christian piety leaves the public realm of national life open to intrusion by the secular norm. What he does not seem to see is that this is the direct result of dispensing with the explicit contents of revelation that, after the encounter, confronts man as the law of God. Without the law, there can only be individual piety. Buber's revelation without content places him in the Pauline tradition.

Ethical Obligation and Revelation

In this connection we should like to take up once again the question of the ethical absolute. We have shown earlier that the absoluteness of the ethical obligation cannot be established dialogically. In addition to what has already been said on this account, let it be also noted that Buber labors here under a fundamental misconception as regards the nature of ethical obligation. In his discussion with Sartre, he says: "One can believe in and accept a meaning or value, one can set it as a guiding light over one's life if one has discovered it, not if one has invented it." [95] It would seem that Buber is of the opinion that values or meanings exist by themselves, not unlike Platonic ideas. One has to discover them (whether dialogically or in any other way need not concern us at the moment). One must perceive them first as values and only then may one believe in them and accept them.

We agree fully with him that to discover a value is not the same as setting it up "as a guiding light over one's life." We would say that the difference between these two is paralleled by the distinction between what constitutes a value and what is the source of obligation for accepting it as a guiding light for one's life. It is possible to acknowledge that a certain course of action is inherently good and yet refuse to accept the obligation to pursue it. The question, what is the essence of the good? is altogether different from the one, why is one obligated to do the good? One does not have to do the good because it is good; one has got to do it, because one is obligated to practice that which is good and not that which is evil. But what is the source of the obligation for doing the good, after one has discovered the good? An obligation is an Ought; it is well expressed in the form of Thou Shalt. A desire that the good shall be is always the source of the obligation. Desiring a good perceived, a man may obligate himself; a society, the state, the family, recognizing a good and wanting it, may obligate its members. Only in this sense can one say that one may accept a value or believe in it after one has discovered it. One discovers a value by grasping its intrinsic meaningfulness; one believes in it by wanting its realization in life. The discovery is accomplished by the intellect; the belief in the value stems from the will. The source of an obligation is always in a will that desires the end to be achieved.

What Buber does not seem to realize is that even if a person were able to perceive the absolute character of a value, he would still not have the absoluteness of a moral obligation. The quality of the obligation would depend on the will that desires the value in question. If a man would discover such a value of essential meaningfulness, if he would then proceed and "set it as a guiding light over his life," it would still be his own decision that would render the acceptance of the value obligatory. It might be an absolutely meaningful value, but the quality of obligation attached to it would be relative to the human desire that "set it up." The absoluteness in an obligation depends on the absoluteness of the will that desires the end in mind. The absolute will is the will of the Absolute. Unless it is explicitly stated to man, it desires nothing from him. The absoluteness of ethical obligation has its source in the absolute will of God revealed to man as His law. Without content in revelation, all ethical obligation is relative.

Law and Continuity

The divine law, or the content of revelation, has its significance for the specifically religious experience of man's relation to God. The relation is never as intimate as Buber wants us to believe; it is never mutual and reciprocal. Most important of all, the moments of the biblical encounter are the rarest in human experience. Buber is aware of the melancholy lot of man that determines that every Thou should, almost immediately, turn into an It. At the same time, he maintains that God is the eternal Thou. When the pure relation does not materialize, it is because man is not present. According to him, man may at any time enter into relation or leave it. Thus the pure relation is presented as the coordinate of solidity and continuity of the entire I-Thou realm. Man and mankind live and prove themselves in the relation or fail outside it.

In this sense, Buber may say that all history is a dialogue between God and man. It means that the I-Thou relation between God and man is expected to be a continuous one. This, of course, is so naive that once again one wonders whether Buber means by the I-Thou relation what the phrase would normally indicate. Even if we agreed that the encounter was a dialogical situation, history could still not be described as a dialogue between man and God, for the simple reason that history endures whereas the encounter does not. People and nations live and act in history, but it is in the rarest moments of their existence that they may pass through the encounter. It is just not true to say that man may enter at any time into the pure relation. Only of Moses is such a statement made in the Bible and even he is not called a partner of God, but "God's slave." Most people all the time of their lives and all people most of the time of their lives must stay outside the relation with the divine Thou. How, then, is continuity to be established between the basic religious reality of the encounter and the wordly reality of human existence? In biblical teaching, the coordinates of such continuity are the contents of revelation with which people leave the encounter. After the departure of the manifestation of God's presence, as a pawn for God's continued concern and love, His law and will for man, remain with man. God is not man's eternal Thou; He is not always accessible. Most of the time He is indeed silent. But His word and His will, once uttered, eternally confront man. Neither man nor nations can stand in living mutual relation with God and enact history; but they can relate themselves in commitment to the word of God and His revealed will, and living in that commitment, they may sanctify life in all its manifestations. One should, however, not mistake the divine word for an It, in the sense in which Buber at times refers to Platonic ideas. The word of God is not only an object of thought. It is a word by which God actually communicates with man; it is a will, actually expressed and made manifest to man. Even though the encounter has long passed, the word remains forever God's word for the human being. There is no I-Thou relation, but there is contact with God by hearing His word and doing His will.

The Biblical Dialogue

Is there, then, no dialogue and no freedom in the context of the religious reality based on the biblical encounter? It is the most dangerously misleading aspect of Buber's philosophy. That it uses biblical and Jewish concepts but interprets them in such a manner that they lose their biblical and Jewish significance. That the original religious experience is an encounter between God and man is the foundation of biblical religion; Buber's interpretation of it as an I-Thou relation of reciprocity is its falsification. A vital aspect of the biblical encounter is revelation; Buber's insistence that revelation has no content is its distortion. We may note the same discrepancy between biblical ideas and Buberian interpretation in the case of the dialogue.

That the whole of life is, in a sense sign language addressed to man, that the concrete situation is given to man by God in order to challenge and to test him, that man is thus addressed by God in every event of his life and has to answer in the human freedom of responsible choice and decision is of course good biblical teaching. What is more, that is exactly how Jews through the ages understood life and history. The authentic Jew approaches every situation of his life with a question in his heart: what is it, my God, you desire of me here and now? But does it mean that he stands all the time in living mutual relation to God? Is he really all the time existentially aware of the divine Presence confronting him as his Thou? It is indeed true that every event of human life contains a challenge to man. But how do I know that the challenge is from God, meant by Him for me? The problem could not be solved on the basis of Buber's dialogical situation. It is not from the concrete situation itself that the Jew derives his knowledge of the challenge, but from what he has learned from the biblical encounter and from what has been revealed to him in that encounter. In the encounter God reveals Himself as the giver of life and its sustainer by giving life to the human being who otherwise could not endure; He also makes known to man that it does matter to Him how man lives and what he does with his life by revealing to man His word, teaching, and command. In the light of this knowledge alone can man approach the concrete situation and know that it is given to him by the Giver, that it addresses him and challenges him on behalf of the Giver, and that the Giver is indeed God. That I am not my own creator, that life is given to me and, therefore, there must be a giver is of course logical. But such reasoning itself cannot identify the giver. It certainly does not show the nature of the giver's interest in human existence in general or in one's own personal life in particular. Standing by themselves, nature as well as history are indeed a mystery, but they do not speak for God. Only after God encounters man and makes known to him His will do nature and history become God's messengers to man. They may speak for God because at first God spoke for Himself in the encounter. Only because of Sinai does a Jew know that every event of his life is God's challenge to him. The confrontation is between man and the Word of God. The concrete situation is not, as Buber maintains, God's voice in disguise. The concrete situation has nothing to say. It is the once-revealed law of God that addresses man all the time regarding each concrete situation. It is God's Word—without the actual experience of his Presence—speaking to all generations, not from the concrete situation, but from the heights of Sinai.

Faith and Freedom

What are we, however, to say about the question of human freedom and responsibility? When Buber asserts that man stands in dialogical freedom in the I-Thou relation with God, he offers us further circumstantial evidence that he does not speak either of the genuine encounter or of the true relation. In the presence of God, there is no freedom. No one who stands in God's presence can deny Him. Of the Decalogue Buber says: "The word does not enforce its own hearing. Whoever does not respond to the Thou addressed to him can apparently go about his business unimpeded. Though He who speaks the word has the power . . . he has renounced this power of his sufficiently to let every individual actually decide for himself whether he wants to open or close his ears to the voice, and that means whether he wants to choose or reject the I of 'I am.' He who rejects Him is not struck down by lightning; he who elects Him does not find hidden treasures. Everything seems to remain just as it was. Obviously, God does not wish to dispense either medals or prison sentences." [96] This too is one of those typically equivocal statements of Buber which are so misleading because they are altogether right and altogether wrong. They are right in their Jewish context and wrong in the Buberian sense. If we change the phrase, "Though He who speaks the word has the power" to "Though He who spoke the word has the power," we stand on Jewish grounds. The freedom and the human responsibility which are thus affirmed are at the core of Jewish faith as it is formed after the encounter. During the act of revelation itself, He who speaks must be heard. He who indeed hears himself addressed by God cannot reject the I of "I am."

Man's freedom is returned to him after the encounter. And since encounters are not everyday occurrences, and since most people never really enter into actual living relation with God, most people are most of the time of their lives free to accept or reject God. After the encounter, as well for all those who never experience the divine Presence as living reality actually confronting them, religion is essentially a matter of faith. For a Jew this means that he commits himself to the implications that follow for his life from the biblical record of God's encounter with men and with Israel. To have faith for him means to believe that God is present all the time even though man hardly ever is able to experience His presence in actuality; that He is concerned about every living creature, even though His concern is most of the time not convincingly made manifest to men; that His law and His will were made known to men and to Israel in His revelations, even though God is silent now and here for me; that the ultimate fulfillment of life is to be found in becoming aware of His presence in living actuality, even though this ultimate experience may never be granted us on this earth. The foundation of religion is the encounter and the revelation; the life and the history of religion is the life and history of faith. The encounter and the revelation are indeed imposed upon man, no less imposed upon him than is life itself. They are given to him, as is life itself. But after the act of giving is completed, man may refuse to accept. Not only is faith not imposed on man, but man's historic experience outside the encounter urges him on to reject all the implications of the encounter. Only in the utmost affirmation of his spiritual independence and responsibility can man commit himself in faith.

Of faith, Buber says that it is the "entrance into this reciprocity [of mutual contact and meeting] as binding oneself in relationship with an undemonstrable and unprovable, yet even so, in relationship knowable Being. . . ." [97] Now, had Buber been satisfied with stating that faith "does not mean professing what we hold true in a ready-made formula," [98] one could easily go along with him. However, it makes little sense to say that faith is entrance into reciprocity "between one active existence and another." One cannot enter into the mutuality of such a meeting by means of faith. Either such contact is real, then there is no need for faith; or else the contact is not real, in which case it will not become real by entering into it with all the power of faith. One cannot enter into a nonexistent relation. Biblical faith is commitment to the proposition that "my Redeemer liveth," that He is present all the time, that He watches man and is concerned about him and that, because of it, man has a responsibility on earth. The man of faith affirms that God is accessible, that He hears when man calls and that He answers in His own way, even though the answer may never be heard by human ears or perceived by the senses. Even if God remained forever silent for him, the man of faith would call again and again and would know that he was heard. Biblical and Jewish commitment in faith is essentially a nondialogical situation. It is living in the divine Presence, even though the Presence is hidden and, most of the time, inaccessible.[99]

IV. BUBER'S METAPHYSICS—THE TWO NOTES OF THE SAME CHORD

In our elucidation of the main features of the Biblical encounter, we had occasion to wonder what kind of an I-Thou relation Buber must have in mind, if in it man is a partner of God, facing Him in freedom and developing in dialogical cooperation with God the meaning of revelation? What kind of an encounter could be accessible to man all the time? What is this "eternal Thou" with whom man is ever able to enter into relation and of whom Buber may say that if man is not encountering him, it is because man is not present? It is our intention to show in this section of our study that these questions are not unrelated to those problems which we raised in the second part of our investigation. There is an underlying trend in Buber's teaching that may explain his confidence in the validity of the dialogical response as well as the sense in which alone one may speak of both the exclusive-inclusive pure relation and the true community of the We; at the same time, it will also reveal the root of his basic departure from the essence of the biblical encounter. This underlying trend is his ontology and metaphysics. Even though Buber often emphasizes that he only reports, that he is only a witness, the fact is that his testimony becomes meaningless without his ontology and metaphysics and therefore, the value of the testimony cannot exceed the value of these.

The Bipolar Experience

Most people use the terms, dialogue and I-Thou relation, without appreciating that they are used by Buber in a very specific sense. In his lecture, *Über das Erzieherische,* for instance, Buber says: "A relation between persons that is characterized in greater or lesser degree by the element of inclusion may be termed a dialogical relation." [100] When two people experience an event in common, if at least one of them, "without forfeiting anything of the felt reality of his activity, at the same time lives through the common event from the standpoint of the other," we speak of inclusion or encompassing. It is the experiencing of the situation from both its ends at the same time, from my own as well as from that of the person who confronts me. It is living through what he lives through; to be here as well as there; to take his place, to be he as it were, and yet to remain oneself. For example, "a man belabors another, who remains quite still. Then let us assume that the striker suddenly receives in his soul the blow which he strikes: the same blow; that he receives it as the other who remains still. For the space of a moment he experiences the situation from the other side. Reality imposes itself on him." Or let us take another example. "A man caresses a woman, who lets herself be caressed. Then let us assume that he feels the contact from two sides—with the palm of his hand still, and also with the woman's skin." This is encompassing. There is nothing perverse or unnatural about it. On the contrary, it is "the bipolar experience," the completion of the turning towards the other, which is "the basic movement of the life of the dialogue." [101] The bipolar experience is the fullness of the I-Thou relation. When Buber was eleven years of age, he was associated in such a bipolar I-Thou relation with his "darling, a broad dapple-grey horse." And since man's relations to house cats and trees can and, therefore, should be dialogical, one ought to aim at such bipolar life with those presences as well.

One should not lose patience with Buber if one wishes to understand him. Even when he sounds absurd, he has his own depth. He is wrestling hard with the problem of human solitude and loneliness, the problem that, according to him, became the stumbling block on the paths of Heidegger and Sartre. Either one can reach over completely to the other, encompass him, take him up into one's own being, or no bridge at all is possible from I to Thou. This is the heart of his teaching, the very core of the dialogical life. The I-Thou relation is not mere solicitude for another, care and concern for the one that confronts me. It is an essential relation, and it is described by Buber in the following words: "In an essential relation . . . the barriers of individual being are in fact breached and a new phenomenon appears which can appear in only this way: one life open to another; . . . the other becomes present not merely in the imagination or feeling, but in the depth of one's substance, so that one experiences the mystery of the other being in the mystery of one's own. The two participate in one another's life in very fact, not psychically, but ontically." [102]

This, then, is the dialogical life: the breaching of the barriers of individuality, the breaking open of the closed units of individual beings toward each other, thus enabling one actually to enter into the substance of the other and be present there: being the one to participate in fact in the other's being. When this is accomplished, a man, experiencing his own reality, also experiences that of the other, who is existentially present in one's own. The question, of course, is how such ontic breakthrough of the barriers and actual mingling of individual beings is to be accomplished? The assertion that such is the dialogical situation is made again and again, but we shall look in vain for an explanation in that part of Buber's work where these assertions are made.

The Dual Rhythm of Cosmic Metacosmic Being

These affirmations of "the philosophical anthropology" must be read in the light of the metaphysics of the *Ich und Du*. Having analyzed Buber's definition of the dialogical situation as between man and man, let us now see how he defines the nature of the same situation as between God and man. Buber himself raises the question, How does one enter into the pure relation? Due to the nature of the subject, the answer is given rather haltingly. All rules and regulations, all religious observances or mystical rites, which purport to prepare one for the relation with the eternal Thou are themselves only objects of human thought. According to Buber, they have nothing whatever to do with the fundamental fact of the meeting between I and Thou. They are Its and belong to the It-world. Regulations and religious practices will not redeem man from his isolation. This can only be achieved by the encounter itself. But how is the encounter to be brought about?

At first, man must know how it is not to be accomplished. One cannot meet the eternal Thou by trying to escape from the world of the senses as if it were a mere sham. This is the world. Nor is the goal we are striving for to be reached by passing beyond the realm of the senses into some state of supernatural experience. All experience,

natural or supernatural, yields again only an It, an object. It will lead
us to thinghood not to the Presence. One might also say, one cannot
conjure up the divine Presence by rules and observances. To attempt
to do that would mean treating God as an It; but God is the only Thou
that never becomes an It. One must know him as the Thou or one
does not know him. Having said how God is not to be encountered,
Buber tries to indicate what is required in order that the relation may
materialize. He puts it in one short sentence. Required is: "the complete acceptance of the Presence." [103] This needs further elaboration.
Unfortunately, it too is given mainly in negative terms. One must give
up one's separation from reality. One must rid oneself of the distorting
urge of self-affirmation which enables man to escape from all encounter
into the possession of things. All this, of course, does not really explain
what is meant by the acceptance of the Presence. Obviously, Buber
cannot mean by it the actual encountering of the Absolute as Thou.
So understood, the phrase would mean that the precondition for entering
into the pure relation is entering into such a relation. The difficulty here
is similar to the one we had to contend with as we discussed Buber's
concept of faith. Indeed, on the basis of other passages in his writings,
we assume that the acceptance of the Presence is not the actual encounter itself, but an act of faith to confront reality, as such, as one
would face a person. Whereas man as a world-using subject is bent
completely on himself, as a person he must undertake the elementary
movement of turning toward reality as one turns to a Thou. Even
before the actual encounter, he keeps himself open for the possibility of
the revelation by the acceptance of all Being as a Presence. What Buber
has in mind is well expressed by what he declares in another place regarding faith. "Real faith, he explains, does not mean professing what
we hold true in a ready-made formula. On the contrary: it means holding ourselves open to the unconditional mystery which we encounter in
every sphere of our life and which cannot be comprised in any formula.
It means that from the very roots of our being, we should always be
prepared to live with this mystery as one being lives with another." [104]
We assume that it is Buber's meaning that if one is prepared to adopt
such an attitude of faith toward Being, one will encounter it as the
eternal Thou. Needless to say, there is an element of risk involved in
such an attitude. One must forgo the satisfaction one may derive from
living in the solid and reliable dimensions of the It-world and one must

put one's trust in the Unknown which will yet reveal itself as knowable in the actualized relation. But why should anyone take such a chance? On what grounds should one adopt such an attitude toward the Unknown?

It would seem to us that Buber's attitude of faith toward the Unknown can be justified only on the basis of his ontology. According to it, the I-Thou relation is at the very origin of being. One may still discover traces of it in the language of the primitive as well as in the early development of the child. The "nuclei" of primitive speech "mostly indicate the wholeness of a relation." The primitive man does not know himself as a separate entity and his neighbor, or the world around him, as something apart from him. His speech testifies to the fact that he sees himself and the incidents of his life always in situations that are relational. Events are experienced by him as "being confronting him" and he is aware of his own situation as, "life with a being confronting him." All separation, all assertion of selfhood and identity, comes later. The same may also be observed in the early life of the child. The child does not discover the world by perceiving the various items in it as separate objects. He reaches out towards it by trying to "grasp" it with his senses and embraces it. He relates himself to what attracts his attention and he discovers it by addressing it. Originally, the child, not being aware of his selfhood, meets the world without being aware of its separateness. "It is simply not the case that the child first perceives an object, then, as it were, puts himself in relation with it. The effort to establish relation comes first—the hand of the child arched out so that what is over against him may nestle under it; second is the actual relation, a saying of Thou without words, in the state preceding the word-form; the thing, like the I, is produced late, arising after the original experiences have been split asunder and the connected partners separated." [105]

Buber is not prepared to accept a psychological interpretation of these phenomena among the primitives and in the development of the child's personality. On the contrary, they can only be understood if one bears in mind their "cosmic and metacosmic origin." "In the beginning is relation" [106] is for Buber a "cosmic and metacosmic" truth. It is, however, only the first point of his metaphysics. The origin of the child is, from the cosmic-metacosmic point of view, not really different from that of all reality. "Every child that is coming into being rests, like all life that is coming into being, in the womb of the great mother, the undivided primal world that precedes form." [107] This resting in the womb of the great mother is the original relation that is retained yet for a while, even after the phase of separation has started. It is reflected, as a manifestation of the cosmic principle, in the initial experiences of the primitive and in the early encounters of the child with the world. There is a cosmic-metacosmic history of Being, which takes place in two movements. The one is separation from the womb of the great mother, the other is turning back toward it. The act of separation is "the process of becoming" or individuation; the turning back toward the womb is the way of finding redemption in Being. The primary words themselves are articulation of this cosmic rhythm on the human level. I-It is the movement of separation, of the becoming of the I as an individuum, a subject, and the emergence of reality as the It-world. I-It is the result of the disintegration of the original unity of the relation which is the beginning. I-Thou corresponds to the movement of turning. The I, as a person, turns toward Being as one turns to the "great mother," to the Thou that confronts one as a person.

Let us allow Buber to speak for himself on this rather difficult point. Says he: ". . . this double movement of estrangement from the primal Source, in virtue of which the universe is sustained in the process of becoming, and of turning towards the primal Source, in virtue of which the universe is released (better translated: is redeemed) in being, may be perceived as the metacosmical primal form that dwells in the world as a whole in its relation to that which is not the world-form whose twofold nature is represented among men by the twofold nature of their attitudes, their primary words, and their aspects of the world." [108] It is true, Buber introduces this paragraph with the word, perhaps. In other parts of his magnum opus this word is completely forgotten. So, for instance, he declares without any qualifications that "the two primary metacosmical movements of the world-expansion into its own being (better translated: expansion into individuality, i.e., existence as I-It) and turning to connection—find their supreme human form, the real spiritual form of their struggle and adjustment, their mingling and separation in the history of the human relation to God." [109]

Buber is dead serious about his ontology and metaphysics. Some of the vital aspects of his teachings are dependent on them. The coming into being of the world is an act of separation and estrangement. All being carries within itself a kind of a memory of the "womb," of "the primal Source"; it is possessed of a desire to return. Such a desire, however, is the flowering of being as spirit. As spirit, all being is yearning for the cosmic binding of itself to the true Thou. There is an ontic longing in all being for its true Thou. This longing is "a category of being"; it is "the *a priori* of relation" or, as Buber also calls it, "the inborn Thou." The inborn Thou is the ontic desire of all being, in its state of estrangement, for reunion with the true Thou. As Kant's categories are the mold of human experience, so for Buber "the *a priori* of relation" is the basis for man's ability to encounter "that which stands over against him" as his Thou. But whereas the Kantian categories are silent on the nature of the *Ding an sich,* Buber's ontological category of the inborn Thou also determines the essential quality of that which stands over against man. It is a Thou. Man does not only have an innate desire for relation, but this desire can be satisfied because whatever "stands over against him" has itself the same ontic longing for its Thou as he himself has. All being, having been separated from the "womb," has the same ontic longing for reunion. This longing is at the root of being a person. All being has thus a personal essence. It is not just a subjective desire within me that induces me to encounter a tree as my Thou. This in itself might be due to a psychological malfunction. It is the nature of Being within me that longs for relation and it is the same nature of Being within the tree that reveals itself in the reciprocity of the encounter. Of course, I must give in to the inborn Thou; I must go out and meet the world as a person, only then will I be able to meet it in its personal reality.[110]

There is, however, one more point which we have to consider before we may complete the analysis of Buber's metaphysics. Since the *a priori* of relation is man's yearning for his "true Thou," how is it that it finds satisfaction in the encounters with finite beings? Buber maintains that in all such encounters the yearning for the true Thou may be only partially satisfied. But partially, at least, it may find fulfillment. This is due to the fact that, according to him, every form of personal being—and that is, of course, all being—is essentially of the same nature. It is the one Presence that irradiates all spheres of existence.[111] Thus, every individual Thou is a symbol, or an image, of the Eternal; every individual Thou represents the eternal Presence. This does not mean that God is only immanent in the world and not transcendent to it; He encompasses all the spheres but he is not encompassed by them. Yet, since all individual presence is a manifestation of the eternal, in saying Thou to any of the spheres and to whatever they contain is like addressing the eternal Thou. In every sphere, in every I-Thou situation, "we look out toward the fringe of the eternal Thou; in each we are aware of a breath from the eternal Thou; in each Thou we address the eternal Thou." [112] Indeed, the purpose of every I-Thou situation is within itself. The contact with any Thou is important, for through it the breath of eternal life touches us. [113]

We may now describe Buber's way to the pure relation. In a state of cosmic estrangement, man is urged by the inborn Thou to find fulfillment in cosmic connection with the eternal Thou. Thus, he enters the world with the desire to meet, and expectant of the meeting. But it is not what he is looking for that he encounters immediately. What he beholds are so many "disguises" of the Presence. With the power of his desire to meet, he at first encounters the Presence in its finite manifestations. All these encounters are, as it were, stations on the way to the ultimate encounter. One knows that this is so, because the inborn Thou finds only partial satisfaction in all of them and thus urges one on—until one comes face to face with the Presence and is at rest again. Of this meeting with the eternal Thou Buber says: "It is a finding without seeking, a discovering of the primal, of origin. His [man's] sense of Thou, which cannot be satisfied till he finds the endless Thou, had the Thou present to it from the beginning; the presence had only to become wholly real to him in the reality of the hallowed life of the world." [114]

The hallowed life of the world is, of course, the life of relation. By entering into I-Thou relations with everything that confronts us, we are more and more encountering Being itself as a presence; thus the eternal Thou, whose presence irradiates all spheres of reality, becomes "wholly real" for us. We see now more clearly what Buber means by saying that I-Thou relations with nature, with human beings, and the intelligible sphere, are the "portals" that lead to the encounter with God. The divine Presence is the only presence in all reality. While it is present all the time, it must become real for man. However, it will become real for man, if man himself is real, i.e., if he is a person and as such longs for participation and speaks the primary word of I-Thou again and again. The divine Presence becomes more and more real for the man who himself becomes more and more real as a person. This is the ultimate significance of the statement that the eternal Thou is always present; it is only man who is not present if there is no relation.

We are now in a position to appreciate what Buber has in mind when he says that the acceptance of the Presence is the prerequisite of the pure relation. It is the acceptance of the thesis that Being is personal, that it should be encountered in the innumerable I-Thou situations with finite beings; for through the contact with each Thou one is touched by the breath of eternal life. This is no longer tautological and it does require entering into "a relation of reciprocity with the Unknown." One does it, however, by acknowledging one's inborn Thou and by going out to "meet the Meeter," at first in his innumerable finite manifestations. If one is prepared thus "to accept the Presence," one will be lead inot the presence of the eternal Thou.

Needless to say, there is a strong pantheistic element in this metaphysics and ontology. Since, according to Buber, God is not only the Being present in all beings, but also transcends them all, we ought to describe his metaphysics as a form of panentheism. Against its background we may now understand what Buber calls "ontic participation," which is characteristic of the "essential relation" and the dialogical life. It is the actual mingling of individual substance with individual substance. The separating walls of individuality may indeed be broken down, since individuality is due to the cosmic movement of estrangement from Being. As such it is unreal. Since all being is essentially one, and since the same Presence irradiates all, the turning toward the other can and should become actual participation in the being of the other. Only because of the pantheistic aspect of his philosophy can Buber maintain that in the dialogical situation a man experiences the mystery of the being of the other in the mystery of his own being. One may even agree that in the light of the underlying ultimate oneness of the Presence which flows through all beings, even the "bipolar experience" may not be as absurd as it would seem at first glance.

The pantheistic metaphysics is the source of Buber's optimism and confidence. He trusts the dialogical situation, he trusts man and the meaning as well as the truth which are dialogically revealed because at heart he is a pantheist. As with all pantheistic philosophy, so with his too, Being and Meaning are identical. So his advice to man is: Be real, participate in all being "ontically," and you will be true. Some of the specific aspects of Buber's teachings, which we presented in the first section of this essay, become only now apparent in their full significance. In revelation, we heard Buber declare, man is revealed unto himself. In the dialogical situation of ontic participation man surrenders his individuality, which emerged in the cosmic movement of estrangement from Being, and becomes real. Only now, does he know his true self. Having become real, his response to the challenge, though given in dialogical freedom, coincides with "the divine law resting deep within man." This follows logically from the original pantheism. It is the same Presence everywhere; ergo, if man finds his "true" self, he discovers "the divine law." He discovers that what he really wants is identical with what God wants of him. Man's own commitment undertaken in freedom and the law of God are one and the same thing. This is the typical way in which pantheism throughout the ages has solved the problem of heteronomy versus autonomy in ethics. As Meaning and Being are one, so are also Law and Being. Law is simply the manifestation of the nature of Being. Therefore, as long as any being is true to its nature, it is also free and yet within the confines of universal lawfulness.

It is this pantheistic commonplace which is also the essence of Buber's solution of the antinomy of freedom and causality, which we described earlier. The deed is waiting for me and as such, it is prescribed for me; yet I have to choose it, declared Buber. It all depends on me, even though I am commissioned to perform my deed. In choosing one's deed, one encounters one's destiny, which is one's completion. Again, freedom and law are one. We could not see how a man deciding on a course of action in dialogical freedom could know that he was choosing the deed destined for him. There is no such problem for Buber. He is pantheistically logical. The deed that is waiting for me is what is required of me by the nature of Being itself. But I myself am a manifestation of the same Presence. Ergo, if I only act like the presence I truly am, I am bound to perform "my deed." Being my true self, I cannot fail to find my deed, which of course will coincide with the divine law. Yet, I shall be free, for I shall be acting with my, and the deed's, true nature, which —rather conveniently—is identical with the divine law. With reference to the Kantian antinomy of freedom, Buber asserts that the conflict between human responsibility and the principle of universal causation cannot be solved theoretically. One must embrace both sides of the paradox. They have "to be lived together, and in being lived they are one." [115] This is, at least, debatable. However, they are indeed one within the metrics of a pantheistic metaphysics.

What is Man?

Let us place the metaphysics in its proper perspective in the history of philosophy. We cannot help being somewhat surprised by the turn Buber's thought was compelled to take. Originally setting out with a number of existential affirmations, he found himself confronted by the need of buttressing them with an ontology and metaphysics which are variations on old themes of classical philosophy. Man's inborn yearning for the true Thou reminds one very much of Plato's anemnesis. The significance of the distinction between the cosmic-metacosmic movements of estrangement and turning is interpreted, almost literally, in the Platonic tradition of the distinction between Becoming and Being. Most obvious, however, is the closeness to Neoplatonism, especially as it found its elaboration by Proclus. The cosmos comes into being in a movement of separation from the One. Since there exists only the One, all reality is an emanation from it. Nevertheless, individual existence is not eliminated. However, as an emanation of the One, the individual reflects the universal. The particular has the same essence as the Absolute, but it is not identical with it. Coming from the One, being of it and yet apart from it, the individual, as well as the cosmos in its entirety, strive to return to their origin. There is one new feature in Buber's ontology. The movement of return is not allowed to be completed fully. With Buber, it cannot go beyond the I-Thou relation with "the primal source." The question that has to be raised now is: What are the consequences for the I-Thou relation of a metaphysics that is essentially pantheistic but is stopped short of the ultimate consummation of the return, the reestablished union with "the womb of the great mother?" More explicitly, the question is: In view of the metaphysics, what is the essence of the I, what is the "substance"—Buber uses the term in describing the essential relation—of particular being?

Buber does insist on the reality and the independence of the I, and this seems to run counter to the pantheistic tendency. But he does not realize that his I in the I-Thou relation is lacking what it most needs, i.e., selfhood. The idea of the "two notes of the same chord" is so deeply rooted in Buber's philosophy that one must apply it to the human being himself, no less than to the human response to the challenge. Since it is the same Presence which shines through all reality, and every individual is in essence a finite "disguise" of the absolute Person, wherein lies the nature of individuality? It is not enough to say in answer to the question: "God comprises, but is not the universe. So, too, God comprises, but is not, my Self. In view of the inadequacy of my language about this fact, I can say Thou in my language as each man can in his, in view of this I and Thou live. . . ." [116] The affirmation, however, emphatic, is no longer sufficient. Too much depends for Buber on his pantheistic ontology. If there is, indeed, a self apart from God, then obviously it cannot be the same presence that irradiates all; then, the "two notes of the one chord," and everything that depends on it, are gone. Buber may, of course, still say that revelation is man's response to a challenge, but unrelated as the response will be to a divine law, it will be a rather meaningless affectation to call it revelation. Neither will it then be possible to see in man's destiny a completion of his freedom. To the extent that his real self will act freely, it may easily be in genuine conflict with the deed that is "awaiting" him. If the I does have selfhood apart from God as the basis for its ability to enter into the I-Thou situation, it is inconceivable how the encounters with finite beings should offer partial satisfaction for the yearning for the eternal Thou, or how these encounters could be considered as "portals" leading to the eternal Presence. The I, in its selfhood apart from God, should be able to meet other selves in their identity apart from God. The acceptance of the Presence may lead to God, if all presence stands for him. But if there is selfhood apart from him, then it is meaningless to say that the attitude of meeting reality as a presence will lead one to God.

Buber does not see that his metaphysics cuts away the ground from under his I-Thou. For him, selfhood and independent existence are the characteristics of the I in the I-It relation, of the I of estrangement and separation. The I in the I-Thou is not really an independent person, but the cosmic yearning for return to the "primal Source," imprisoned in a finite vessel. The innate Thou, the so-called *a priori* of relation, this category of being, does not inhere in a person but is the essence of personal being. There is no selfhood in its own right which yearns for the Thou; there is only a cosmic-metacosmic yearning in finite shape. This finds its expression quite clearly where Buber describes "the fundamental difference" between the two primary words. According to him, one may see the distinction between them best illustrated in the spiritual history of the primitive, whom we had occasion to mention earlier in our discussion. As we have heard, the original situation of the primitive is relational. It is a state that Buber calls *vorgestaltlich,* i.e., one in which the

primitive has not yet learned to recognize forms about him in their individuality. Everything is experienced as relational, comprehending
him as well as that which confronts him. At this stage, neither of the
two has as yet separated itself out of the relation. The I-Thou, says
Buber, is not composed of an I and a Thou. The I-Thou precedes the I.
The primitive man speaks the primary word of I-Thou in "a natural
way," i.e., even before he is able to recognize himself as I. The I-It, on
the other hand, is a composite word. The "natural event" that is the
foundation of the I in the I-It realm is the separation of the human body
from the surrounding world. The body, in its perceptions and experiences, comes "to know" itself as differentiated from its surroundings.
However, the differentiation is not a confrontation, which is possible only
on the spiritual level. The original interaction between the human body
and the world around it is not relational; it is a situation "of pure juxtaposition." Hence, the character of an I cannot be implied in it. Only
after the I, originally comprehended in the I-Thou situation, has separated itself as an independent entity, may it associate itself with a separated human body and awaken "there the state in which I is properly
active." The I that stepped forth declares itself to be the bearer, and
the world around about to be the object, of the perceptions.[117] This is
another version of the basic theme with which too we are already
familiar, that in the beginning is relation.

That the I-Thou precedes the I should be seen in its full significance
for the understanding of the person with Buber. If the essence of the
person were indeed what the word says, no I-Thou relation could precede man's awareness of himself as I. If personal existence meant selfhood and individuality, no one could be part of an I-Thou situation
without having known oneself a person first. Only because for Buber
the person is essentially the inborn Thou, i.e., the finite form of the
cosmic yearning for the true Thou, is it possible for man to speak "the
primary word I-Thou in a natural way." There is no need for an I to
be the bearer of the longing for return; the longing itself is the I. Actually, this is not only so in the primitive state. Buber's person is of
necessity empty of personal reality. To be conscious of oneself as a
person is the end of the I-Thou situation. One is always alone with
one's self. The moment the I knows itself as a self, he is no longer participating; he becomes the I of I-It. Only the I of separation, the I of
I-It, has selfhood and personality according to the inherent logic of

Buber's position. However, this I, as the result of the basic pantheism, has to be rejected by Buber. This is the full significance of Buber's statement that all reality is participation and relation. If, indeed, there existed a form of personal being as bearer of the yearning for the Thou, then such personal being, even when disloyal to its innate yearning, would still be real.

Nor are these consequences which follow from the metaphysics affected by anything that Buber has said in his writings about philosophical anthropology. In *Das Problem des Menschen,* and with obvious reference to a statement in *Ich und Du,* discussed earlier by us in this section, Buber does say: "It is true that the child says Thou before it learns to say I; but on the height of personal existence one must be truly able to say I in order to know the mystery of the Thou in its whole truth." [118] Even stronger, he declares, in *Urdistanz und Beziehung* that the principle of human existence is a twofold one. The first is that of separation and the second, that of entering-into-relation. The first is a precondition for the second. For, obviously, I can enter into relation only with someone that exists at a distance from me, that "has become an independent vis-à-vis" for me.[119]

It would seem to us that, notwithstanding the emphasis on the I and on selfhood as a prerequisite for the relation, they still remain empty of contents and reality. We know well what Buber means by "knowing the mystery of the Thou in its whole truth." It is a knowledge gained by "ontic participation" in an other; it is experiencing the mystery of the being of the other in the act of experiencing the mystery of one's own being. But this, as we saw, is only possible because "the same Presence irradiates all being" and because individuality is not real. The entering-into-relation is so defined that it can be carried out only because self-being is not of the essence of man's nature. Actually, the twofold principle of human existence, distance and relation, is the anthropological counterpart of the cosmic-metacosmic principle of separation and turning. The only reality selfhood possesses in the *Urdistanz* is its being apart for the sake of entering "into ontic participation." In itself and by itself the I is not real. It is the conclusion one has to draw not only from the metaphysics but also from the anthropology. Man is real only if and as he enters into "essential relations" with the entire realm of existence. Man can attain to self-being only if every possible relationship to the world around him becomes reality for him, i.e., if every one of his relations to life becomes essential.[120] Buber also formulates it in the following manner: "Speaking anthropologically, man does not exist in isolation, but only in the completeness of the relation between one and another." [121] In other words, man exists only in the act of "ontic participation"; he is real only in essential relations. However, essential relations in Buber's sense are only possible because man has no essential identity of his own. It is rather interesting to note that in the context from which we have just quoted, Buber speaks of an inborn urge of self-realization. What, however, seems to be granted at first glance is immediately withheld by the words: "It would be a mistake to speak here of individuation alone. Individuation is only the necessary personlike mold of all realization of the nature of man. Not the self as such is ultimately essential. . . ." [122] The truth is that, on the basis of Buber's philosophy, the self is not only not ultimately essential; it is lacking essence altogether. As he puts it very well, the self, or individuality, is only the particular mold for the realization of being human. And the realization of being human consists in not being an individual but existing in "ontic participation" in other beings. The inborn urge for self-realization, which every man is supposed to carry within himself, is the anthropological parallel to the inborn Thou of the metaphysics. Examine it as one may, the I which—according to Buber—enters into the relation with the Thou has no substance; it is a finite vessel that contains a measure of the cosmic yearning for reality by returning to the "primal Source."

Relation and Relatedness

We may now be in a better position to appreciate the significance of our criticism of Buber's concept of the exclusive-inclusive pure relation as well as of his definition of the true community. At the same time, the ultimate roots of Buber's disagreement with the biblical encounter will become uncovered.

The result of our investigation of Buber's notion of the I has been that it is empty of personal substance; it has no genuine selfhood. By means of his idea of ontic participation in all being, Buber overcomes man's isolation and solitude by eliminating man's personal reality. But where there is no selfhood, where the I has no personal substance which he may rightly call his very own, there can be no relation either. Only an I existing in all actuality as a clearly definable and separate person can confront and meet another I of the same category. In his pantheistic predilection, Buber confuses relatedness with relation. What he calls an I-Thou relation is in truth a situation of relatedness. Being, in its finite mode, relates itself to the rest of being in order to overcome separation. In the condition of relatedness, an original harmony and connectedness is restored. If Buber's interpretation of the secret of primitive speech is correct, it would still not reveal, as Buber thinks, that primitive man experiences reality in an I-Thou situation of relation. Where there is no genuine separateness, there can be no genuine relation. It would, however, yield a good example of relatedness in an essentially impersonal situation. This is certainly so in the case of the early development of the infant. To call it an I-Thou situation preceding I-awareness is meaningless. What is taking place at this stage of human growth is the attempt on the part of a distinctive being, not yet conscious of its personal existence, to relate itself to the world around it. Forms of connectedness may thus arise, but no relation.

In this connection Buber's misinterpretation of Spinoza's *amor dei* is rather enlightening. Since the love with which God loves Himself is, according to Spinoza's pantheism, identical with the love with which man loves God, Buber believes that the *amor dei* means the encountering of the reality of God. Says Buber: ". . . it is truly an encounter, for it takes place here in the realization of the identity . . . of His love and ours, although we, finite natural and spiritual beings, are in no wise identical with Him, who is infinite." [123] Now, it is of course perfectly correct to say that man, the finite natural and spiritual being is not identical with God, who is infinite. Yet, he is a mode of the infinite; and only because of that, because he has no independent personal existence in his own right, is his love for God identical with God's love for Himself. There is no possibility for a genuine encounter with God within the system of Spinoza. The very identity of God's love with man's love, the pantheistic "two notes of the one chord," excludes the encounter. There is no I-Thou relation here. There is, of course, a relatedness between the infinite substance and its finite modes. The *amor dei* is an expression of this relatedness. It is worth noting that in the postscript to *I and Thou,* Buber defines personal existence in terms of Spinoza's philosophy. He does add to Spinoza's two attributes of the Infinite a third one, that of "personal being." However, of it he says: "From this attribute would stem my and all men's being as person, as from those other attributes would stem my and all men's being as spirit and being as nature." [124] In other words, finite person is a mode of the absolute Person. This is in keeping with his concept of the one Presence which shines through all being. As for Spinoza, so for Buber, personal existence has no reality. The personal for both is the particular, which is the Absolute in its mode of finitude. Buber, however, conceives it more in the dynamic sense of Neoplatonic pantheism. The particular, which he calls the person, has "history." It starts out as the inborn Thou, a finite form of cosmic yearning for the true Thou, and ends up as yearning satisfied in what Buber calls the true relation, which, however, is a restored form of relatedness between the absolute Person and one of his finite modes.

Let us now have another look at the specific nature of Buber's pure relation. He maintained that it was both exclusive as well as inclusive. We could not make much sense of it, because we took his concept of the I-Thou relation literally. As long as we assumed that the I had personal selfhood and validity as such, it could not be conceived how even in the pure relation the I could preserve all its other I-Thou relations intact. But Buber's I-Thou relations are really forms of relatedness between the finite modes of the one Presence. It is, therefore, understandable that Buber should assert that this life of relatedness may be preserved in the relatedness of a particular final mode of the Presence to its primal Source, which, in its turn, comprises all its modes of finitude. If one is ontically participating in the Being of all beings, one is *eo ipso* also participating in all particular being. This is also the clue to the mystery of the true community. As we saw, it just made no sense to say that the true community was constituted by the people living in mutual relation with a living Center and, at the same time, in mutually living relations with each other. It was not possible to see how all members of a people or a society could at the same time establish such a mutual relation to the living Center; far less was it possible to understand that human beings, with their very limited capacity for I-Thou relations, could stand to each other in such rich forms of I-Thou relations that they would constitute a community or a holy people. All this was well reasoned on our part, because we took Buber at his word. This, however, we can no longer do. Since his I-Thou relations are in their essence forms of relatedness between various manifestations of the same Presence, it may be possible to make the metaphysical assertion that the same "I" may indeed be related in innumerable ways to Being in all its manifestations, which is essentially the same everywhere; just as one might affirm, with the same metaphysical plausibility, that the numerous finite modes of the Presence might conceivably be related to the "living Center" or "the womb of the eternal mother" or "the primal Source." Buber's true community is as little a genuine community as his relation is genuine relation. The true community as Being has completed the second movement of its cosmic-metacosmic history, i.e., having turned to its source after the movement of separation from it and having related itself to it by an act of ontic identification.

Since, however, the I is no genuine person, neither can its Thou be truly personal. Buber's eternal Thou is as little convincingly personal as the One of Neoplatonism or Spinoza's infinite substance. It remains forever "the womb of the eternal mother." The "eternal Thou" is the goal of the cosmic yearning of being, estranged from its origin, for the primal Source. It is true, Buber does not seem to be much concerned about that. In the preface to his book on Moses, for instance, he makes the remark: "It is a fundamental error to register the faith with which I deal as simple 'monotheism'. . . . Whether the existence of a Unity exalted over all is assumed in one's consideration, is not decisive but rather the way in which this Unity is viewed and experienced, and whether one stands in an exclusive relationship to it which shapes all other relations and, thereby, the whole order of life." [125]

It would seem to us that the matter is just not that simple. Buber, of course, is not a mere agnostic concerning the nature of the Unity; nor does he only testify to the nature of an experience of encounter and relation with it. He definitely rejects the idea of "a Unity that is exalted over all" and his entire testimony is meaningless without the acceptance of the existence of a Unity that permeates all and whose being is ontologically the being of all beings. But a Unity so conceived does have its implications for the relationship. What Buber is testifying about is not a genuine confrontation between an I and a Thou, but a "plugging-in" by the particularized modes of being to the mainstream of Unity. Speaking of the pure relation, Buber once explains: "Who wishes to make division and define boundaries between sea and streams? There we find only the one flow from I to Thou, unending, the one boundless flow of the real life." [126] Buber ought to realize that what he is talking about all the time is indeed "the one boundless flow." He ought to appreciate also that in "the one boundless flow of real life" there can be neither a genuine I nor a genuine Thou. There is no encounter, no genuine "meeting with the Meeter." There is either relating oneself to the flow as part of it or stepping out of it and becoming unreal in the separation of selfhood. No wonder he knows nothing of the fear and trembling of the biblical encounter. Only a real person can be afraid. His eternal Thou does not threaten man's I in the encounter, for what Buber calls encounter is at best the absolute Person's self-encounter with the finite modes of his self. Can there be, in such a situation of relatedness, a genuine dialogue? The freedom of which Buber speaks is, in reality, man's freedom to persevere in a state of separation; the response to the challenge, on the other hand, is knowing oneself as part of "the one boundless flow of real life." The response is not an answer, but an act of self-recognition as being one and the same with the "challenger." Where there is no genuine personal distinctiveness, there can be no dialogue. Buber's "two notes of the same chord" cannot imply a true dialogical situation. The pure relation which he propagates is a form of ontic connectedness, which, if achievable, would yield the restored unity of Being. Needless to say, such ontic connectedness would indeed "shape all other relations and thereby the whole order of life." Only, it would do so by making effective and manifest the ontic order of Being. To call it an ethical or spiritual order would be justified only on the grounds that a particular mode of the all-pervasive Unity, in this case a man called Martin Buber, wills to do so.

Conclusion

Quite obviously, it has not been our intention to develop a Jewish position as regards the weighty issues which are treated by Buber in the area of his teachings which we have reviewed. Judaism does have to articulate its own point of view in relationship to the problems of human existence as raised in modern philosophy. It is to be regretted that Buber's philosophy cannot be accepted as the sorely needed modern articulation of the Judaism of the ages. The distinction between I-Thou and I-It is indeed fundamental and vital. However, by speaking of "the possibility and reality of a dialogical relation between man and God, i.e., of man's free partnership in his "dialogue between heaven and earth," as Buber does,[127] he places himself outside the historically authentic Jewish tradition. When Buber maintains that "the same Thou that goes from man to man also descends from the Divine to us and ascends from us to him," [128] he is much closer to Christian teaching than to Judaism.

It was the sameness of the Thou that constituted Kierkegaard's dilemma. It is understandable that against the background of the Christian tradition, the deity could become so intimately humanized and personalized that a Regina might well turn into "the object" standing between a man and his true love. Buber, of course, believes that he has been more successful in solving the dilemma. It is "the same Thou" in the deity as well as in the Reginas, but they do not exclude each other. He does not humanize the deity, he deifies Regina by making her a finite mode of the all-pervading Unity. Unfortunately, in this manner poor Regina loses, at least metaphysically, all the charms of personal identity.

The Jew does turn to God, addressing Him endearingly with the almost impudent *Gottenyu*. He does call Him with the word Thou. He knows that God is present, that He hears and answers. He prays to a living and personal God. But the distinction between creation and Creator, between creature and Creator is irremovable and insurmountable. In the light of this basic distinction, one would have to define the I, the Thou, the It, and the We, as well as the human I and the divine Thou and the relationship between them all. There is encounter between God and man; it is the very essence of biblical religion. But it is fundamentally different from the I-Thou encounter and the dialogue which are of such importance between man and man. Because of that difference, love for God cannot compete with love for man. And perhaps, just because one cannot hug God as one hugs a fellowman, or participate in him ontically, one should show one's love for Him by loving His creatures and His creation.

CHAPTER 4

Faith and Law

1.

Ever since the Christian apostle, Paul, subjected the concept of the law to his devastating criticism and opposed to it the idea of faith, faith and law have become related to each other antithetically. It is assumed that he who lives by his faith is in no need of the law, and he who lives by the law is lacking in inwardness of faith. The Western Jew, who is on all sides surrounded by the traditions of Western civilization, is continually exposed to the impact of this antithesis and often accepts its validity almost subconsciously. From the Jewish point of view, however, this manner of confrontation between faith and law is the result of a misunderstanding of the function of the law and, with it, of the very purpose of Judaism. The law is not an end in itself; it is a means to an end. The law shows a way and teaches a deed, "the way that they should go and the deed that they should do." According to the Talmud, the teaching of the law is of decisive importance because it leads to the deed. The Torah is the guide to the Jewish way, it prepares man for the Jewish deed. The emphasis on the law is due to the emphasis on the *Ma'aseh*. It is for this reason that the law in Judaism is known by the term *Halachah,* which, because of its derivation from the root *haloch,* to walk, is best rendered as the discipline for going along one's way as a Jew. The confrontation is not between faith and law but between faith and deed. The question is not what importance one attaches to the law in relationship to faith, but what significance one ascribes to the deed as compared to faith.

Having reached this point, we have to be on our guard. What do we mean by faith? The faith of Judaism? Certainly not. Within Judaism the conflict between faith and law or between faith and deed does not

138

arise. That "the righteous lives by his faith" was not a discovery of the
Christian apostle, Paul. Using those words, he only quoted the Jewish
prophet Habakkuk. That the words of the prophets were not lost on
Judaism, one may judge by the talmudic interpretation that the six
hundred and thirteen commandments of the Torah were summed up in
the one principle of Habakkuk, that of living by one's faith. Faith in
Judaism requires that the deed be done in accordance with the will of
God as made manifest in His law. He who rejects the law rejects the
deed. But since the deed is prescribed by a law whose acceptance is
based on faith, the rejection of the deed implies a rejection of the faith
too. Rejecting the deed, the Christian apostle did not choose faith but
formulated a new concept of faith. The antithesis is, therefore, not
between faith and law but between the Christian concept of faith and
the Jewish concept of law. But again, since the Jewish concept of the
law and the deed is not to be separated from the Jewish concept of
faith, the confrontation between faith and law is based on a confusion
of issues. In truth, the antithesis is between faith and faith—which, of
course, should not be a bit surprising.

One may discuss the relationship between faith and deed in Judaism
successfully with the help of the understanding of the new concept of
faith that emerged from Christianity's rejection of the law and of
the deed. The source of the rejection was not a new insight into the
nature of faith but rather a new evaluation of life, of human existence.
With the depreciation of the law, the deed—to which it leads—was
devalued. The deed was degraded because one had lost faith in the
meaning of the works of man. At the root of it all was despair over
man and the world. In the philosophy of the Christian apostle, man
and the world stood in the sign of hopelessness. This meant, of course,
not only the rejection of the law but also the rejection of the old faith.
According to Judaism, faith in God extends to God's creation too.
Because he trusts in God, the Jew knows that God's evaluation of His
creation, *ki tov,* that it is good, is valid forever. It applies to man no
less than to the rest of creation. Man, too, is good, because he is
capable of goodness, because he may well serve the purpose which God
intended for him in his creation. Because of this, his life, in all its
creaturely existence, is significant; it carries on itself the marks of divine
approval. Because of it, what he does, how he lives does matter; the
human deed is all-important. When this faith was lost, the human deed,

too, became meaningless. Those who were overwhelmed by a sense of hopelessness over man and history needed a new faith that held out hope in an other-worldly salvation.

What are the characteristic features of such a faith? It is a faith most intimately private and personal. It aims at the closest possible relation between man and his Maker. Since it is altogether spiritual, and a flight of the soul from the indignities of bodily existence in the valley of darkness, one should better say that this faith is a relation of trust between a soul and God. The human being in his wholeness may not enter into the relation; the body, man's biological reality, is left outside. Furthermore, in pure faith the soul "detaches" itself not only from the body but also from other human beings. Dedicated as one is in faith to the exclusive concern for one's soul and its bliss, one clings to God in solitude, as a being apart, alone with the Alone. Whatever is happening between God and the individual soul is outside the dimension of space and time. Man in his biological reality and society in its this-worldly historicity are unredeemable. The result is a kingdom of God which is not of this world, a religion which is essentially indifferent toward history and society. There is no room left here for the deed, nor any function for the law.

Not such is the faith of Judaism. Since its trust in God embraces an attitude of confidence in His creation, as man turns to God he is led to life by his faith. The relation, however intimate, is never truly private, for it is open to the world and man's responsibility in it. It is by his faith that the Jew learns of his place in the world. He may seek God in loneliness, but once he has found Him he stands in the midst of life. He draws near God not as a soul but in his full humanity: "The soul is thine, and the body, Thy work." He longs for redemption not as a spiritual being but as a human being. Man in all his creaturely existence is to be redeemed. Redemption is an event in history. This world is to be established as the Kingdom of God. The deed, man's daily life in space and time, must find its place in the Kingdom; it builds the Kingdom. The deed is the act of the integrated human being. It is not performed by the soul, nor can it be done by the body alone. It comes into existence through the coordination of the spiritual and material powers of man. It is through the deed alone that man may relate himself to God in the fullness of his humanity. The deed, being the stuff out of which history is made, is never private; it is always public, as history itself. The true dimension of the deed is between man and man. It is always performed among people. The faith that motivates the deed links the Jew to God; the dimension of the deed joins him to mankind. The faith may be private and individual; the deed is public and social. The deed is an act of faith in God and an act of faithfulness toward man; it is trust in God and responsibility toward man. The faith needs no law. But the faith leads to the deed and the deed is never without a law, without an understanding of what is required, of what ought to be. Nor is the deed the act of an individual; it is that of man in community with other men. The deed of a community must be informed by a law for the community. A faith in God that leads to the deed in the presence of God asks for a law of God.

There is, in truth, no genuine confrontation between faith and law; there is no choice between them. If one starts out with a philosophy of despair and is willing to abandon life in its biological and socio-historical fullness to its doom of futility and meaninglessness, one is bound to seek salvation in some otherworldly spiritual redemption. One has not chosen faith and rejected law; one has rejected life and thus needs no law. One is left with one's faith. But he whose faith in God includes faith in the value of God's creation, he must do and live in the presence of God, he must do so in the company of men, together with his fellow-men. He embraces the law as he embraces the life which reaches him from God. He has no choice. He must do so if he wishes to live by his faith. Indeed, others may desire to be *saved* by their faith; he alone *lives* by his.

2.

There is, however, another sense in which faith and law may be considered antiletical to each other. The confrontation between them may be seen as a conflict between authentic subjective inwardness and conformity to an external objective norm. In this form, the antithesis has been accentuated in our days as a result of existentialist thinking. Faith as the realm of the most intimately personal requires personal involvement. It is an act of free individual commitment. In its very essence, it is altogether subjective. Law, one the other hand, stands for heteronomy. It is objectively given, and that means it is imposed from without. By its very nature, law is impersonal and, as such, destructive of individuality, the lifeblood of faith. In our opinion the antithesis, so considered, is due to the dilemma which is at the very heart of the existentialist position. To view the relationship between faith and law within Judaism as one of insoluble conflict is due to the unresolved existentialist dilemma which casts its misunderstood shadow on the Jewish canvas. What is the nature of this dilemma?

Subjectivity is truth, said Kierkegaard, and, of course, he was right. Without vital involvement of the whole human being in it, without living commitment to it, truth is meaningless. Yet, at the same time the principle that subjectivity is truth may also be very wrong. Kierkegaard's main concern was the "how" of man's involvement in truth. He was rather indifferent toward the "what" of truth. He believed that if only the "how" were right, the "what" of truth would follow automatically. In fact, however, personal involvement is not enough. One may be most truly committed to something that is utterly untrue and false. Kierkegaard's indifference toward objectivity may prove disastrous. Martin Heidegger, in his pursuit of authentic being, ended up in the Nazi camp. The existentialist emphasis on the individual and the personal is important, but it is not enough. Objectivity, too, is needed.

The second aspect of this existentialist dilemma derives directly from the human situation. At this point, existentialism is self-defeating. It insists on the importance of the individual, and, because of that, it must also insist on the importance of the deed. Living one's own life authentically demands that the existentialist commitment issue into action. But only faith, i.e. affirmation without action, is purely individual. With action one breaks through the category of the individual—Kierkegaard called this his discovery—into the public, the communal. All action takes place in the midst of people. If one desires to live, one must take cognizance of the nonindividual, nonpersonal, the other. Calling himself the individual, how little satisfying was Kierkegaard's life with other people! Here existentialism is up against something purely objective— the objective givenness of other people; indeed, the objective givenness of reality, including the individual subject.

We may sum up the existentialist dilemma by saying: if the necessary concern for the nature of the "what," to which a person commits himself, requires a decent respect for objectivity, the givenness of the human situation, in which the commitment is enacted makes the encounter with objectivity inescapable.

The significance of the dilemma of our theme now becomes obvious.

In the light of the nature of the dilemma, faith and law can no longer be considered antithetical to each other in an unfriendly manner. The subjectivity of faith in purity is untenable. If such subjectivity remains unrelated to objectivity in some adequate fashion, its very subjectivity may render faith either futile or dangerous. Since faith, if it is truly existential, requires the deed, the demand for objectivity in faith as well as in the deed is in truth a demand for law. Without subjectivity of affirmation, faith is hollow; without objectivity and lawfulness of contents, faith is truly blind.

Martin Buber and Franz Rosenzweig, the two outstanding Jewish existentialists, have attempted to resolve the dilemma. Martin Buber, of course, does not accept the traditional notion of a revealed law. Instead, he knows of the silent, wordless address of God that speaks to man from every experience of his life. Man is called to respond, and he responds with his deed. It is the deed that man chooses from among the numberless possibilities of his concrete situation. He alone must choose and do in complete freedom of commitment. Thus, the commitment is altogether subjective. Yet, the deed that follows also has its objective side. Among the innumerable possibilities of the concrete situation there is the one deed that is waiting to be done by man, that "means" him, that is intended for him. It is as if God had planted it there in order to be selected by man in his own unique situation. While it all depends on man, man is called to "his" deed, which is "his" even before it is undertaken by him. At times, Buber even speaks of the law of God. But it is not a law which is thrust upon man from without; "it rests deep within him." It is up to man to awaken it when the "call" reaches him. Thus, by discovering his own innermost being he also embraces the law of God. The subjective commitment and the objective law become one when man chooses the deed. They are like "two notes that are one chord." In this manner, Buber hoped to have solved the conflict between autonomy and heteronomy.

We are, however, unable to accept his solution. Since revelation, according to Buber, is a call to man, a challenge as it were—to find the deed and to do it—but otherwise is without contents, we remain completely in the realm of pure subjectivity. It is man alone who makes the decision; it is he alone who chooses the deed and judges that it is the deed that "means" him; it is but he who discovers the law of God at rest deep within him; it is only on the strength of his personal authority that he declares it to be the law of God within his heart. At every point everything depends on one's subjective affirmation.

These subjective affirmations and commitments are sufficient for Buber. They are all there is. He has not really moved one step beyond Kierkegaard in this respect. It is still subjectivity that is acknowledged as truth.

Franz Rosenzweig, in his famous essay about the law which he addressed to Martin Buber, attempts a different solution. Unlike Buber, he acknowledges the law. His problem is how to make it relevant for the contemporary situation, for today. If, for Buber, in the dialogical situation man seeks to respond by discovering "his" deed and doing it, for Rosenzweig the task of the Jew is to make the law "his" law, the law for himself. But the law becomes my law if I have to carry it out, not because I am orderd to do so by some outside authority, but because I, in the fullness of my being, cannot leave it undone. One does not execute the law because one wills it, but because one is able to execute it. The law itself must turn into strength with the power of one's individual being. In order to achieve this, it is necessary that the modern Jew, estranged from Judaism and from his people as he is, should once again become a link in the chain of the generations. Thus, the law itself may turn into Jewish vitality within him. He will carry out the law because he will act with the newly gained strength of his whole being. He will do it in order to give expression to his innermost nature. He will do what he can because he can do no other. Out of existential need, the ability to do so will become a necessity. It should, however, be understood that Rosenzweig, who found the way back to Judaism, spoke from a situation of estrangement to a generation of estranged Jews. His position is not a solution to the philosophical or theological problem; it is, rather, advice—and probably very good advice—in the accidental historical situation of an attempted return to Judaism. Philosophically speaking, even with Rosenzweig we remain caught in the net of subjectivity. The strength that enables us to carry out the law because we are able to do it flows to us as it lists. It comes when it comes and as it comes. We accept it, we do not examine it, we do not judge it. It is our strength; it is we. We carry out the law, because in possession of the ability to do it, which is identical with our very being, we cannot leave it undone. But we do what we can, what we are able to do.

Thus, we carry out the law selectively. We do only what we are able to do; only *that* do we have to do existentially. However, we have no objectively valid principle of selection. The selection is not determined by our will, but only by our ability. Now, ability to do is, of course, not physical ability; that may be always present. It is existential ability that, when turned into the fulfillment of the law, gives meaningful expression to our whole being and that, therefore, must be employed if we wish to be ourselves. While there is a law which is given to the Jew, it is valid only when he is able to make it his own. The validation of the law is altogether subjective. Rosenzweig envisages not only "selection" from the inherited law but even the increase of the law by the institution of new laws through the inability of leaving that undone which one is able to do and, therefore, must do. Rosenzweig is, of course, much closer to what we consider to be the authentic Jewish position. In essence, however, he has not advanced far beyond Kierkegaard either. What he is saying in fact is that the "how" of our involvement with the law is more important than the "what," that if only the "how" is truly personal and subjective it is bound to lead us to the objectively valid "what." This, however, is more than questionable. The core of the existentialist dilemma remains unresolved.

3.

It would seem that the individual, as individual, must reach beyond the individual in order to find truth not in subjectivity alone or in objectivity alone, but in the meeting of subjectivity and objectivity. In Judaism, the point of meeting between the two is the law.

What type of faith is that of the Jew? Notwithstanding the Christian apostle Paul, it is wholly personal. Who can doubt it who knows of the life and work of the endless galaxy of Jewish giants of faith—men and women wholly committed to Judaism—finding in it the entire meaning of their lives, choosing it daily anew, discovering the ultimate of personal fulfillment in giving themselves to it without reservation? Yet, these people of faith did not experience the law as an impediment to the subjectivity of the "how" of their commitment. If one wishes to understand the relationship between faith and law in Judaism, one should not ask those to whom the law has become a meaningless yoke or a chain of slavery. The law in Judaism is not what it is to those who reject it but what it means to those who—often in full awareness of its critiques

—accept it and strive to live by it. Only the Jews of faith-and-law can testify to the nature of the relationship between the two. For them, the law is naturally incorporated in their faith of unqualified personal commitment. The law itself, the *mitzva,* is the inexhaustible source of religious inspiration; it is the joy of the heart that enriches the very subjectivity of human existence and renders it personally more meaningful. "Sweeter also than the honey and the honeycomb" is the law for the Jew of faith-and-law. For him, the *simcha shel mitzva,* the joy that he derives from doing the will of God, is the highest form of existential fulfillment. In the *simcha shel mitzva,* the "how" of the truth is valid, yet the "what" of the truth has its source in the acceptance of the objectively given law and command. How is this to be explained?

From the religious point of view, man and law have something in common which is essential to both: the law is God's law, and man, too, is God's. He is God's man. This is not to be understood only in the external sense that he *has* to do the will of God, that he *has* to submit to a superior power, that he has to obey. That man is God's is an ontological statement about man—such is his being, such his nature. Man is God's existentially. God is given to him, to his individuality. Such is the nature of human subjectivity that it can realize itself only by taking due cognizance of the objectively given reality that is God. Such is the essence of man's individuality that it may find fulfillment only in the presence of God. Thus, the very subjectivity of faith requires living in the sight of God and doing the will of God.

Especially existentialist thinkers speak of faith as if it were a personal relation between one subject and another, between an I and a Thou. This is a mistake. In the actuality of the encounter between God and man, in the I-Thou relation, there is no need for faith. However, such actualization of the relation is extremely rare. Only exceptional people experience it at exceptional moments of their lives. But beyond the I-Thou relation, God remains the objectively given reality that forever accompanies man's individual existence. Faith acknowledges this fact by affirming the relation between God and man beyond the actuality of the I-Thou situation. In the act of faith the law represents the objectivity of the givenness of God for man's individuality; by means of the law the relationship is sustained beyond the actualization of the Divine Presence; by doing the will of God man remains Godward turned, related to Him, and only thus fulfilling the ontic meaning of his God-

given and God-anchored subjectivity. In the act of faith the law is
God's messenger, His representative. It is in this sense that a midrashic
interpretation has the boldness to say of each of the *arba minim* (the
four plants) of the Succot festival: *"Ze ha'kadosh baruk hu,* it is the
Holy One, blessed be He." (*Midrash Rabba,* Vayikra 30:9) Acknowledging each *mitzva* as God's messenger to man, the Jew of faith is in
contact with God by fulfilling His commandment.

Man is God's we have maintained, and, of course, so too is the law.
The proper understanding of this concept may further clarify the idea
that the law is the meeting point of subjectivity and objectivity. The
true significance of the God-given law is not that it is imposed from
without. Theonomy is not heteronomy. God knows man; God considers
man, his essenial nature. He considers not only man in general, *i.e.,*
mankind, He knows man the individual, every individual in his uniqueness and in the uniqueness of his situation. Thus, when He revealed His
law to Israel, He directed it to all Israel, to every individual Jew, in his
situations at all times. This is the meaning of the midrashic teaching,
that all the souls of all generations yet to come were assembled at Sinai
to receive the Torah together with the contemporary generation of Jews.
Because it is God's law, it possesses the quality of being able to confront
man in full consideration of his subjective nature. Because it is divine
law, because God does consider man, the human subjectivity of faith
and the objectivity of the law complement each other.

If our thesis is correct, while the form of the law is uniformly established for all times, its meaning, its address to the individual must be
inexhaustible. It carries its own single message to every individual in
the singleness of his own condition. The form is objective; the meaning
of its contents is subjectively directed to each man in his time, to his
individuality, by the One who knows him and gives him His law *because*
He knows him. According to midrashic interpretation, on the occasion
of the revelation at Sinai each one of the assembled received the Torah
in a manner commensurate with his strength and receptive capacity.
We see the eternal validity of the Torah in this its quality of revealing
itself to everyone according to his own condition. The objectivity of
form hides riches of meaning that are capable of speaking ever anew
to the present man in the contemporary situation. This is the meaning
of the old rabbinic teaching that one should read the Torah as if it
were given today. One should read it in this manner because it is indeed
directed to us each day anew.

There is, of course, tension between the subjectivity of faith and the objectivity of the law. But the tension is necessary. It is the creative irritant in the continuous unfolding of meaning and contents. By means of the tension, each generation—and every individual Jew—discovers the layer of meaning in the law God intended for it, for him. Not all is given. The meaning intended for us must be discovered by us and made our own in the fullness of our individuality within the frame of the God-given objectivity of our situation, in which our very subjectivity, too, has its root and origin.

CHAPTER 5

Reconstructionist Theology: A Critical Evaluation

I.   THE THEOLOGY OF RECONSTRUCTIONISM

There can be little doubt that wide sections of modern Jewry are engulfed by a deep spiritual crisis due to the conflict between traditional Judaism and the secular civilization of the age. On the American Jewish scene, Reconstructionism represents the school of thought whose chief preoccupation has been the interpretation of the meaning of this conflict and that has devoted its intellectual energies almost exclusively to its resolution. The movement, led vigorously by its founder, Mordecai M. Kaplan, has now achieved sufficient self-assurance to claim to offer "the only alternative to Orthodoxy and Secularism." [1]

Is this claim justified? Does Reconstructionism indeed offer a way out of the present predicament of our destiny? We shall have to consider the main teachings of Reconstructionist religious philosophy and then inquire into their objective validity.

We shall have to consider the main teachings of Reconstructionist religious philosophy and then inquire into their objective validity.

Rejection of Supernaturalism—Transnaturalism

Reconstructionism links the cause of the spiritual crisis of our time to the supernatural element in traditional religion. The modern mind is unable to accept supernaturalism. As long as religion is associated with the supernatural, modern civilization will remain secular. According to Reconstructionist thought, supernaturalism is "gone with the wind" never to return again. If religion is to be saved at all, it will have to be "wedded to naturalism." [2] Therein lies the solution to the problem.

149

Reconstructionism undertakes the task of purifying Judaism from its admixture of supernaturalism.

Occasionally the attempt is made to use the term "supernaturalism" in a specific way: as the belief that God may at will suspend the laws of nature in order to reward those whom He loves and punish those who have earned His wrath.[3] However, it is obvious that the inherent logic of Reconstructionism does not allow it to stop at the negation of the supernatural in this limited sense only. The stumbling block is not just the concept of "God as miracle worker" or "as a reservoir of magic power to be tapped whenever they [the believers] are aware of their physical limitations."[4] The idea of the supernatural as such is objectionable. According to Dr. Kaplan, modern science has invalidated "the distinction between natural and supernatural."[5] For the Reconstructionist, the idea of God as a transcendental, omnipotent, all-kind and all-wise Supreme Being that confronts the world and man as their Creator has no meaning. Modern man, so he maintains, is able to conceive the godhead only as immanent in the world; modern man is incapable of entering into relationship with the supernatural.[6] His concern is with life on this earth exclusively; there is no other. His goal is self-fulfillment, which may also be called, salvation—not, of course, in its traditional other-worldly meaning, but as this-worldly self-transcendence through the realization of man's inherent potentialities. Religion must help man "to live and to get the most out of life." This it can do only if it teaches him "to identify as divine and holy whatever in human life or in the world about him enhances human life."[7] The forces in us and around us which make "for health, happiness and progress"[8] are the manifestations of the divine. The God idea may be seen as the sum total of the process which in man and in nature contribute to human salvation. Reconstructionism asserts that this new concept may rightly be considered as reinterpretation of the traditional one, for it "can function in our day exactly as the belief in God has always functioned; it can function as an affirmation that life has value."[9]

At this point, however, the question might be asked: since the supernatural is rejected, what need is there for religion at all? In view of the fact that man's purpose in life is this-worldly self-fulfillment, could he not strive for it without having to identify as divine those forces that assist him in his endeavor? Why should we not be satisfied with a purely secular form of self-realization? In answer to such and similar questions the concept of man's striving for salvation is elaborated. Man is inspired to transcend the inheritance of his evolutionary origin from the brute by certain ideals and values which are of the spirit. Even though they are not part of the world of objective facts, they are no less real than the world of the senses. However, naturalistic science cannot account for values and meanings. It is for this reason that "secularism is not enough." [10] Human salvation depends on the realization of man's ethical aspirations. As man yearns to transcend his "subhuman tendencies," he is really raising himself above the dominion of the natural laws of the scientist. On account of that he is in need of "a transnatural religion." Transnaturalism is, then, the "alternative" that Reconstructionism submits as the union between religion and scientific naturalism.

Transnaturalism is defined as "that extension of naturalism which takes into account much that mechanistic or positivistic science is incapable of dealing with. Transnaturalism reaches out into the dominion where mind, personality, purpose, ideals, values and meanings dwell. It treats of the good and the true." [11] The distinction between fact and value is, of course, a very old and valid one. Our question, however, has still not been answered. If one so pleases, one may call the reaching out into the realm of meanings and values by the term "transnaturalism." But why transnaturalist *religion?* What is gained by it? May this recognition of a realm of ends and purposes as an aspect of reality not be adequately expressed within the scope of some secular humanism or ethical culture movement? However, Reconstructionism avers that "a godless humanism" [12] is an inadequate interpretation of life, because "it fails to express and to foster the feeling that man's ethical aspirations are part of a cosmic urge, by obeying which man makes himself at home in the universe." [13] Man needs the awareness that something in the very nature of the universe answers to his desire for self-fulfillment. This applies not only to man's individual happiness, but also to his endeavor for "maximum social cooperation," which is inseparable from salvation. It is maintained that "a religionless humanism fails to provide. . . . a motive for 'dedication to mankind.' That motive can come only from seeing in mankind potentialities which are in rapport with the creative principle in the cosmos—with God." [14] Without being able to see that his efforts at self-realization are indeed in keeping with the inherent nature of reality, man could not maintain himself in defiance of the endless temptations, failures, and disappointments which forever beset his path.

Godhood as a Cosmic Process

Reconstructionism does not find it difficult to show how "the inner drives of man" are a manifestation of cosmic reality. As is well known, man is not a self-sufficient being, independent of the rest of the world. "Human nature is part of the larger world of nature." [15] Whatever constitutes his being reflects powers outside him in the universe, the source whence he derives his existence. His very will for self-fulfillment is part of the cosmic will to live and is characteristic of all living things. Ethical inclinations and purposeful aspirations reveal aspects of reality because human nature itself has its place in the universal scheme. We have to learn to view the drives and urges of man for self-transcendence "as no less an integral part of the cosmic structure of reality than the life-drive and the sex-drive. . . ." [16] In the very choice of goals as we strive for salvation, we are impelled by the cosmic powers that have formed us and that sustain us. These powers we identify as divine, because they alone make life meaningful and valuable. The divine reveals itself in us in our own urge for self-realization. The very purpose of speaking of God as "the Power that makes for salvation" is "to identify the particular human experiences which enable us to feel the impact of that process in the environment and in ourselves which impels us to grow physically, mentally, morally, and spiritually. That process is godhood. It reveals itself in those particular experiences." [17]

Needless to say, if godhood is the cosmic process that impels man to grow, the "cosmic urges that are manifest in him also represent the will and the law of God for him. A deity that is immanent in nature and in man cannot communicate his will or law in a specific act of personal revelation." The law of God is revealed to man in man's "own best vision of his capacity for rendering service to the cause of humanity." [18] It follows from the Reconstructionist premise that "we cannot see the will of God in any one specific code of laws. Only in the spiritual life of man as a whole, only in the complex of forces which impel man to think in terms of ideals and seek to implement their ideals through laws as well as through social institutions can we discover the will of God." [19] This is a new interpretation of the old adage, *vox populi vox dei*. From the Reconstructionist point of view one might say that while the Torah is of course not *min ha-shamayim* as tradition understands the term, all law that aims at cooperation represents a form of divine self-revelation, brought about through the instrumentality of man's "best vision." By relating man's higher aspirations to cosmic nature and bestowing the name of God on "the totality of all those forces in life that render human life worthwhile" religion becomes the source of values and meanings, whereas science "describes objective reality." [20]

It would of course matter little by what name we called the cosmic forces whose self-revelation we discern in man's idealistic impulses. Name-calling is often a mere game of semantics. The religious significance of identifying those forces as the process of godhood lies in the fact that by doing so we affirm our confidence in the validity of the meanings and purposes for which they are responsible. By recognizing godhood in everything that impels man "to grow," we express our confidence that, indeed, he will grow. The "process of godhood" assures the Reconstructionist of the possibility of the realization of man's yearning for salvation. He calls this process "God" because he defines the term as the Power inherent in the universe that, by the very fact of its activity in the human soul, "endorses what we believe ought to be and that endorses that it will be." [21] The word "God" is for Reconstructionism a symbol that expresses "the highest ideals for which men strive and, at the same time, points to the objective fact that the world is so constituted as to make for the realization of those ideals." [22] This may be called the faith of Reconstructionism. To argue from man's position as part of nature for the recognition of the cosmic roots of his strivings is one thing; to conclude that, because of their being rooted in cosmic forces, they are bound to find fulfillment is quite another. It implies an act of faith in the cosmos.

The Faith of Reconstructionism

Let us see what must be assumed in such an act of faith. Not only does the Reconstructionist believer reason from man placed in the context of "a larger nature" to his relatedness to universal life, but he assumes on account of this relatedness a kind of "preestablished harmony" between his impulses and the cosmic urge. He must further assume some form of built-in harmony between the order of nature, as described by science, and the powers that are responsible for the human drives that manifest values and purposes. Unless the realm of nature and that of the spirit are coordinated, there can be little hope that the material conditions in the universe will ever allow the realization of man's aspirations. Reconstructionism is aware of what is implied in its belief in the possibilities of human salvation. It interprets faith in the sovereignty of God as "faith that in mankind there is manifest a power which, in full harmony with the nature of the physical universe, operates for the regeneration of human society." [23] Underlying this assumption is the concept of unity among all the cosmic forces. Unless they are purposefully interrelated, no purpose can prosper in the universe. The cosmic drives, active in man and society, in nature as well as in the realm of the spirit, must be related to each other in an all-embracing universal harmony; otherwise the fulfillment of man's striving for self-realization is left to mere chance. Only on the basis of a concept of universal oneness does it make sense to affirm that the world is so constituted that what the human mind recognizes as valuable will indeed come to be for the sole reason that it ought to be. Reconstructionism perceives God "as the apotheosis of the interrelated unity of all reality; for it is only such unity that is compatible with life's worthwhileness." [24] Only by virtue of its purposefulness can life have meaning.

No doubt, man does have some experience of life's unity. Personality itself may be looked upon as the result of a unifying process in the world. Man's own creative urge as well as his appreciation of value are manifestations of life's general trend towards unity. Meaning achieved in an act of creativity is always a deed of unification. However, such experiences testify mainly to a *tendency* toward unity, to an effort in life "to achieve and express unity, harmony and integrity." [25] There is, however, a long way from such tendencies to the affirmation of actual harmony between man and the universe, and among all the cosmic powers themselves. How is such affirmation justified? The father of Reconstructionism assures us repeatedly that the concept of "the interrelated unity of all reality," which alone "spells God" for him, is based on an intuition—on the intuition "that human life is supremely worthwhile and significant." [26] The belief in God, accordingly, means to subscribe to "the certain assumption" that the nature of cosmic reality endorses and guarantees "the realization in man of that which is of greatest value to him." "It is an assumption that is not susceptible to proof," says Dr. Kaplan, but if we believe in it, we believe in God. [27]

Thus, the basic Reconstructionist concept of life's worthwhileness, which to affirm is "the function" of the idea of God, becomes a matter of intuitive assumption. This implies also that it cannot be "demonstrated" that self-fulfillment, the goal of Reconstructionist religion, will ever be attained. What alone may be said concerning it is that "faith must assume it as the objective of human behavior, if we are not to succumb to the cynical acceptance of evil, which is the only other alternative." [28] One should, however, not be misled by this quotation into believing that the faith that is meant here is only the result of a tragic choice between itself and the despair of cynicism. Such a faith would indeed be nothing but á mere opiate. In one of the finest passages of Reconstructionist literature, part of which has already been quoted in connection with Dr. Kaplan's rejection of secular humanism, one reads: "Without the emotional intuition of an inner harmony between human nature and universal nature, without the conviction, born of the heart rather than of the mind, that the world contains all that is necessary for human salvation, the assumptions necessary for ethical living remain cold hypotheses lacking all dynamic power.... It is only this emotional reaction to life that can make humanity itself mean more to us than 'the disease of the agglutinated dust." [29] Notwithstanding the recurring echo of the alternative of despair, there is no doubt that the intuition of Reconstructionist faith is presented as an actual experience of deep emotional intensity.

Chaos and Cosmos

Having followed thus far the analysis of the Reconstructionist thesis, the question may no longer be put off: What is the status and the meaning of evil in the Reconstructionist world view? Since the emergence of values and purposes in man and society are attributed to the interrelated complex of helping cosmic powers which we identify as divine, shall we be justified in identifying evil in the world as the self-revelation of some diabolical cosmic forces that "unmake" man's striving for salvation and unity? In view of human experience with nature as well as in history, it would not seem to be an unwarranted conclusion. Shall we then assume a Manichean "universe" in which the two principles of good and evil are locked in struggle with each other? Reconstructionist thinking does not countenance such a solution. It does not agree to the spelling of the word evil as Evil. According to it, evil must not be granted status side by side with "the goodness of life which is its godliness." Evil does not exist in a positive way, so Reconstructionism avers. Evil is a mere negation, a chance, an accident. It is "inevitable only in the logical and passive sense that darkness is the inevitable concomitant of light." Evil is mere unshaped and unformed *Tohu va-Vohu*, that phase of the universe which has not yet been invaded by the creative energy, not yet conquered by will and intelligence, not yet completely penetrated by godhood. The creative energy, which is the element of godhood in the universe, is all the time at work, in man and in nature, forming cosmos out of chaos.[30]

Such an interpretation of evil must be paralleled by an appropriate interpretation of life's worthwhileness. Life is worthwhile in spite of all that mars it. It is worthwhile not so much because of the actually realized good in it, but mainly owing "to the infinite potentialities that are still latent and that will in time come to fruition." [31] Latent potentialities can, of course, never be demonstrated. It is again a matter of intuitive faith, a knowledge of the heart rather than of the mind.

Whatever the value of this interpretation of evil may be, it is obvious that the Reconstructionist credo has been badly jolted. Even if one is not prepared to grant evil positive status, the mere existence of chaos beside the process of godhood necessitates a new definition of the concept of the deity. A god that "like an artist" struggling with the passive resistance of a block of marble, step by step, forms cosmos out of the meaninglessness of chaos, is obviouly lacking the attribute of infinity or perfection. As long as there is evil, there is chaos; and chaos exists because godhood has "not yet penetrated it." But a deity that needs time to do his job is of necessity limited in his capacity. This, indeed, is recognized to be one of the consequences of the Reconstructionist position. The Reconstructionist interpretation of evil involves "a radical change in the traditional concept of God. It conflicts with that conception of God as infinite and perfect in His omniscience and omnipotence." [32] However, we are assured that there is really no need for such an idea of the godhead. A concept which symbolizes "the sum of the animating, organizing forces and relationships which are forever making a cosmos out of chaos" is quite sufficient. It is such a concept that the Reconstructionist has in mind when he speaks of "God as the creative life of the universe." [33]

This, of course, gives us an entirely new idea of the deity. As our awareness of the divine aspect of reality is derived from the meaningful and purposeful contents of the universe, divinity must manifest itself in the cosmos. The cosmos, however, is continually growing. As the cosmos expands, so does its divine quality develop with it. We ought, therefore, to conclude: the more cosmos, the richer the potency of the creative life of the universe that is identified as God. We have actually netted a god that is neither perfect nor infinite; one that, though finite in his effectiveness, is infinite in the possibilities of further development; one that grows more and more perfect as it forces cosmos upon the face of chaos.

Enthusiasm for Living

The extremely original idea of the Reconstructionist godhead illustrates dramatically how much Reconstructionist intuition must accomplish in order to establish the worthwhileness of life. We see now that the belief in the unity of all reality, which alone could guarantee the realization of man's nobler aspirations, involves belief in cosmic powers that are finite in potency as well as in wisdom. No one is, of course, in a position to evaluate the vastness of universal chaos as compared with the finite amount of creative life which, at any moment, may be immanent in the cosmos. Whether the potency of a finite godhead may not be after all exhausted in its struggle with the passive resistance of the *"tohu and bohu"*; or whether the process of cosmic godhead may not occasionally lead to a blunder of universal magnitude and thus allow chaos to regain its lost terrain—such questions receive no adequate attention. Apparently, it is felt that the emotional reaction of faith in life is convincing enough to silence such questions.

One of the strongest statements of Reconstructionist faith seems to be directed against such and similar carpings of the intellect. Toward the end of one of Dr. Kaplan's major works on Reconstructionist theology, once again the question is asked: "Whence do we derive this faith in a Power that endorses what ought to be?" And the answer is given in the following words: "Not from that aspect of the mind which has to do only with mathematically and logically demonstrated knowledge. Such faith stems from that aspect of the mind that finds expression in the enthusiasm for living, in the passion to surmount limitation. . . . The fact that many lack this enthusiasm does not invalidate the truth [of the faith] any more than the fact that it took the genius of an Einstein to discover the principle of relativity should lead us to cast a doubt upon its truth. This enthusiasm is man's will to live the maximum life. Just as the will to live testifies—in an intuitive not, a logical sense—to the reality of life, the will to live the maximum life testifies to the realizable character of such life." [34]

We must confess that we are not quite able to see how "the enthusiasm for living" can be considered an "expression" of an "aspect of the mind," since this enthusiasm is also equated with "man's will to live the maximum life." Be that as it may, the passage quoted indicates that "the enthusiasm for living" is the cornerstone of the Reconstructionist philosophy of religion. Without it, there can be no faith in the power that endorses what ought to be and guarantees that it is also realizable. This enthusiasm must therefore be the source of the conviction, "born of the heart and not of the mind," of the harmony between individual strivings and cosmic urges and, finally, the origin of the intuition of the unity of all reality. As one realizes that the entire scheme of Reconstructionist salvation depends on "the enthusiasm for living," one can hardly suppress the thought that the far-reaching cosmic conclusions of the Reconstructionist heart represent no less a bold "leap of faith" than the boldest ever performed by Karl Barth and his disciples.

At this point, one is induced to recall the way the founder and leader of Reconstructionism pokes fun at an author who has stated that a sense of sureness, "a sense of overmastering certainty which grips the spirit," is the characteristic mark of supernatural revelation. After the summary dismissal of the illogicality of such notions, one was entitled to look forward to something more tangible than "emotional reaction," "intuitive affirmation," and "enthusiasm for living" to form the foundation of Reconstructionist religious faith. Should one, perhaps, use Dr. Kaplan's own words with which he contemptuously rejects the sense of sureness and overmastering certainty of supernatural revelation and say regarding the intuitive convictions of Reconstructionism that "one takes exception, as a modernist must, to the folly of making sureness a criterion of truth, since stupidity is almost invariably sure of its own wisdom?" [35] We shall not follow Dr. Kaplan's example. We believe that a sense of sureness need not always be wrong, only because at times even fools seem to possess it; just as we hold quite confidently that the value of the most enthusiastic enthusiasm will not be proved by the argument that it took the genius of an Einstein to conceive the theory of relativity.

Suffice it that we have traced the place of intuition and enthusiasm in the structure of Reconstructionist thought.

In bringing to a conclusion this presentation of Reconstructionist theology, we may point out that its characteristic feature is a mood of optimism, of "trust in life and in man." The optimism is intuitively derived from "the quality of universal being," which is called divine and is identified with godhood. One may say that Reconstructionist thought is a variation on the religious theme of the seventeenth and eighteenth centuries; it is a form of natural religion. The very title of Dr. Kaplan's latest work, *Judaism Without Supernaturalism,* reminds one of that classic of eighteenth-century deism, *Christianity Not Mysterious,* authored by John Toland and published in 1696. The "natural light" by which the deists were guided was, of course, reason, which possessed the dignity of logical necessity and universal validity. Reconstructionism, however, is familiar with the intellectual climate of the twentieth century. Its "natural light" is provided by the insights of experimental science and psychology. Reconstructionism is, therefore, guided by human experience, by aspirations, urges, yearnings, drives. Universality is acquired by granting these manifestations of human nature cosmic status as the expressions of a cosmic vitality. In such an atmosphere reliance on intuition and on an enthusiasm for living is, perhaps, understandable. At the same time, one is also reminded of certain specific forms of natural religion which were in vogue in the seventeenth and eighteenth centuries. In particular, one is induced to recall the English philosopher, Shaftesbury, who, in his writings published in 1711, placed at the center of his thought the principle of enthusiasm for life and living. He, too, derived the meaning and worthwhileness of life from a universal harmony. Not unlike Reconstructionism, Shaftesbury, too, saw the meaning of religion in the enhancement of personality which may be achieved because man knows himself at one with the interrelated unity of all reality. For Shaftesbury, too, the interrelated unity of reality is the divine aspect of reality. It follows logically from such a position that, like Dr. Kaplan, the Englishman, too, is compelled to deny the reality of evil. If evil existed positively and actively, and on the worldwide scale in which it does seem to exist from the point of view of commonsense observation, what would become of the enthusiasm for living?

It should also be noted that in Reconstructionism we are confronted with a form of pantheism. By identifying certain processes in man and the world as divine, we identify the divinity with the world and, indeed, with man. In a striking passage it is stated: ". . . we must not identify the sovereignty of God with the expression of the will of a superhuman, immortal, and infallible individual personality, but with that Power on which we rely for regeneration of society and which operates through individual human beings and social institutions." [36]   In untold other passages we are assured that God is a cosmic vitality, the creative urge in the universe; that man is in God and God is in man. Godhead is immanent in nature and in humanity; its sovereignty is exercised through man and society.[37]

We should then say that transnaturalism, the religion of Reconstructionism, is a pantheistic faith of optimism, conceived in a twentieth-century setting, in the traditions of eighteenth-century natural religion. According to its own testimony, its reasoning is not conclusive; but it feels very strongly that its tenets are securely anchored in convictions "born of the heart rather than of the mind," in a number of intuitions, and—ultimately—in an enthusiasm for living.

II. CRITICISM

One should, perhaps, not attempt to reason with intuitions and enthusiasms. In themselves they are matters of purely personal concern and those who say that they have them may well be trusted to speak the truth. However, transnaturalism is presented to us as a reinterpretation of Judaism and we are asked to accept it as "the only alternative to Orthodoxy and secularism." For one who is not a Reconstructionist the way to take the Reconstructionist solution of our spiritual dilemma seriously is to investigate its philosophical and theological validity. In this attempt we shall at first turn our attention to the self-consistency of Reconstructionist religious philosophy. We shall do this under three headings: the problem of evil, the problem of freedom, and the problem of unity.

The Problem of Evil

The interpretation of evil as chaos and of good as the purposive urge that forms cosmos from chaos is a thought for which one is not prepared by the premises of Reconstructionism. Among these premises we find the idea that modern science, in revising our picture of the universe, has abolished the distinction between the natural and supernatural as well as the dichotomy between the physical and the metaphysical.[38] This would seem to be one of the main reasons that Reconstructionism is so impatient with the supernatural in religion, which is, usually, so strongly supported by metaphysical speculations. Having thrown out the supernatural, Reconstructionism is forced to establish a new distinction, that between cosmos and chaos or, as one might also say, between nature and subnature. The relationship between the two is not altogether unlike that which—according to Reconstructionist interpretation—existed in traditional religions between the natural and supernatural: cosmos forces its will and its intentions on chaos.

There is, of course, a difference. Chaos is mere resistance, absence of meaning. Its only weapon of self-defense against being penetrated by the cosmic urge is its inertia. Chaos can be overcome and conquered, but not so nature. Nature has laws and order; it has positive existence. But why should it not be mastered by a more powerful supernature? The answer is, of course, that supernature does not exist. No one has ever seen it. We know for a certainty that science has "invalidated the distinction between natural and supernatural." But does science approve of the distinction between natural and subnatural? Has anyone ever encountered the *"tohu* and *bohu"* of Dr. Kaplan, the neutral, negative inertia of the unformed "resistant?" What people know from actual experience, the only witness admitted in the Reconstructionist court, is evil and wickedness, sorrow and suffering, failure and sin, prevalent in history and nature on a far more impressive scale than the goodness of life that, according to Reconstructionism, is godliness. It is possible to interpret evil as mere chaos, the mere absence of goodness; but to do so is good, old-fashioned metaphysics. The Reconstructionist distinction between chaos and cosmos, or, as we may say, between subnature and nature, is no less a metaphysical supposition than the distinction between natural and supernatural. He who rejects the one cannot cling to the other.

The very idea that evil is a mere absence of goodness "as darkness is the inevitable concomitant of light" has, of course, a long and glorious history. It originated in Neaplatonism in the third century and ever since it has been made use of in numberless philosophical systems. (In the history of Jewish philosophy Saadia Gaon, in the tenth century, was its most distinguished spokesman.) But Neoplatonism is purest metaphysics. It denies the very existence of nature, in the sense in which Reconstructionism uses the term. According to Plotinus, there is only the One and everything else is emanation of its substance. In this context evil represents a logical inconsistency. How can it exist, if everything is an emanation of the divine substance of the Infinite? And so its existence is denied. It is only in this way that the idea of evil as the mere absence of good may be used and has been used. It is always the logical requirement of an originally purely metaphysical interpretation of reality. Only the power of metaphysical thought has ever dared to deny the reality of evil in defiance of overwhelming human experience. Such defiance, however, makes little sense, if one starts out with naturalism, as Reconstructionism does, and acknowledges experience, within the framework of nature, as the only arbiter of truth. In actual life we find some goodness and a great deal of disgustingly positive and sickeningly real evil. This is the material the Reconstructionist has with which to work and with it he has to justify his intuitive affirmation of the worthwhileness of life and his enthusiasm for living. He dare not deny experience, since his entire *raison d'être* is derived from experience.

When ideas are made to serve in contexts for which they were originally not intended, they often take revenge on their despoilers by involving them in the most absurd illogicalities. The consequences of the denial of the positive nature of evil are an interesting example in case. It is not easy to define exactly the area of the Reconstructionist "chaos." Fortunately, there are a few passages in classical Reconstructionist writings that are quite explicit. We read, for instance, that earthquakes and volcanic eruptions, devastating storms and floods, famines and plagues, noxious plants and animals "are simply that phase of the universe which has not yet been completely penetrated by godhood." [39] In another context again we are told that the divine quality of life is not to be seen in tempests, conflagrations and earthquakes, but "in 'the still small voice' in which the patiently creative and constructive forces of life find expression." [40] These statements make it quite clear that if evil was denied positive status, it meant that the destructive powers in the universe were neutral toward concepts of value; they were mere resistance to and not active opponents of meaning. However, the intention was not to deny its status as nature. No doubt, Reconstructionism cannot be blind to the fact that tempests and earthquakes, noxious plants and animals, belong to the dominion of nature and are subject to its laws and orderliness no less than its more pleasing and constructive manifestations. From the scientific point of view, the existence of toadstools, cobras, and man-eating tigers is no less natural than that of strawberries, kittens, and babies. We now realize that the distinction between chaos and cosmos is not between subnature and nature, but between two manifestations of nature itself: nature that makes for human survival and salvation—we call it cosmos because it is penetrated by the purpose of the constructive life forces; and nature, as exemplified in tornadoes, cobras, and man-eating tigers, not so conducive to human survival and salvation—we call it *tohu* and *bohu* because it has not yet been "conquered by will and intelligence."

This is meant to be taken seriously. Not only do the two forms of nature follow logically from the Reconstructionist concepts of chaos and cosmos; we find the idea so stated explicitly. Reconstructionism identifies "as divine the forces in the physical environment that make for physical survival and well being." [41] This is clear enough. Forces in the physical environment that do not make for man's survival and well-being are not divine; they are not yet invaded by purpose; they are not of the cosmos, but of chaos. It is also emphasized that "the creative powers in the physical world" alone are the manifestations of godhood. Needless to say there are others too which are not creative and, therefore, not divine. But that which is not divine is not purposive, not directed toward a goal which is worthwhile—it is chaotic. Chaos too is nature, no less than cosmos. Chaos is the merciless order of causal connections, utterly indifferent to the outcome of its own processes; whereas cosmos is the condition of the natural order, after having been compelled to admit purpose and meaning. The one is blind, the other, guided nature. It is, of course, unlikely that naturalism could consider such a distinction anything but mere foolishness. To us it would seem to be the most bizarre product of an extremely fertile metaphysical imagination or—shall we perhaps say?—intuition.

The Problem of Freedom

The most serious objection to the distinction between chaos and cosmos, between the blind order of natural law and the one guided by purpose and plan, comes from another quarter.

One of the premises of Reconstructionist thinking is that one "cannot believe that God performs miracles and at the same time believe in the uniformities of natural law demanded by scientific theory." [42] The uniformities of natural law cannot be suspended or disturbed. However, one cannot help wondering what happens to these uniformities when "the creative urge" of the universe breaks into their domain with purpose and plan. What an infinite, omnipotent God could not be believed to be capable of accomplishing is now assumed to be successfully performed by a creative impulse in the cosmos that, as we have seen, must be thought of as finite and imperfect. It is true that the creative urge is conceived as being immanent in the world, whereas the omnipotent and omniscient Supreme Being is transcendental to it. In both cases, however, the problem is the same: How can the lawful orderliness of nature be made to obey a purposeful will without interfering with the "uniformities" of natural law? It makes no difference whether the purpose emanates from an immanent cosmic urge or a transcendental divine will; its origin in each case is seen in something that is external to the dominion of "the immutable laws of cause and effect." In each case we are confronted with the conflict between the order of nature, held together by the unbreakable bonds of its laws, and the order of the spirit guided by the chosen goals of an intelligent will. The order of nature is the realm of necessity; that of the spirit the realm of freedom. No matter how one imagines the power of the spirit, immanent or transcendent, the problem is unchanged: How can purpose, conceived and pursued in freedom, penetrate the unconquerable fortress of necessity?

Reconstructionism fully appreciates the fact that the conquest of chaos by purposeful intelligence is an act of freedom. It is, however, doubtful that it realizes the magnitude of the problem of the possibility of freedom as it arises on the basis of its own naturalistic premises. We are assured that there is a principle of creativity in the universe. This principle is responsible for "the continuous emergence of aspects of life not prepared for or determined by the past." Needless to say that a principle that is active independently of what is prepared for or determined by the past is free from the iron yoke of the law of causality that dominates nature. It is a principle of cosmic freedom that is said "to constitute the most divine phase of reality." [43] The same creative urge that is forming cosmos from chaos in the universe is also at work within man as he is struggling with the *tohu* and *bohu* within himself.

The ethical life of man is itself a manifestation of creativity.[44] In fact, in accordance with the Reconstructionist deduction of the divine from human experience, it is principally man's awareness of alternative courses of possible action, and his power to choose between them, that grant us the knowledge of a creative principle free from what has been "prepared for or determined by the past." It is because of this creative impulse, experienced by us, that we are entitled to speak of its cosmic correlative—since man himself is "part of a larger nature"— as the divine power that makes for freedom. The creative urge within man, which reflects corresponding cosmic powers, is the freedom that is "at the root of man's spiritual life, and is the prime condition of his self-fulfillment, or salvation." [45]

This is nobly said. Undoubtedly, freedom is to the life of the spirit what air is to our bodily existence. The question, however, is, how is freedom possible in the context of a reality that is dominated by the determinism of irrepressible laws?

Reconstructionism does make a number of bold affirmations in favor of freedom. The attitude of naturalistic determinism that "looks upon everything as the effect of everything else" is derided as an obsession.[46] The idea that the realm of natural law is not amenable to the influence of freedom and responsibility is likened to "a resurgence" of the old belief in fate of Greek antiquity. According to such an idea the realm of nature is the modern concept of fate. This is said in the best tradition of A. N. Whitehead's *Science in the Modern World*. But how does Reconstructionism meet the power of the sinister empire of nature-fate? The most significant passage on this issue that we are able to discern runs as follows: "But no more fatal error can be committed than that of overlooking the element of personality. There is in every human being something irreducible which renders him a monad, a world in himself, a microcosmos . . . the individual is a center of reference, an end in himself and fully responsible for what he does with his life." [47] This is indeed edifying. Unfortunately, one cannot solve the decisive problems of human existence by homiletics. Having started out with the premise of "the immutable laws of cause and effect," the Reconstructionist road points clearly to determinism and the denial of freedom. If Reconstructionism nevertheless wishes to affirm freedom, it must show how freedom and necessity may be accommodated in the same system.

When Whitehead drew our attention to the idea that in modern thought the concept of the natural law has taken the place of the old Greek concept of fate, he also showed us how to cope with the resulting problem by giving us one of the imposing metaphysical systems in the history of philosophy. But he who, because of "the uniformities of natural law," rejects the belief that God may perform miracles, cannot logically assert the creative principle of freedom merely by affirming its existence very firmly. It is fine to hear that the human personality is a monad, a world in itself, a center of reference. However, we should like to know how this monad may be responsible for its life in the context of "the uniformities of natural law." Reconstructionism overlooks the point that in relationship to the uniformities of nature every ethical deed is a deed of freedom, indeed, a miracle; and perhaps an even greater "miracle" than the suspension of a natural law by the intervention of the will of a Supreme Being. As Kant has already shown, freedom is transcendental to the order of nature.[48] It is essentially supernatural. We may say then, that the Reconstructionist distinction between chaos and cosmos is not, as we first thought, a distinction between subnature and nature, nor one between two types of nature, as it appeared to us on second consideration, but the good old "dichotomy" between natural and supernatural, the rejection of which is one of the premises of Reconstructionism.

We are led to the same conclusion about the implied supernaturalism of Reconstructionist thought, if we consider that cosmos-forming creative urge which is "the element of godhood in the world."[49] It is the urge that is responsible for the intelligence and the will that forever seeks to invade the chaos. It introduces meaning and plan into the world. It is the "divine process" which brings into being "personalities, men and women, with souls," liberating them "from tohu and bohu, the void of meaninglessness and purposelessness."[50] As we have noted already, the Reconstructionist theologian prefers to talk of "the divine process," "the creative urge" which is godhood, of God as the power in the universe that makes for one thing or another, in order to emphasize that what he understands by the deity is, not transcendentally apart from the world, but immanent in reality as its "constructive" and meaningful aspect.

It would seem to us that all this terminology is mere semantic juggling with words which have become empty because the ideas which they are supposed to convey are not properly understood. The founder of Reconstructionism does not realize that intelligence and will, purpose and plan, meaning and value, are not the manifestations of urges and processes, or of impulsions or powers, however universal and cosmic they may be imagined to be. Intelligence and will are not conceivable without intellect and soul; purposes and plans are conceived by minds; and meaning and value are meaningless and valueless unless they are related to some individual being. Therefore, to speak of cosmic powers as being responsible for cosmic intelligence, will, and purpose, implies a cosmic intellect, a universal mind. Since such cosmic intellect, according to the theory, faces chaos with the intention of penetrating it by the imposition of a purpose of its own, the cosmic intellect must be transcendental and prior to both chaos and cosmos. It is supernatural; and, as a mind associated with a will and purpose, it must be imagined in some terms of personal existence.

Of "freedom and responsibility of which human nature is capable" Reconstructionism maintains that they are the natural manifestation, on a self-conscious level, of the cosmic principle of polarity; freedom standing for selfhood and responsibility, for cooperation. However, neither selfhood nor cooperation has any meaning without self.[51] If freedom and responsibility should indeed be the manifestation of a cosmic principle, then it must be the principle of cosmic selfhood cooperating with other selves; or, paraphrasing what we heard Reconstructionism call the human personality, a cosmic monad or, perhaps, even Leibniz's "monad of monads." No doubt this would still not be the God of traditional religion. Reconstructionism's "divine aspect of reality," which we have now unmasked as a cosmic personality is, as we recall, neither infinite nor perfect. We may, therefore, say that implied in the Reconstructionist concept of godhood is a finite, Platonic demiurge, which is apart from the cosmos it forms. We have landed again in supernaturalism, so much despised by the Reconstructionist.

In order to avoid a possible misunderstanding, we shall take another glance at the statement that freedom and responsibility "are the natural manifestation, on a self-conscious level," of a cosmic principle. The phrase, "natural manifestation on a self-conscious level" suggests ideas borrowed from the evolutionary theory of ethics. Evolutionists speak of levels of evolution, among which self-consciousness is the latest and highest. They would see in freedom and responsibility the manifestation of evolutionary progress on the level of self-consciousness. However, no

evolutionist of rank will today look for correlatives to human freedom
and responsibility in the cosmos. He knows that in order to do so he
would have to assume one of two alternatives. Either the cosmic correlative produces all the levels of evolutionary development, including
consciousness, freedom, responsibility, and purpose by consciously directed activity, or else by some unselfconscious, purposeful drive. In
either case one would have to conclude that all ethical values are latently
present in the evolving cosmic powers just as all the qualities of a
plant are dormant in the seed. If ethical values are evolved by some
conscious cosmic power, they must be forever present in a transcendental
cosmic mind. If, on the other hand, they are brought into being by
some unselfconscious cosmic drive from a condition of immanent possibility into a state of actuality, one would still have to posit the potentiality of the ethical life in the cosmos as "preformed" by a transcendental
cosmic consciousness. This was indeed the meaning of evolution in the
pre-Darwinian days. Evolution was seen as the unfolding of latent
possibilities, which were originally planted in the cosmos by the Creator.

This position has been abandoned by the post-Darwinian evolutionary
theory, especially by its latest representatives. From the scientific point
of view, the evolution of latent possibilities that are inherently present
in the universe is mere metaphysical speculation with suspiciously
theological implications. Modern evolutionary theory, even though it
recognizes the evolutionary validity of ethical concepts, will not acknowledge any cosmic correlatives to ethical values, no "powers that make
for freedom and human salvation." The evolutionary principle is able
to explain the rise of ethics by means of adaptive functions which work
automatically within the context of causation. As one of its ablest
present-day representatives writes: ". . . We have the glorious paradox
that this purposeless mechanism [of evolution], after a thousand million
years of its blind and automatic operations, has finally generated purpose—as one of the attributes of our own species."[52]

All the Reconstructionist affirmations of a universal urge that forms
cosmos from chaos with will and intelligence are a relapse into pre-
Darwinian concepts of a metaphysical evolutionary theory. One might,
however, say in defense of Reconstructionism that it does not understand
the supernaturalist implications of such metaphysics. In order to save
its affirmation of the harmony between individual strivings and cosmic
urges, Reconstructionism may attempt to take refuge in some mysterious
élan vital or *évolution créatrice*. If so, Reconstructionist teachers will be

well advised to make peace with some metaphysical and supernaturalist philosophy, for neither of these Bergsonian principles have any status outside metaphysics and the supernatural.

Freedom and Reconstructionist Pantheism

As freedom and responsibility, purpose and plan, related to a cosmic canvas, lead back into entanglements with the metaphysical and the supernatural, so does Reconstructionist pantheistic immanence, in its turn, undermine the foundations of all purposeful human endeavor undertaken in a spirit of responsibility and as an act of free commitment to a worthwhile goal. We have noted that Reconstructionism regards the powers which within man make for ethical action as the extension of cosmic reality. From this point of view, the ethical life of man is intensely impulsive. We heard it described as "no less integral a part of the cosmic structure of reality than the life-drive and sex-drive." [53] Wisdom, cooperation, and creativity are presented as the natural offsprings of universal urges. They "too are hungers" which are "irrepressible until they are satisfied." The idea of right is really "a form of might, an overpowering impulse" to do the right. Man's ethical aspirations are viewed as "part of a cosmic urge." Social ethics must conform to "certain fundamental laws that are as intrinsic to human nature as the law of gravitation is to matter." [54]

The entire ethical life of man is thus conceived in terms of urges and drives, impulsions and compulsions, which, on the level of self-consciousness reflect corresponding cosmic activities. This, of course, is inherent in the logic of Reconstructionism. No Reconstructionist ever encountered cosmic powers which make for life's worthwhileness. His experience is only with the worthwhileness of individual lives. The ethical aspirations of man might be sufficient material to base on them a religionless humanism; they were, however, turned into the foundations of transnaturalist religion by looking on them as manifestations of cosmic powers, representing the divine aspect of universal reality. We saw how this was accomplished. It is, therefore, necessary for Reconstructionism to interpret man's ethical life as rooted in drives, urges, irresistible impulses, and hungers which give man no rest until they are satisfied. It is an almost biologically determined ethics. Unfortunately, ethical drives built into the cosmic structure are the blight to all personal ethics. The ethical deed is the fruit of freedom. Actions that are prompted by irrepressible impulses and hungers which cannot be denied are not performed in free commitment to an ideal. The teachers of the Talmud were bold enough to state that "everything is in the power of Heaven except the fear of Heaven." [55] The closer the bond between man's ethical aspirations and the cosmic powers in which they originate, and which become manifest in them, the less free the human deed which results from such aspirations; and the less free the deed, the less ethical will it be adjudged. Yet, Reconstructionism cannot sever the bond and dissolve the identification. For unless we see the ethical strivings of man as the activity of the cosmic reality of which he is part, we know nothing of "the divine aspect of universal being," the belief in which is the essence of Reconstructionist religion. Reconstructionism is faced here with a dilemma. Either freedom is taken seriously as being at "the root of man's spiritual life," [56] in which case his ethical strivings are not the manifestations of the activity of any cosmic powers and Reconstructionism cannot identify the divine aspect of reality; or else, the strivings are the activity of the cosmic process of godhood in man, then freedom has become an empty phrase, and ethics a nobler aspect of biology.

Reconstructionism does not seem to be aware of the problem and affirms enthusiastically both freedom and the immanent ethics of a cosmic mechanism which works with the forcefulness of hungers and other natural drives for the realization of the good. It would seem that whenever man performs an ethical deed, he acts in freedom as well as under the pressure of some cosmic compulsion. He himself desires this-worldly salvation and sets his goal accordingly, "but neither the quest for salvation nor the choice of goods is entirely man-determined." [57] As we have already learned, "human nature is a part of the larger world of nature. . . ." Such ideas render the extent of personal responsibility extremely vague. Obviously, man cannot be made responsible for what is not "man-determined" within him but is the action of a cosmic urge through him. If as "moral agents we are *inwardly impelled* to consider the consequences from the standpoint of their destroying or enhancing the value of life," it will be difficult to censor an agent who does not act morally. The very fact that he does not consider consequences may be an indication that he is not sufficiently impelled by the powers that make for responsible behavior. His very action proves that "the consciousness of the power and the responsibility to choose the right in the face of temptation" [58] were not really "irrepressible" within him, as they were supposed to be according to the Reconstructionist affirmation.

The nature of the problem may perhaps be best illustrated by the Reconstructionist reinterpretation of the concept of sin. Man's failure to live up to the best that is in him is sin because "it means that our souls are not attuned to the divine, that we have betrayed God." The best that is in man is the divine in him, the function of cosmic forces in the soul of man. We "identify" it as God because it is identical with "that aspect of reality which confers meaning and value on life and elicits from us those ideals that determine the course of human progress." [59] If this is indeed true, one cannot help wondering how it is possible ever to know that a person has failed to live up to the best that is in him. Whenever a person does not come up to our expectations, may it not be due to the fact that what we consider the best in man has not been "elicited" in this man with sufficient forcefulness so as not to let him fail? Instead of accusing him of "betraying God," may it not be that the poor soul was let down by "the divine aspect of reality," a supposition all the more within the realm of possibility since the Reconstructionist process of godhood is itself finite and imperfect? In vain is it maintained that the fact that the same man often does not fail proves that he is responsible for his failures. Since "the best in man" is due to the activity of cosmic powers, the extent of their presence and effectiveness may only be gauged by the strength of the ideals that they "elicit." Occasional successes and repeated failures will allow us the one conclusion that the cosmic forces which make for salvation are indeed extremely limited and not very consistent. Such a conclusion would not be unjustified, especially if one recalls that the creative powers are all the time locked in struggle in every human being, no less than in the universe, with the resistance of the chaos that "invades his soul." Every failure may be due to the finitude of the creative urge that, momentarily, may be lacking in power or wisdom to overcome the *tohu* and *bohu* which is "not of man but in man."

It is a mere running around in a circle to say that our task is to cultivate the sense of responsibility and "not one of calling into being something that does not exist." [60] Every task is a responsibility. The responsibility of cultivating a sense of responsibility is itself part of our sense of responsibility. Since, however, responsibility is among those "certain fundamental laws that are as intrinsic to human nature as the law of gravitation is to matter," the fundamental law of cultivating the sense of responsibility will either function, as any decent law should, or it will not function. No matter what happens, it will have as much bearing on ethics as has the law of gravitation.

The issue at hand may also be stated by saying that Reconstructionism became entangled with the implications of the pantheistic element of its teachings. Every form of pantheism is destructive of individuality. Individuality is a mere sham or shadow, as in Hinduism or a mode of the infinite substance as, for instance, in Spinozism. In either case, it has no reality or value of its own. Pantheism is inherently deterministic. There is no "ought", only an "is." All reality is a manifestation of divine nature, which is what it is of intrinsic necessity and could not be anything else. From this point of view, freedom is a mere illusion as is also all personal ethics. Notwithstanding the title of his chef d'oeuvre, i.e., *Ethics*, Spinoza had to regard human actions and desires "exactly" as if he were dealing "with lines, planes, and bodies." [61] Such is the inescapable logic of pantheism. Human aspirations and actions are "part of the larger world of nature." They are manifestations of cosmic reality which cannot be affected by the illusions of the sham that we like to call personality. Since there is neither freedom nor personal existence in reality, good and evil "indicate nothing positive in things considered in themselves." [62]

All these implications of pantheism also apply to Reconstructionism. If God is in man and man is in God, the human personality cannot be an irreducible monad, a world in itself, an independent center of reference, as Reconstructionism also teaches. If human strivings are the "revelation" in man of the activities of cosmic urges, if they reflect the cosmic structure of reality, if they are irrepressible hungers, impulses, and fundamental laws, as Reconstructionism has to assert, freedom cannot be "at the root of the soul," which Reconstructionism also affirms, so that it may make room for ethics within the scope of its world view. Reconstructionism is not aware of its inconsistencies. It has no appreciation of the logical implications of its own position.

The Problem of Unity

We have discussed above the problem of the possibility of freedom in a world which is ruled, according to the premise, by the flawless "uniformities" of the causal nexus in nature. The problem is greatly aggravated by the assumption that freedom is not only possible, but that its aspirations will ultimately be realized. We have heard the *Ani Ma'amin* of Reconstructionism that the world is so constituted that its "divine aspect" not only endorses what ought to be, but also guarantees that what ought to be will indeed be realized. We noted that such a belief implies a strong faith in a universal harmony between the order of physical nature and the realm of values and ideals. It is the idea of the "interrelated unity of all reality," which we had occasion to analyze earlier in our presentation. Without such universal harmony, man's striving for self-fulfillment or salvation would be a hopeless undertaking. It would seem, then, that not only does Reconstructionism affirm a faith that freedom is possible, notwithstanding the uniformities of natural law, but that freedom and necessity are in harmony with each other; that physical nature and the moral order are somehow attuned to each other; that they represent the "interrelated unity of all reality."

Judged by the premises of Reconstructionism, such an affirmation—with all due respect to the "heart of which it is born"—sounds rather fantastic. From all our experience we know that the laws of nature are indifferent to the considerations of right and wrong, that the causal nexus is the deadly enemy of freedom and teleological guidance. This indeed is the Reconstructionist position on naturalism. Ideals and values are recognized to point to a phase of reality of which "natural law does not take account." How then, is it possible to conceive of the natural and the moral order as being in harmony with each other? According to Hermann Cohen, the agreement between the causal order of nature and the teleological nature of ethics is *das Urproblem,* the fundamental problem of all systematic philosophy.[63] Spinoza, having identified nature with God, had to eliminate the concept of freedom and purpose from his system and reduce the distinction between good and evil to a mere subjective illusion. Fichte, on the other hand, who saw God in an active moral order, beheld the universe exclusively as the manifestation of that order. Kant was the outstanding personality in the history of philosophy who made it his major task to reconcile the order of nature with that of ethics. He was struggling with the problem in his three *Critiques*. His philosophy of "practical reason" demanded that what ought to be is possible of realization, or else human salvation would be inconceivable. It is a concept which is often used by Reconstructionism itself. As long as the order of nature and the realm of ethics remain alien to each other, such a concept will make no sense. Kant, of course, realized that the principle of their harmonization or unity could not be found in either of them but had to be sought outside them. In this manner he was led to the major "postulate of practical reason," the existence of an omnipotent, omniscient, and perfect Being, who alone—as the Supreme Lord of the universe—would have the power to make the uniformities of the causal order submit to guidance by the purposefulness of the "categorical imperative." The need for the "practical postulate" of a Supreme Being, transcendental to both the order of nature and that of ethics, is all the more significant, since Kant himself insists that "theoretical reason" is unable to prove the existence of God, and can acknowledge the idea only as a "regulative principle" of reasoning.[64]

Reconstructionism, of course, need accept neither Spinoza's or Fichte's or Kant's solution of the problem. However, it must offer some solution if it desires to be taken seriously. It is not enough to affirm intuitively that the realm of causal necessity is in harmony with purposeful ethical aspirations. On the basis of the Reconstructionist premise of identifying godhood with cosmic processes, the affirmation contains a logical contradiction.

In one important passage the founder of Reconstructionism quotes Thomas H. Huxley as having said: "Ethical nature may count upon having to reckon with a tenacious and powerful enemy as long as the world lasts." The quotation is taken from Huxley's famous Romanes Lecture of 1893. One might say that in it the speaker was discussing the Kantian problem of the discrepancy between natural and moral order from the point of view of the evolutionary naturalist. Huxley's conclusions, right or wrong, deserve serious treatment. Not so, however, in the opinion of Dr. Kaplan. Having practically stumbled on the problem, he orders it out of court by one of his many edifying affirmations. After berating one of the fathers of evolutionary theory for treating cosmic nature as if it were " a new name for the old Satan," he continues: "In reality, however, it is incorrect to assume that cosmic nature is 'red in tooth and claw,' and that the ethical strivings of men lie outside nature and constitute as it were a world by themselves. If there is any metaphysical significance to the doctrine of the unity of God, it is that the ethical and spiritual strivings should be considered as belonging to the same cosmos as the one in which there is so much that is evil and destructive of the good." [65]

These are noble words which, however, Reconstructionism is not entitled to use. Reconstructionism has no right to take recourse to the doctrine of the unity of God in order to prove the unity of the cosmos. Only the supernaturalist can do that. For him, God is the Supreme Being that transcends the world, confronting it as its Creator and Sovereign. Indeed, the significance of such a doctrine of the unity of God has always been that from it followed the unity of all created reality. The world is one as the creation of the One God. With such a faith, the supernaturalist may confront all the disharmony in the cosmos. But the Reconstructionist rejects the concept of the One God, the Creator of the universe. For him, God is an immanent aspect of reality; it is identical with the cosmic processes themselves. As we have seen, the Reconstructionist recognizes the "interrelated unity of all reality" as "the divine aspect of reality" or, as we have also heard it put, godhood is "the sum of animating, organizing forces and relationships which are forever making a cosmos out of chaos." The Reconstructionist cannot, therefore, argue from "the doctrine of the unity of God" in order to prove the unity of reality. He has to move in the opposite direction. He can only affirm the unity of God by establishing first the "interrelated unity of all reality." Dr. Kaplan's argument runs in a circle. First it affirms intuitively the unity of all reality. Identifying, then, such unity with the "divine aspect of reality," it concludes from the affirmation the unity of God. When, now, anyone should point to the wide areas of disharmony in reality, the answer is given rather indignantly: "But you are wrong! Haven't we proved the unity of God? Everyone knows that the unity of God signifies the interrelated unity of all reality." Since, however, on the Reconstructionist assumption the immanent godhood of the world is "identified" as the "interrelated unity of all reality," Dr. Kaplan has logically proved only that the intuition of the interrelated unity of all reality signifies the interrelated unity of all reality.

The truth is that relying completely on naturalistic experience as Reconstructionism does, one has no possibility of discovering the unity of all reality. In experience we encounter multiplicity, diversity, and disharmony. There are small areas in which a unifying tendency may perhaps be discerned, as there are others of chaos and conflict. We are aware of ethical striving in man and we also know of nature "red in tooth and claw." If they belong to the one cosmos, even though their respective orders of freedom and necessity are exclusive of each other, who dare affirm it on the basis of naturalism? The very idea of a cosmos is a metaphysical concept. It is either the fruit of a monistic and deterministic pantheism or of a supernatural ethical monotheism. The logic of the Reconstructionist position, however, leads to a modern polytheism. The polytheist of old, too, was an empiricist. He observed and encountered the plurality of powers in nature and in himself. By personifying these powers, he came to know them as gods. Reconstructionism starts out as well with man's naturalistic experience of strivings, drives, impulsions, within himself and in society. In trying to understand them, it searches for their "cosmic correlates." The Reconstructionist is, of course, not a primitive polytheist; his feet are firmly planted in the world of modern sicence. He does not "personify" these powers; he identifies them as divine. Since, however, the interrelated unity of all reality is unsupported by naturalistic experience, the Reconstructionist is left with a plurality of powers that, if not gods, ought properly to be referred to as *processes* of godhood and divine—and, occasionally, with greater justification, chaotic—*aspects* of reality. "Process of godhood" and "divine aspect of reality" in the singular, have no logical justification in the Reconstructionist context.

The attempt to reinterpret Judaism comes to grief on the failure of Reconstructionism to establish meaningfully the unity of reality. Reconstructionism maintains that only by "dissociating Jewish religion from supernaturalism can the universal significance of its ideals and values be made apparent and the Jewish contribution to the world order take effect."[66] It is exactly such dissociation that cannot be brought about. Jewish universalism is essentially anchored in the supernaturalist concept of the unity of God. As has been made clear by Hermann Cohen in his *Die Religion der Vernunft*—"The Religion of Reason"— the world of experience is not one. The idea of the One God constitutes the world as a unity, a universe. And what is true of the world is even more so of human beings. In actual experience we find only tribes, races, and nations. The very concept of the unity of the human race, the idea of mankind, has its origin in ethical monotheism. The concept of the One God, the originator of the one universe as well as the source of moral law, alone makes known to us the multitude of people as the brotherhood of men.[67] We can do no better than to quote the observations of Max Scheler on the same subject. In his work, *Vom Ewigen im Menschen,* he writes

> Actually as well as logically it is correct to say that the assumption of the unity . . . of the world is only to be derived from the assumption of an only God its Creator. . . . The world is world (and not chaos) and only one world, when, and because, it is God's world—when, and because, the same infinite spirit and will is powerfully active in all Being. Just as the unity of human nature is ultimately not based on the proven natural characteristic of man, but on the image of God which he shows; and just as mankind as a whole is mankind when all individuals and all groups are united with each other, legally as well as morally, by means of their bond with God, so is the world one world only because of the unity of God.[68]

The rabbis in the Talmud were expressing the same thoughts in the midrashic style when they remarked: "Why was man created alone?" (Or, as we may paraphrase the question: Why does, according to the Torah, only one Adam stand at the beginning of human history?) And the answer is given: "So that no man may say to his fellow: My father was greater than your father (and therefore, being of nobler descent, I am superior to you)." [69] The equality of the human race is established by its issuance from the one act of creation by the One God.

In vain does Reconstructionism declare that it is "one of the main functions of religion in the modern world to curb aggressive nationalism, by insistence on the essential unity of human society." [70] Aggressive nationalism is certainly bad and Reconstructionism is always well-meaning. However, having rejected the traditional concept of God as the transcendental Supreme Being and Creator, Reconstructionism has failed to provide a valid foundation for the essential unity of human society. Such essential unity has never been a matter of experience. On the contrary, the whole of history testifies to the actual inequality of men and the disunity of the human race. To quote a Reconstructionist text, "mankind is not all of one piece. It is divided among peoples, communities and families." [71] In this respect too the implied logic of the Reconstructionist position is a modern version of the old polytheistic one. Neither the concept of one humanity nor the ideal of equality could emerge in a polytheistic world in which people and nations claimed their descent from the various gods. Mankind was as much divided as its gods were many. The gods, have, of course, departed; the division and the disunity have remained. The Reconstructionist is confronted with a multiplicity of races which he explains as having developed from an animal ancestry as a result of the activity of "cosmic powers." Search as one may, one will not find unity and equality on such a basis. The different races may indeed represent different evolutionary trends. The Cro-Magnards and Grimaldis, as well as their latter-day children, may be the offsprings of cosmic forces acting in a pluralistic world. The actually experienced inequality of men may logically reflect the nature of a multiple cosmic reality. Any other conclusion is not justified on the basis of the Reconstructionist world view. The attempt of Reconstructionism to reinterpret Judaism by dissociating the universal significance of Jewish ideals from their source in the One God, the Creator, must be considered a complete failure. Having rejected Jewish monotheism, Reconstructionism has not provided a convincing foundation for Jewish universalism. It does not understand the age-old truth, which represents "the Jewish contribution to the world order," that before one may speak of the brotherhood of man one must acknowledge the fatherhood of God. Without it, all ethics is mere utilitarianism and politics.

III.   EVALUATION

Having analyzed the logical implications of the main concepts of Reconstructionist theology and religion from the angle of their own consistency, we shall now attempt to offer a general evaluation of both Reconstructionist transnaturalism and its starting point in what Reconstructionism considers present-day naturalism.

From the Ego to the Cosmos

The method of transnaturalism, as we saw, is a simple one. We know of the existence of personality, of human ideals and ethical strivings. They are no less real than the material aspects of life, yet naturalism cannot account for them. Transnaturalism is able to explain them by viewing them as the manifestations of cosmic powers that are responsible for their existence. These powers are identified as "the divine aspect of reality," since they tend to render human life worthwhile. It is the function of the idea of God to assure the worthwhileness of human existence. From the striving of man for self-transcendence transnaturalism concludes not only the existence of certain cosmic powers but also the nature of cosmic reality, which is seen to be such as to guarantee the ultimate fulfillment of man's aspirations.

It would seem to us that notwithstanding the fact that man is seen as "part of a larger nature," any conclusions drawn from his own aspirations for self-fulfillment or salvation to the nature of cosmic reality is not logic but a form of megalomania. A contemporary astrophysicist, in trying to convey an idea of the proportion which exists between our earth and the rest of the universe, uses the following comparison. If the major railway terminal of a large metropolis represented the size of the cosmos, then one particle of dust floating around in its atmosphere would represent the earth. In relationship to the world man is the inhabitant of such a particle of cosmic dust. What conclusions may be drawn from his aspirations to the structure of reality? The founder of Reconstructionism does attempt to answer this question in a very few words: "But does not the very ability to think in cosmic terms render physical measurements and proportions irrelevant? . . ." [72]

We cannot agree that he has met the objection. Though the idea was already voiced by Saadia Gaon, and, in addition, also has a Kantian ring about it, we do not know what is meant by "the ability to think in cosmic terms." Man, we would say, is able to think only in human terms; in terms of the human intellect he is even able to think of cosmic extension and structure. Be that as it may, we are in hearty agreement with the insight that physical measurements and proportions are irrelevant. Value and meaning of the smallest order are superior to mere physical bigness of the largest size. Mere physical bigness is nonsensical. All this is, however, beside the point. The objection that Reconstructionism has to meet, but does not, is as follows: Is the universe empty of meaning and does its vastness, surpassing all human imagination, represent nothing but bigness? Then the little sense and purpose which are noticeable in the human inhabitant of the particle of cosmic dust, our earth, is indeed the greatest conceivable miracle. However, it would be a miracle illogically set in an ocean of cosmic meaninglessness, completely out of harmony with the structure of reality. Or else, beside its physical brilliance, the universe does incorporate significance in true cosmic terms, then all conclusions from the nature of human strivings as to how reality is constituted are bound to be fallacious.

It is of little use to say, as if anticipating such objection: "We do not need to pretend to any knowledge of the ultimate purpose of the universe as a whole. . . . But it is an undeniable fact that there is something in the nature of life that expresses itself in human personality, which evokes ideals, which sends men on the quest of personal and social salvation." [73] As so much of Reconstructionist reasoning, this is begging the question. For the question is: What is the status of this "something in the nature of life" in the context of cosmic reality? May it not be that this something is a cosmic flaw, that from the point of view of the structure of all reality "the evoking of ideals which send men on the quest of personal and social salvation" was a regretable oversight? Personal and social salvation are of great human importance. Reconstructionism, however, has not proved that there exists a correlative to them in the nature of reality which has positive significance in terms of that reality.

Reconstructionism regards life as the supreme value: for "if life itself is worthless, no object on earth can have any value." [74] This would not be illogical, if the meaning of it were that life had supreme value for most men. Unfortunately, what is meant is "the life of the universe of which our lives are but a part." The supreme value is supposed to be objective, cosmic value, "from which all others are derived." Since our lives "are but part of universal life," Reconstructionism expects human life "to yield cosmic meaning." To speak of the life of the universe and human life as if both belong in the same category and were one and the same phenomenon is not justified. On the contrary, all our scientific knowledge suggests that life, as we know it on this globe, is completely out of step with the life of the universe. The Second Law of Thermodynamics is one of the concepts of science in which the human mind has revealed its ability "to think in cosmic terms." According to it, the life of the universe consists in an irreversible process of cosmic dying. Like a wound-up clock, the universe is "running down" by the inevitable increase of entropy. Evolution, which scientifically speaking is responsible for life on earth, is a process running in the opposite direction. Entropy implies, as it were, the continuous degradation of the universe from higher forms of organization to lower ones, until, by the equal distribution of heat, all activity is brought to a standstill and universal *rigor mortis* ensues. Evolution, on the other hand, works from lower forms of organization to higher ones; from death to life, as it were. We are certainly not competent to pass judgment on the significance of the relationship between global evolution and the universal law of entropy. From the writings of scientists, however, one is able to gather that, in cosmic terms, life as we know it is an insignificant side-show, enacted in a tiny corner of the universe. It was rendered possible, so it would appear, by the mere accidental coincidence of a certain state of entropy in the universe and the mechanically determined, no less accidental, conditions on that cosmic particle of dust, our earth.[75] One of the great astrophysicists of this century, Sir Arthur S. Eddington, has occasion to describe the rise of human life in the following manner: "Nature seems to have been intent on a vast evolution of fiery worlds. . . . As for Man —it seems unfair to be always raking up against Nature her one little inadvertence. By a trifling hitch of machinery—not of any serious consequence in the development of the universe—some lumps of matter of the wrong size have occasionally been formed. These lack the purifying protection of intense heat or the equally efficacious absolute cold of space. Man is one of the gruesome results of this occasional failure of antiseptic precautions." [76]

This is how man looks when considered in "cosmic terms." It is foolish to draw any conclusions from his own strivings as to the structure of cosmic reality. Notwithstanding the fact that human nature is part of a larger nature, it is preposterous to discern in human nature a manifestation of the structure of cosmic reality. Reconstructionist religion is far from being "the triumphant exorcism of Bertrand Russell's dismal credo 'Brief and powerless is man's life. On him and all his race the slow sure doom falls pitiless and dark,' " as it maintains.[77] However dismal, from the scientific point of view Russell's credo makes more sense than Reconstructionist transnaturalism. We agree that the idea of God implies "the absolute negation and antithesis of all evaluations of human life which assume that consciousness is a disease, civilization a transient sickness, and all our effort to lift ourselves above the brute only a vain pretense." [78] The traditional Jewish belief in God does mean all that, but not the Reconstructionist "intuition of God." We are familiar with this intuition by now. It begins with our experience of human strivings for self-fulfillment and ends with "the assumption" of a cosmic reality so "constituted as to endorse them and to guarantee their realization." The Reconstructionist intuition of God is the conclusion from man to the structure of reality which is identified as divine. The intuition has as much significance as the conclusion makes sense. Man cannot derive status from his position in the cosmos, but from his relationship to the Lord of the cosmos. The idea was poetically expressed by the Psalmist, when he exclaimed:

> When I behold Thy heavens, the work of Thy fingers,
> The morn and the stars, which Thou hast established;
> What is man, that Thou art mindful of him?
> And the son of man, that Thou thinkest of him?
> Yet Thou hast made him but little lower than the angels,
> And hast crowned him with glory and honor.[79]

This makes sense. The Psalmist recognizes the insignificance of man when judged as "part of a larger world nature," an evaluation borne out by modern science, and sees that the only source of human dignity may be found in the fact that the son of man is the child of God. Reconstructionism, however, which knows only man and a larger world of which he is a part, but not a universe that "Thou hast established," has but one way to ascertain the glory and honor of man, i.e., to derive it from his place in the cosmos. As we have seen, judged by its cosmic position, human life certainly does not yield any "cosmic meaning." The question that in such a case may it not be "the course of wisdom to pursue a policy of 'eat and drink and make merry, for tomorrow we die?' "[80] proves nothing to the contrary. Such a course of wisdom may indeed follow from the inherent logic of the Reconstructionist world view.

Reconstructionist Pananthropomorphism

The Reconstructionist method of drawing conclusions from the higher aspirations of man to the structure of universal reality is tantamount to fashioning the cosmos in the image of human aspirations and values. The cosmic "correlates" are nothing else but the projection of man's wishes and desires into the cosmos. This is the origin of the distinction between cosmos and chaos. From the point of view of nature there is no distinction between "tempests, obnoxious plants and animals" and the, for man, more agreeable manifestations of nature. When Reconstructionism calls the constructive powers of nature "the creative urge" and identifies as chaos that aspect of reality which may doom human aspirations, it introduces purely human value concepts in the determination of the nature of reality. Outside human consciousness and strivings we find only facts and not values. The life of the universe of which we are part and which is "the supreme value because from it all other values are derived" is the projection of the Reconstructionist "enthusiasm for living" onto the cosmic canvas.

By learning to view man's nobler desires as an "integral part of the cosmic structure of reality," Reconstructionism attempts to give human values universal objectivity; however, all it accomplishes is the view of a world seen through the rose-colored glasses of human ambitions. When it "identifies" the powers that make for those nobler impulses in man as the divine aspect of reality, far from discovering God, it has merely deified certain aspects of the human personality. Ludwig Feuerbach was not right in generalizing that the idea of God represented nothing but the deification of human nature; nevertheless, the Reconstructionist inflation of human aspirations into cosmic proportions, their projection into the universe where they are discovered as divine, proves that his theory is not always wrong.

When Reconstructionism speaks about God, it is really moving in a circle, starting with man and concluding with him. This is nowhere more amusingly illustrated than when it attempts to offer a "reinterpretation" of the biblical idea of man's having been created in the image of God. We have already discussed the quotation in which reference is made to "the something in the nature of life" which becomes manifest in the existence of human personality, evolving in man ideals and the quest for salvation. It is maintained that by identifying that "something" with God, "we are carrying out, in modern times, the implications of the conception that man is created in God's image. For such an identification implies that there is something divine in human personality in that it is the instrument through which the creative life of the world affects the evolution of the human race." [81] The truth is, of course, that the aspect of reality responsible for the emergence of human personality is referred to as "the creative life of the world" only because man attaches value to personality. The "something in the nature of life" which is responsible for "evoking" ideals and for sending man in quest of self-fulfillment is identified as God only because man approves of his own ideals and of the quest. This is the deification of human values. No wonder Reconstructionism discovers something divine in the human personality. It starts out with the projection of human personality into the universe as "the something in the nature of life" which is responsible for it. In this state, human personality is deified. It is then rediscovered in man as "something divine," which it is because we called it so right from the beginning. Such semantic juggling, however, has nothing in common with the conception of man's creation in God's image. It is its very opposite; it is God's creation in man's image. This is the essence of the Reconstructionist "intuition of God."

Whenever Reconstructionism speaks about God, it is in reality speaking about man. When man sins he betrays that which is "best in him." On *Rosh Hashanah,* the Reconstructionist, standing before the bar of judgment, judges himself "in the light of whatever truth experience has revealed to him." [82] The true meaning of the acceptance of God's kingship is to attain faith in man.[83] To serve God is to strive for self-fulfillment.[84] By the holiness of God religion means to convey the idea that life is the supreme value.[85] The "main problem of Jewish religion" is defined as the task to discover "a common purpose, which makes for the enhancement of human life" and to which Jews as a people are willing to be committed so passionately "as to see in it a manifestation or revelation of God." [86] This is quite logical. The divine is in man because man deifies "the best in him." When, then, he is passionately devoted to a cause which enhances life, such commitment and devotion is divine revelation for it represents the best in him. All the while man is gyrating around himself; or, better still, around his best potentialities. He serves and worships his noblest aspirations. In practicing transnaturalism, he is forever engaged in an intellectually incestuous mystical communion with his deified super-ego.

In our presentation of Reconstructionist theology, we pointed out that transnaturalism was a form of pantheism. In the light of our analysis and evaluation, we now have to qualify this appellation. In the history of philosophy we distinguish between acosmic and atheistic pantheism. Acosmic pantheism is, for instance, that of Spinoza. Its origin is a metaphysical vision of the Infinite God whose very infinity leaves no room for a cosmos. Identifying nature with God, Spinoza denied not God but nature. It is for this reason that he was called the God-intoxicated philosopher. (The philosophy is, of course, contrary to Judaism because it eliminates creation and the Creator.) It is obvious that Reconstructionism has nothing in common with this type of pantheism. The other form of pantheism beholds, again in a metaphysical inspiration, the wholeness of nature and identifies God with it. Not such is the Reconstructionist position, which is based on the naturalistic rejection of metaphysics. The Reconstructionist starting point is not a vision of the wholeness of nature but man, his aspirations, drives, and values. Insofar as man approves of his goals and impulsions, they are projected into the cosmos and become inflated into cosmic urges revealing the structure of reality. The viewing of these aspects of reality as divine does identify God with the cosmos, but with a cosmos shaped in the image of human aspirations and interests. Reconstructionist transnaturalism should, therefore, not be called pantheism. It is the most radical manifestation of anthropomorphism. It should properly be known as pan-anthropoism. It is much too original a religious philosophy to be considered a mere "revaluation" of traditional Jewish concepts. If one should use Dr. Kaplan's own criterion for what constitutes revaluation, one would have to say that transnaturalism shows not the least trace of a "psychological kinship with what the ancients did articulate." [87] Christianity as well as Islam are by far closer to Judaism than Reconstructionist religion.

"Wedding Religion to Science"

As indicated in the opening sentences of this study, the task of harmonizing the valid results of scientific theory with the truth of religion is indeed of vital religious importance. All the more is it to be regretted that the Reconstructionist endeavor "to wed religion to science' has to be considered such a dismal failure. It should be obvious that it has not been our intention to offer another solution to the problem of the conflict between naturalism and traditional Judaism, one perhaps from a supernaturalistic viewpoint. Nor did we make any attempt to defend supernaturalism against Reconstructionist criticism. We investigated Reconstructionist theology and religion on its own philosophical and theological merits and found it very much wanting. At the same time, it is rather a pity that Dr. Kaplan should have been so impatient with, and intolerant toward, the supernaturalist element in Judaism and treated it with utter intellectual contempt. Impatience, intolerance, and contempt are, of course, the historic privileges of all prophets of new religions in their attitude to the old one that they "revaluate." Yet, had he possessed only a small suspicion that the believers in a supernaturalist religion need not all be intellectually incompetent, he might have felt induced to take another good look at his own naturalism. Such a second look, we believe, might have prevented him from failing so wretchedly in his transnaturalist "reinterpretation" of Judaism.

We shall, therefore, attempt to review those principles of "the new scientific world view" which seems to be mainly responsible for the Reconstructionist rejection of supernaturalism. These are essentially: "the uniformities of natural law demanded by scientific theory," also referred to as the scientific thought or insight of "the assumption of the universality of natural law"; the immutable laws of cause and effect"; and "that inner necessity which compels things to be what they are." [88] Anyone can see that these principles are completely in "gear with the thinking of the average intelligent person at the present time." [89] This is as it should be from the Reconstructionist point of view. The "average intelligent person at the present time" is the supreme authority to whose thinking Professor Kaplan bows in the spirit of childlike faith. It is, however, surprising that these concepts of the uniformity of nature are also claimed as being 'in keeping with the most advanced ideas of reality." [90] The facts are quite to the contrary, as any average intelligent person may easily find out for himself by doing some elementary reading in contemporary scientific method and philosophy.

In the light of modern scientific theory, the reference to "that inner necessity which compels things to be what they are" must be considered the vestigial remnant of some obscure mysticism. The statement could have been made meaningfully—as indeed it was, though perhaps not exactly in those words—by Spinoza. However, it is fair to say that the spectacular development of modern science began when scientists stopped explaining natural events by inner necessities that compel things to be what they are. We shall not go wrong in stating that the ghost of inner necessity as a principle of scientific explanation has not shown itself in any responsible quarter for at least the last hundred years. As to the uniformities and the universality of natural laws, it is now realized that there is no foundation for them either in experimental or theoretic science. The quantum theory, Heisenberg's principle of indeterminacy, the incalculable "jumps" of the electrons from orbit to orbit, prove that the good old principle of *natura non facit saltus* was a mere illusion. Natural laws of today show no such uniformity. Quantum mechanics and wave mechanics, the indeterminism of events in the atomic structure, and the statistical laws of microphysics made an end to "the assumption" of the universality of natural laws. In the wake of all these new developments, the concept of the immutable laws of cause and effect" governing nature is gone.

An outstanding scientist draws a number of fundamental conclusions "from the mere fact of the atomicity of radiation, coupled with those well-established facts of the undulatory theory of light." Among them we find, for example, these:

"So far as the phenomena are concerned, the uniformity of nature disappears.

"So far as our knowledge is concerned, causality becomes meaningless.

"If we still wish to think of the happenings in the phenomenal world as governed by a causal law, we must suppose that these happenings are determined in some substratum of the world which lies beyond the world of phenomena and so also beyond our access." [91]

We fully realize that there are many who do wish to think of the happenings in the phenomenal world as governed by a causal law. However, following the discussion between eminent scientists on the subject of the principle of causality, on which uniformity and universality depend, it is safe to say that it is not really possible to disagree with the factual statement made by the late Professor Eddington that "the law of causality does not exist in science today—in that body of systematic knowledge and hypothesis which has been experimentally confirmed." Eddington is careful to point out that this does not mean that modern science has proved that the law of causality is not true of the physical universe, but that "present-day science is simply indifferent" to the law of causality. "We might believe in it today and disbelieve in it tomorrow; not a symbol in the modern textbooks of physics would be altered." [92]

We do not pretend to be able to settle the issue as between the scientists. However, one thing is certain: the uniformities and the universality of the laws of nature are not only not demanded by scientific theory but they are not even used in "the body of systematic knowledge which has been experimentally confirmed." The division between determinists and indeterminists among scientists is not a matter of science, but one of philosophy; it is based essentially on theoretical speculation. In our days, the principle of causation itself has become a metaphysical concept. He who affirms it as an explanation of universal order can adduce no proof that may be experimentally secured. As Jeans says, he *supposes* that the happenings in the phenomenal world "are determined in some substratum of the world which lies beyond the world of phenomena, and so also beyond our access." But he who deals with substrata of the world which lie beyond the world phenomena is dangerously close to the border of the supernatural. The truth is that modern science excludes as little the Will of God "of the ancients" as a possible substratum to the world of observable phenomena, as it confirms the principle of causation as such as a determining metaphysical background. The worst one may say about the Will of God as being responsible for the world of phenomena is that science is no more indifferent toward it than it is toward Dr. Kaplan's immutable laws of cause and effect.

These new insights, which were only quite recently gained by scientists, corroborated what was accepted by critical philosophy ever since the days of Hume. Independently of any particular advances in actual scientific knowledge, critical philosophy since Hume has shown that experience can never serve as the foundation of the principles of causation and the universality of natural law. In his *Science and the Modern World,* A. N. Whitehead has maintained that Hume's criticism of these principles has never been answered by experimental science. If science nevertheless proceeded to treat causation and universality as if they were validated principles of experience, this was based "on a widespread instinctive conviction" of the existence of an order of nature. Hume was right, "but scientific faith has risen to the occasion and has tacitly removed the philosophic mountain." [93] We shall be in a better position to evaluate the significance of the Reconstructionist ideas about the order of nature if we recall the source of "the scientific faith" in that order. Says Professor Whitehead: "My explanation is that the faith in the possibility of science, generated antecedently to the development of modern scientific theory, is an unconscious derivative from medieval theology." [94] This, of course, needs some elaboration. The true meaning of Hume's criticism consisted in the rejection of the theory of induction. Since the days of Bacon, induction had been the main tool of scientific logic. Unfortunately, the theory of induction presupposes the existence of an order with a uniform system of organization. Only on the *a priori* assumption of such a uniform cosmos was it logical to conclude that events belonging to the cosmos would be controlled by the same laws. The task was to discover the laws. However, without the *a priori* assumption of a uniform cosmic order, induction would prove nothing. As Whitehead puts it, "induction presupposes metaphysics." [95] Medieval theology did have a theistic metaphysics from which the concept of a uniform order of nature was derived; modern experimental science, however, rejected any *a priori* assumptions of a natural order and based itself on the observation of "brute facts." The reliance on the principle of induction, which is valueless without the corresponding metaphysical assumptions, was indeed an act of faith in the orderliness of nature which was "an unconscious derivative from medieval theology." The point worth noting is that the principles of causation and universality never had any scientific validity; they were affirmed as a matter of faith, unconsciously borrowed from the system of a supernatural theism. (When some scientists realized the intellectual implications of such a situation, scientific positivism was born.)

We can do no better than quote here an illuminating passage from J. W. N. Sullivan's *The Bases of Modern Science:*

> The general medieval outlook made the assumption that Nature was rational a reasonable one. Since both Nature and man had the same author, and Nature was designed to forward man's destiny, it was not unreasonable to suppose that the workings of nature should proceed in a manner intelligible to the human mind. Later, when science gave up this basis for the rationality of Nature, there was nothing to replace it but a pure act of faith. Science replaced the medieval scheme by a different one, but the new scheme did not contain within itself any grounds for supposing that it must be successful. Science itself provides no ground, beyond the pragmatic one of success, for supposing that Nature forms an orderly and coherent whole. Science, therefore, rests not upon a rational basis but upon an act of faith. The scientific belief in the rationality of Nature is seen to be, historically, an inheritance from a system of thought of which the other terms have been discarded.[96]

The inevitable conclusion is that modern science cannot scientifically explain its own spectacular success, which pragmatically confirms a faith that has its origin in a scientifically rejected metaphysical and theistic system.

It is the irony of the Reconstructionist declamation about the immutable laws of cause and effect and the universality of natural law that these laws are purest metaphysical principles, historically and logically derived from supernaturalist religion. At a moment when experimental science, for the first time in its history, may be intellectually true to its nature and be "indifferent" to the principles of causation and universality, Reconstructionism still blindly believes that they are "demanded by scientific theory." Because of its faith in their scientific rationality, Reconstructionism rejects supernaturalist theism. In reality, the laws of university and causation made sense only in the context of a supernaturalist religion, whence they were unconsciously lifted by an irrational scientific faith. Truly, the Reconstructionist insight into the modern world view is the acme of scientific-philosophic innocence.

Since the Reconstructionist view of naturalism is so extremely naive and outdated, nothing but failure was to be expected from its "wedding of religion to naturalism." Any one who undertakes the task will have to attempt to harmonize a mature naturalism with a mature supernaturalism (and not the old-wives' tale of supernaturalism with which Dr. Kaplan is bickering all the time). The moment is not at all unpropitious. With the brilliant progress made by scientists in describing phenomena with mathematical exactitude has come a continually deepening realization that the more exact our description, the more mystified our understanding of what is being described. Matter has been equated with energy; the notion of substance has been replaced by behavior. And energy is that something that behaves in a certain way, of whose existence we know because it so behaves. No one, of course, has the slightest notion what it is that behaves. Discussing such concepts of Newtonian physics as mass, force, weight, J. W. N. Sullivan, whom we quoted earlier, says that whereas Newton considered them "objectively existing entities," we know now "that these terms are not names of entities, but are concise descriptions of behavior. They tell us nothing about what is behaving. This is true of all terms used in physics." [97] Needless to say, that neither do they tell us why the unknown It behaves as it does. "Our most advanced ideas of reality," on which Reconstructionism imagined it could build its own structure, are not unlike the theology of the medieval philosopher. As to reality, we know that it is, but we do not know what it is. We do not know it by its essence, but only by its actions. We know what it does, but we do not know why it does it.

Furthermore, it appears that it would be even more correct to say that science does not even describe the behavior of the unknown reality, but only the pattern which results from such behavior; the relationship that exists in a field between unknown events performed by unknown actors. Modern science deals with group structure, which can be described without specifying the material used or the operations by which it was composed. [98]

Eddington sums up the resulting situation in the following words:

> Our present conception of the physical world is hollow enough to hold almost anything. . . . What we are dragging to light as a basis of all phenomena is a scheme of symbols connected by mathe-

matical equations. That is what physical reality boils down to when
probed by the methods which a physicist can apply. A skeleton
scheme of symbols proclaims its own hollowness. It can be—nay
it cries out to be—filled with something that shall transform it from
skeleton into substance . . . from symbols into an interpretation of
the symbols.[99]

Reconstructionism can make no contribution to the task indicated in
the above words. Whereas its conception of the physical world, filled as
it is to the brim with the deadwood of outdated ideas, is not hollow
enough to hold anything meaningful, its conception of the spiritual world
is much too hollow to provide it. Only from the fullness of the spirit
will the cold skeleton of physical experience be clothed with life and
saving dignity.

CHAPTER 6

Dr. A. J. Heschel's Theology of Pathos

Pathos and Sympathy

In his work, *The Prophets,* Dr. A. J. Heschel has undertaken the task of analyzing and interpreting the prophet's consciousness of God. He distinguishes between two aspects of the prophet's awareness of God: an objective one and a subjective one. The objective aspect is due to the reality of God that the prophet meets and which, in its objective quality of givenness, transcends the prophetic consciousness. By the subjective aspect Dr. Heschel means the individual response of the prophet to the reality of God as he encounters it. The investigation of the objective side of the prophet's understanding of God is the theme of prophetic theology; its subjective nature may be called prophetic religion.

The reality of God known to the prophet is, of course, not the idea of God discussed by philosophers. The prophet's knowledge of God is not derived knowledge, something acquired by the logical methods of syllogism and induction. The prophet knows God from direct confrontation with the divine presence; he knows Him from "fellowship" with Him, by "a living together" with Him. His knowledge of God is intuitive. It is not knowledge about God but rather an intuitive understanding of God, the kind of understanding that binds a lover and his beloved to each other. God in Himself, in His Being, is the subject matter of metaphysics. God is encountered by the prophet in "His directedness to man." Because of the nature of the prophet's understanding of God, the prophet does not teach us ideas about God but reveals to us God's relatedness to man. The reality of God is experienced by the prophet as God's care and concern for His creation. "Man stands under God's concern" is the basic message of all prophecy.

192

These are, of course, familiar thoughts, well understood by all who have some knowledge of biblical theology or religious philosophy. The originality of Dr. Heschel consists in expanding these ideas into, what he calls, a theology of pathos. God is not only concerned about man, He is also affected by man. God is involved in the human situation. He is involved in the history of mankind. "Whatever man does affects not only his own life, but also the life of God insofar as it is directed to man." [1] God is passible; He is affected by what man does and He reacts according to His affection. He is a God of pathos. He is "emotionally affected" by the conduct of man. [2] In his customary eloquent manner, Dr. Heschel declares:

> To the prophet . . . God does not reveal Himself in an abstract absoluteness, but in a personal and intimate relation to the world. He does not simply command and expect obedience; He is also moved and affected by what happens in the world and reacts accordingly. Events and human actions arouse in Him joy or sorrow, pleasure or wrath. . . . Quite obviously, in the biblical view, man's deeds may move Him, affect Him, grieve Him or, on the other hand, gladden and please Him. This notion that God can be intimately affected, that He possesses not merely intelligence and will, but also pathos, basically defines the prophetic consciousness of God. [3]

Divine pathos, thus conceived, is presented as a theological category *sui generis*. [4] It is a mystery, which cannot be grasped rationally, that the Creator of heaven and earth, the transcendent God, should be concerned about man and that He should be affected by the conduct of man. But only in the light of the mystery can one fully appreciate "the theological connotations" of the prophetic insight of the divine pathos, the essential significance of God's involvement in history. [5] Because God is the God of pathos, the concept of God as the Wholly Other must be rejected. "The Holy is otherness as well as non-otherness. . . . To the prophets, the gulf that separates man from "God is transcended by His pathos. For all the impenetrability of His being, He is concerned with the world and relates Himself to it." Pathos is "togetherness in holy otherness." [6]

In the subjective aspect of prophetic consciousness Dr. Heschel discovers prophetic religion. He calls it religion of sympathy. It is the pathos of God that is communicated to the prophet in the encounter with the divine presence. The mission of the prophet is to convey God's pathos to man. It is not conceivable that the prophet should be able to do that in inner detachment. He is aware of the divine pathos. But he cannot be aware of it merely intellectually. For one cannot have merely intellectual awareness of "a concrete suffering or pleasure." The very fact that the prophet fulfills his mission of intimating God's pathos to the people implies "an inner identification" with such pathos. He feels God's feeling. The prophets react to the divine pathos with sympathy for God. In contrast to the stoic sage, who may be defined as *homo apatheticos,* the prophet is *homo sympatheticos.* Sympathy is "a feeling which feels the feeling to which it reacts." The prophet is so deeply moved by the divine pathos that "his interior life" is transformed by the pathos of God. The prophet is "theomorphic." He is aware of "God's cares and sorrows"; he communes with the divine "in experience and suffering." In solidarity with "the pain of God," his communion with God is one of compassion for God. Because of his sympathy, the prophet "is guided, not by what he feels, but rather by what God feels. In moments of intense sympathy for God, the prophet is moved by the pathos of God." [7] We may express the essence of Heschel's theory in one sentence: According to his theology of pathos, human action evokes divine pathos; according to his religion of sympathy, divine pathos evokes prophetic sympathy. Man affects God and God affects the prophet. In the dialogue between God and man, God responds with pathos; in that between the prophet and God, the prophet responds with sympathy.

The Problem of Anthropopathy

It is not difficult to see that the boldness of Dr. Heschel's thought consists, first, in taking literally all biblical expressions that ascribe to God emotions of love and hatred, joy and sorrow, suffering and pleasure; secondly, in letting the prophet share in these emotions of God and feel them as God's feelings. One may of course wonder what becomes now of the age-old problems of Jewish theology and philosophy. Most of them are ignored by Heschel's affirmations. There is, however, one that he does not venture to ignore. It is the question of anthropomorphism or rather, since it is the pathos of God that comes under scrutiny, anthropopathy. The question of course is: by ascribing emotions to God, by allowing Him to be affected by man, by conceiving Him as capable of joy and sorrow, pleasure and pain, don't we form Him in the image of man?

Wrestling with the problem, Dr. Heschel observes that there are four
rules by which one may ascertain the presence of anthropomorphic
concepts in a religion or theology. The "equivalence of imagination and
expression; the unawareness of the transcendence and uniqueness of
God; the adjustment of God's moral nature to the interests of man; the
endeavor to picture or to describe God in His own existence, unrelated
to man." The Bible is well aware of the transcendence and uniqueness
of God. There was, therefore, no danger that the anthropomorphic
expressions might be taken literally and thus bring about an equation
between expression and imagination. He who attempts to describe the
essence of God in its absoluteness is trying the impossible in human
language. The prophets, however, speak of God always in His relatedness to the world; it is divine acts that they picture, not divine substance. Needless to say, in the Bible God is not made to subserve the
selfish interest of man. On the contrary, biblical expressions of pathos
are always morally determined and convey "a sense of superhuman
power, rather than resemblance to man." In spite of the anthropomorphic expressions, God in the Bible is quite obviously not thought
of as being anthropomorphic.

What then is the significance of the anthropomorphic presentation of
the divine pathos? All expression of pathos in the Bible "are attempts
to set forth God's aliveness." However, in this undertaking we should
recognize "the greatest challenge to the biblical language," which has
to reconcile God's transcendence with "His overwhelming livingness and
concern." Confronted with such a challenge all words are of necessity
inadequate. Any attempt at adequacy of expression is mere pretension
or delusion. On the contrary, by consciously making use of inadequate
language, one "drives the mind beyond all words." "The prophets had
to use anthropomorphic language in order to convey His nonanthropo-
morphic Being." Pathos is "a thought that bears resemblance to an
aspect of divine reality as related to the world of man"; it is not "a
personification of God, but . . . an illustration or illumination of His
concern." Expressions of pathos should be understood "as allusions
rather than descriptions," as "understatements rather than adequate ac-
counts." As such they are "aids in evoking our sense of His realness."
In truth, however, "the nature of divine pathos is a mystery to man."
In reality, Isaiah's declaration concerning the thoughts of God applies
equally well to God's pathos, so that we may paraphrase it as: "For My

pathos is not your pathos, neither are your ways My ways, For as the heavens are higher than the earth, so are My ways higher than your ways, and My pathos than your pathos."

We are inclined to believe that Dr. Heschel has not succeeded in the solution of the problem. No student of the Bible who was ever willing to take the anthropomorphic expressions literally ever imagined that God was human. Those "greater and better men" than Maimonides, to whom the *Ravad* refers in a famous passage, who believed that God existed in bodily form, knew Him of course as the Creator of heaven and earth, superhuman and transcendent. If God had bodily form it was of course divine and not human, just as, in Dr. Heschel's defense of anthropopathy, God's pathos is divine and not human. It is only now that we have reached the threshold of the problem. Those "greater and better men" did not see what was logically implied in the fact that the distinction between the Infinite and the finite, between the Creator and the creation, was an absolute one. They imagined that by refining and elevating concepts derived from human experience one could reach the Infinite, that by idealizing aspects of creation one can think or imagine the Creator. The essence of Maimonides' criticism of the positive attributes of God is that all our concepts are derived from our finite experience; we can associate with them only finite meanings. No matter how much we might magnify or purify them in trying to apply them to God, we either associate some positive meaning with them, in which case we shall be describing something finite that will have no relevance to God, or else we shall be using words without any meaningful positive contents.

A very good example to illustrate the point is provided by Dr. Heschel himself when he maintains: "Absolute selflessness and mysteriously undeserved love are more akin to the divine than to the human." [8] Now, we know what is meant by selflessness—something quite human. Absolute selflessness may of course mean a superlative form of selflessness. We still know what is meant by it and it is still quite human. If, however, we take the phrase literally as the selflessness of an absolute being, we no longer are able to associate with it any meaning, unless we take recourse to a theory of negative attributes. To say that absolute selflessness is more akin to the divine than to the human is of course true, but it is a meaningless tautology. Since absolute selflessness and "the mysteriously undeserved love"—whatever that may mean in its absolute sense—are divine by definition, they will of course be divine and not human. According to Dr. Heschel divine pathos "consists of human ingredients and a superhuman *Gestalt*." [9] It is, however, just because of it that it is either anthropopathy or it is a word with which no meaningful positive contents can be associated. We either see the human ingredient and the superhuman *Gestalt* will be an idealization of the human and, thus, remain human after all; or else, we shall concentrate our attention on the superhuman *Gestalt* and the human ingredient will dissolve into incomprehension.

With what little success Dr. Heschel explained away anthropopathy may be seen by the fact that his major proposition, that of a religion of sympathy, makes sense only on the basis of anthropopathy. We saw that sympathy is the prophet's response to the divine pathos. At times he feels for God, at others he feels with God. He feels God's feeling and he shares in it. It is even said that "the true meaning of the religion of sympathy" is "to feel the divine pathos as one feels one's own state of the soul." [10] In the light of such interpretation of sympathy can one take Heschel's statement seriously that the divine pathos is superhuman? If it were indeed so, that, just as concerning the thoughts of God, one may also say concerning His pathos that His pathos is not man's pathos just as man's ways are not His ways, could the prophet indeed feel the pathos of God as his own state of soul? Can man grasp the thoughts of God, can he make God's way his own? Since Heschel, paraphrasing the words of Isaiah, maintains that as the heavens are higher than the earth, so are God's ways higher than man's ways and so is God's pathos higher than man's pathos, how can he, in presenting his religion of sympathy, also affirm that the "prophet is the person who holds God's love as well as God's anger in his soul"? [12] Could any man hold God's love and anger in his soul, if God's pathos were as removed from human emotions as "the heavens are higher than the earth" and as God's ways are higher than man's? Divine pathos, according to Dr. Heschel's theology is a mystery as well as a paradox. (In fact it is a mystery in a twofold sense, which we need not elaborate here.) Yet, according to his religion of sympathy, he is compelled to declare that "pathos, far from being intrinsically irrational, is a state which the prophet is able to comprehend morally as well as emotionally." [13] Without such comprehension the religion of sympathy is lost completely. But if God's pathos were as different from man's as is

God from man, the mystery of the divine pathos would remain morally as well as emotionally incomprehensible. In Dr. Heschel's presentation, God's pathos is much more sublime than that of man; it is, as he says, "always morally conditioned and required"[14] which of course is not quite human. The difference, however, is only one of degree—that is why the prophet may feel it as his own—and not one of kind. It is exactly what is meant by anthropomorphism and anthropopathy.

The Dilemma of Divine Wrath

There is, however, at least one specific form of divine pathos that not even Dr. Heschel is able to accept in its literary sense as he does with the other manifestations—it is the pathos of divine wrath. It appears that while he finds it quite in order that "God's participation in history finds its deepest expression in the fact that God can actually suffer,"[15] he recoils somewhat from the idea that God can be very angry. He seems to feel that anger is a somewhat surprising emotion for God and, thus, he is not satisfied with what he says in the general analysis and interpretation of pathos, but singles out the *Ira Dei* for an elaborate separate treatment. (Another specific form of pathos which is discussed separately is God's concern for justice.) In its explanation, he proceeds essentially along two lines. First, he desires to show us that anger is itself an expression of God's concern for man; second, he tries to explain the meaning of divine anger so that it may not be morally objectionable.

Along the first line of approach toward the solution of the problem Dr. Heschel argues cogently that without God's responsiveness to man anger would be impossible. If God would not care for man, if He were indifferent toward him—and especially toward the evil inflicted by man on his fellow—His anger could not be kindled against man.[16] It is of course correct that divine concern for man is the *conditio sine qua non* for the possibility of divine wrath. If God would not consider man, the possibility of responding to him would never arise. This in itself, how-ever, does not justify the outburst of anger in God, if we understand by anger what the word is normally assumed to mean. Even in man, anger is not too laudable a quality. According to the Talmud, he who is angry is like one who serves an idol. Is it conceivable that God should indulge in it? All the eloquence of Dr. Heschel is of little avail on this point. "The anger of the Lord is a tragic necessity, a calamity for man and a grief for God. It is not an emotion He delights in, but an emotion He deplores." [17] Almost as much may be said of human anger as well. The average human being does not delight in his fits of anger, he deplores them; they are a source of grief to him and, if his specific situation is such that he cannot learn to control them, he may well regard them as "tragic necessity." Nor does it help very much to say that the "intrinsic significance" of anger is "pain in the heart of God." [18] Pain is not anger. Pain may at times cause a person to get angry; but God too? One will find no solution that way. More important is what Dr. Heschel says about what is meant by divine wrath. Divine anger is not an uncontrolled outburst, as in man. God controls His anger, He is its master. It is not "anger for anger's sake," it has a meaning. It is a warning to man, when he is guilty. Its purpose is to bring about repentance. Its desired consummation is its own disappearance. It is "instrumental," it is applied in the best interest of man himself in order to guide him. "His wrath can be unbearably dreadful, yet it is but the expression and instrument of His eternal concern." [19] The idea is also formulated differently by describing anger as "suspended love." One may say that to God wrath means "suspended mercy or love withheld;" it is only to man that it becomes manifest as "doom, destruction, agony." [20] Finally, the theological significance of this interpretation is summed up in the words: "Just as God is absolutely different from man, so is divine anger different from human anger." [21]

This part of the argument does make sense. One is, however, rather surprised to find it in a discussion of the theology of pathos. What Heschel says now is that divine anger and wrath are neither anger nor wrath. "Instrumental anger" is but an educational gimmick. A father, who in complete mastery of his anger, by its consciously controlled manifestation toward his son, guides him in the son's best interest, is not angry but loving. "Instrumental anger" is a pretense of anger and an act of love. Nor is "suspended love" anger. In fact, in keeping with his interpretation, there is no need whatever for Dr. Heschel to call divine anger "love withheld." Since the suspension is motivated by God's "eternal concern" for man, the suspension itself becomes an act of love and compassion. This need not surprise us. Since God is absolutely diffrent from man, His anger too will be absolutely different from man's anger. It could very well be that what is absolutely different from human anger is God's love. One cannot help wondering however what would become of the entire theology of pathos and the religion of sympathy if one would apply the same method of interpretation to the other emotions of God. What if one applied to them the principle of God's absolute difference from man?

It is worth noting that both the theology of pathos and the religion of sympathy are based on the insight that the prophet "refers to God, not as absolute, but always as related to the people." The prophet does not interpret "divine Being" but "divine interaction with humanity." [22] This is fundamental for the thesis of Dr. Heschel. One must not relate divine pathos to divine being. One cannot connect pathos with divine essence or substance. "It seems inconceivable that the Supreme Being should be involved in the affairs of human existence." [23] Yet, it is so. The relationship between pathos and Being is a mystery and a paradox. Pathos is, therefore, not an attribute of God; it is divine action directed to man. In fact, only because pathos cannot be rationally connected with divine Being is the prophet able to respond to it with sympathy, comprehending it, as we saw, "morally and emotionally." This is affirmed for every other form of pathos except for the pathos of anger. Dr. Heschel does not say: "It *seems* inconceivable that the Supreme Being should be involved in the affairs of human existence angrily. Yet, it is the experience of the prophet and it is a mystery and a paradox." What he says concerning anger is that it is inconceivable that God should be angry. He now becomes a rationalist and refers to the absoluteness of divine Being in order to explain what is meant by the pathos of anger. How can anyone imagine that with God anger could mean anger. Is not God absolutely different from man? To God, His anger is really love, an instrument of His care and concern for man.

One can see that Dr. Heschel does not relish the idea of an angry God but, at least intellectually, he rather appreciates the thought of a suffering God.

A Theology of Pathos?

At this stage of our inquiry, we have to pay some attention to the reasons that in the past have prevented the rise of a theology of pathos. We recall the great intellectual struggle of Maimonides against the idea of ascribing any emotions to God. God could not be affected from without; nor could He be moved by emotions. "All affection is evil," he declared. There was also the problem of divine events and actions. The concept of God as complete actuality excluded the possibility of any change in God. Change always implies the realization of a potentiality. How could one conceive of a change of mind in God, if everything within God is actual and perfect? Maimonides discusses at great length and with great ingenuity the question of the act of creation. If God ever existed without a world, then the act of creation is the result of a decision in God. But what could have moved God to create the world when He did what was not present within Him in all eternity? What new consideration could have arisen within Him, if His Being is absolute and perfect?

One cannot help remembering with a high grade of uneasiness the great mental struggle of Maimonides with such and related problems as one follows Dr. Heschel's description of the form in which divine communication to the prophet takes place. Its most important aspect he identifies as inspiration. Inspiration is the form of the act of communication, pathos is its contents. Where there is inspiration, there must also be an inspirer. "Inspiration happens to the Inspirer as well as to the human person." Actually, inspiration is an event that occurs *in* God before it can be experienced by the prophet. God is normally silent and aloof but inspiration is communication directed by God toward man. Therefore, in order to communicate, God must turn "from the condition of concealment to that of revealment." But before He turns, He has to reach a decision to turn in order to communicate. So that the event that must take place within God before any prophecy is possible has two phases: the phase of decision and the phase of turning. But why should God desire to turn? The answer may easily be "inferred from the act itself, from the character of eventuation." God has "an inclination to tropos." Because of his inclination to turning, He has a need to reveal His pathos to the prophet. The "tropos tendency of the Eternal" is the ultimate ground of prophecy. What makes possible the prophetic act within the prophet's consciousness "is an act that happens beyond his consciousness, a transcendent act, an *ecstasy* of God. . . . In its depth and intensity the act takes place in the transcendent subject, but is directed toward the experiencing prophets." Therefore, inspiration is not something that happens to the prophet; "inspiration is a moment of the prophet's being present at a divine event." [24]

Is Dr. Heschel able to lift the veil from the intimate details of the private life of the Almighty and allow us to glance at the depth and intensity of the drama of divine ecstacy? What has become of those theological problems of old that beset a Saadia Gaon, a Yehuda Halevi, a Maimonides? Dr. Heschel does not overlook them altogether. According to him, they had their origin in certain Greek concepts that are alien to the Bible. In Greek thought emotions are a disturbance in the soul. Even a man had to strive to master them. If they were unworthy of man, how much less could they be attributed to God! Not so, however, in the Bible. There we do not find the dichotomy between body and soul. The spirit and the passions are integrated. The heart is the seat of the emotions as well as the intellect. Far from disparaging the emotions, great deeds are performed in the Bible by "those who are filled with *ruach,* with pathos." It is, therefore, not unbecoming to God to have pathos, to feel emotions. As to the problem of divine involvement in actions and events, it arises from an ontological presupposition that is also typically Greek, i.e., the idea that God was "true being," which—by definition—is unchangeable. It is the basis of the Jewish and Christian scholasticism of the Middle Ages, which, following the Eleatic premise, conceived God as perfect and, because of it, immutable. Not so the God of the Bible. "The God of Israel is a God who acts, a God of mighty deeds. The Bible does not say how He is, but how He acts. It speaks of His acts of pathos and of His acts in history. . . . Here the basic category is action rather than immobility. . . ." [25]

We readily agree with the main burden of these thoughts. What Dr. Heschel presents here as insights of his "depth-theology" is of course the well-known distinction between the God of Abraham, Isaac, and Jacob and the God of Aristotle; between the personal God of Judaism and the philosophical idea of the Absolute. It is correct to say that the conception of God as detached from the world and from man is "totally alien" to the biblical mind. What Dr. Heschel is seemingly unable to realize is that by simply proving this point one has not formulated a theology. The historic origin of certain concepts of philosophical thought are interesting and informative but, nevertheless, beside the point of discussion. That the notion of God as a perfect Being is not of biblical origin, that it "is not the product of prophetic religion, but of Greek philosophy" [26] only beclouds the basic issue. The truth is that even though the Bible calls perfect "only" His work and it never refers to

God as the Absolute, absoluteness is implied in the biblical concept of God as is as well perfection. If Dr. Heschel thinks otherwise, let him say so. The God of Abraham, Isaac, and Jacob is not the God of Aristotle, but certainly includes the philosopher's concept of absoluteness. The personal and living God of Israel is not so at the expense of perfection or true being; it is personal and living, even though it is perfect and all-transcendent.

No doubt Dr. Heschel agrees with that. He ought to realize that merely to contrast the personal aspect of the biblical concept with the philosophical concept of the absolute is no Jewish theology. Jewish theology begins when one realizes the implications of the presence of both aspects, that of the absolute and of the personal, in the biblical concept of God. As we have learned earlier in his discussion of anthropopathy, Dr. Heschel observed that "the greatest challenge to the biblical language was how to reconcile in words the awareness of God's transcendence with His overwhelming livingness and concern." Paraphrasing his own words we might say that the fundamental challenge to Jewish theology through the ages has been how to reconcile the awareness of God's transcendence with the awareness of God's livingness and concern, which are one in the Jewish concept of God. It is this challenge that gave no rest to the outstanding Jewish philosophers and theologians of the Middle Ages; it is this challenge that is completely ignored by Dr. Heschel. Until he is able to render the presence of pathos in the Absolute meaningful or sensible he cannot speak of a theology of pathos.

It is true that he does not emphasize the basic irrationality of emotional engagement on the part of the Creator of heaven and earth. He calls it a mystery and a paradox. But to call something a mystery and paradox is no theology either. Occasionally, Dr. Heschel tries to make the mystery more palatable. He explains the prophet's "theology" in the following manner: "His presence pierced the impregnable walls of His otherness. The dilemma was overcome by abstaining from any claim to comprehend God's essence, His inmost being, or even to apprehend His inscrutable thoughts, unrelated to history, and by insisting upon the ability to understand His presence, expression or manifestation. The prophets experience what He *utters,* not what He *is.*" [27] It is for this reason that pathos must not be seen as an attribute of God. An attribute would be describing the divine essence in detachment.

Pathos does not reveal anything about divine nature in itself. It is an "attitude," an act, a relationship, a divine situation, which is changeable as the divine essence could not be.[28]

We do not agree that it is possible to overcome the dilemma in this way. Assuming that, indeed, the prophet experiences only what God utters, what He does in relationship to man, only His manifestations directed to man, the question of what He *is* remains inescapable. What He does and utters is of vital importance to man only because of what He is. The "overwhelming livingness" of God that touches the prophet in the relationship is overwhelming only because it is God who enters into the relationship. The words and acts of a mountain spirit—assuming there be such creature—will count for very little, notwithstanding their being directed to man, because of what mountain spirits are in their essence. The life-giving significance of God's relatedness to the world is not in the act of relatedness but in the fact that it is God who relates Himself. It is the very essence of God, God as He exists in His absoluteness and perfection, that determines the value of His care for man. It is not possible to separate the essence of God from His pathos. The prophet does not have sympathy with pathos; experiencing God's pathos, he sympathizes with God, the Absolute and Perfect, the Supreme Being, the Creator of heaven and earth. The theological dilemma is therefore inescapable. It cannot be overcome by abstaining from any claim to comprehend God's essence. Of course, one may well take the position that it is all a mystery, but one should not speak of a *theology* of pathos.

This in itself need not weigh too heavily in the scales against associating God with pathos. Perhaps it is a mystery; and there is no possibility for formulating a theology of pathos. Even though pathos may not be considered a theological category *sui generis,* it may still be regarded as a basic religious category. Except that one may call something a mystery after one has established unequivocally its rationally inexplicable existence. What is the basis of Dr. Heschel's affirmation that God is a God of pathos? As far as we are able to ascertain, it seems to be based on, at least, one point of deductive reasoning and on the biblical text. The logical deduction runs like this. According to the Bible, the greatness of God is seen in the fact that "man is not an abstraction to Him, nor His judgment a generalization." God knows man, the individual human being, and judges him as an individual. "Yet in order to realize a human being not as a generality but as a concrete fact, one must feel

him, one must become aware of him emotionally." [29] This would make
sense if God's pathos could be explained logically. But since what we
gain by the argument must be called a mystery, why don't we call for
a mystery a step sooner? Why not reason in the following manner: It
is inconceivable that the Supreme Being should be passible. Therefore,
there could be no such thing as divine pathos. At the same time, God
realizes man as "a concrete fact." However, in order to do that one
must feel him, one must become aware of him emotionally. But God is
free of pathos. Ergo, God's realizing man as a concrete fact and not
as an abstraction is enveloped in mystery. We believe that our way of
reasoning is much more valid than that of Heschel. For Dr. Heschel
commits the unforgivable fallacy of equating the human way of realizing
a fellowman as a concrete fact with the way of God. Man's way of
"knowing" a fellow being as a person depends on feeling and emotion.
Could not conceivably God's way be different from that of man? Surely,
our mystery is much more logical than Dr. Heschel's.

However, there are also biblical texts. In numerous passages the
Bible does associate love and hate, anger, sorrow, joy with God. If
we take the references to God in those passages literally, the Bible does
seem to speak of a God of pathos. This, however, raises the question of
biblical interpretation. Shall we say that whenever the literary meaning
of a text does not make much sense, we—who acknowledge the book
as divine revelation—are confronted with a mystery? This has been
neither the halakhic nor the aggadic, neither the philosophical nor the
theological tradition of Judaism. Whenever the literal meaning was
logically or morally unacceptable, the text was interpreted so as to yield
meaningful teaching. In a single case Dr. Heschel does follow this
well-trodden path. In our analysis of his interpretation of the wrath of
God, we were able to show how "anger" became "suspended love," an
"instrument of God's eternal concern." By implication, he also seems
to reject any actual anthropomorphism. But why? How come he does
not equip the Almighty with a body too? The anthropomorphic references to God in the Bible are hardly less conspicuous than the anthropopathetic expressions. Using Dr. Heschel's own method of reasoning,
it should not be difficult to prove that God has a body. We shall first
quote a rather significant passage from the discussion of anthropopathy.

We are inclined to assume that thought and sympathy, because
they are found in man, are limited to man. However, with the

same logic it may be maintained that being, because it is characteristic of man and matter, is limited to them. Sight, because of
its being a faculty of man, is not to be denied to God. Yet, there
is an absolute difference between the sight and the thought of God
and the sight and the thought of man. God compared with man is
like the potter compared with the clay. [Quotation from Isaiah
follows.] For My thoughts are not your thoughts, Neither are your
ways My ways, saith the Lord. For as the heavens are higher than
the earth, So are My ways higher than your ways, And My thoughts
than your thoughts. Isaiah 55:8-9

The nature of the divine pathos is a mystery to man. What
Isaiah (55:8f.) said concerning the thoughts of God may equally
apply to His pathos: For My pathos is not your pathos, neither
are your ways My ways, says the Lord, etc.[30]

Let us now replace the word pathos, or its equivalent, by the word
body and see what we get.

We are inclined to assume that body, because it is found in man, is
limited to man. However, with the same logic it may be maintained that
being, because it is characteristic of man and matter, is limited to them.
Sight, because of its being a faculty of man, is not to be denied to God.
Yet, there is an absolute difference . . . (as above).

The nature of the divine body is a mystery to man. What Isaiah said
concerning the thoughts of God may equally apply to His body: For
My body is not your body, neither are your ways My ways.

There is hardly anything in Dr. Heschel's arguments for the divine
pathos that could not be used in pleading for a bodily form of divine
existence. Yet he rejects the literal interpretation of anthropomorphic
expressions just as he interprets away the literal meaning of anger, in
relationship to God. This makes sense. But until such time that he is
able to show that the possibility of the Supreme Being, the One God,
Absolute and Perfect, makes good sense too, his profusely eloquent
dissertation on God's "emotional engagement to man" cannot be taken
seriously.

A Religion of Sympathy?

It is not easy to decide what is more objectionable, the "theology of
pathos" or the "religion of sympathy." The very idea of the prophet's
feeling the feelings of God, of his establishing emotional harmony with
God, of his feeling the divine pathos as he feels his own state of the

soul, consummated by the insight that "in sympathy man experiences God as his own being," notwithstanding the dignified mystical connotations of the thought seems very foreign to Jewish religious teaching and experience.[31] Even if one could accept the theology of pathos, one would have to reject most emphatically this religion of sympathy.

However, let us see what the proofs are for Dr. Heschel's theory. As in the case of the theology, so with sympathy too, there is an indirect argument and there are also biblical passages which are adduced; and as in the case of the theology neither form of the argument proves anything. As to the indirect deductive reasoning, it is maintained that it serves the purpose of solving the riddle of the ruthless wrath with which the prophets often castigate and condemn their own people, whom they love so much. How could Hosea, for instance, ask: "Give them, O Lord—What will Thou give? Give them a miscarrying womb and dry breasts?" How is the, at times, unbridled fury of Jeremiah against his own people to be understood? It is the prophet's pathos of wrath that Dr. Heschel desires to explain. It is sympathy with the divine pathos that fills the prophet with anger of such intensity that he is unable to control its outburst. The psychological process is explained in the following manner: ". . . sympathy derives from an understanding of the situation and pathos of God. The divine evokes a similar pathos in the prophet."[32] Because of his "personal concern for God" the prophet focuses all his emotions on the given pathos of God. When he absorbs God's pathos of anger, he becomes filled with anger against the people who caused God pain. Dr. Heschel maintains that sympathy is the key to the psychological understanding of the prophet. "It enables us to understand the zeal of the prophet who knows himself to be in emotional harmony and concord with God; and the power of his anger, which motivates him to turn away from his people whom he loves so dearly."[33] In other words, you cannot blame the prophets. In God's anger, which is communicated to them, they recognize God's suffering. They feel God's suffering as their own. They are unable to control their wrath against their people who caused God such suffering.

Once again Dr. Heschel explains a lesser mystery with a far greater one. Granted, the limitless wrath with which the prophets often face their people is a riddle. But it is much more logical to bear with this riddle than to try to explain it with the far greater riddle of a mysterious divine pathos that is intuited by the prophet so that he can feel it as his very own. There are also many more reasons why this psychological key of sympathy opens no doors to the understanding of the prophet. There is, for instance, this question. If the prophet's anger by itself is inexplicable, even more so must be God's anger. Or are we to assume that the prophet loves his people more dearly than God does? And now we recall that Dr. Heschel is of the opinion that above God's anger is His love. God is not really angry. His anger is only suspended love. If then the prophet is filled to overflowing with God's suspended love, what he feels with God is God's instrumental care and concern. The prophet's anger must, therefore, not be taken literally. Somehow, it has to be interpreted as suspended love, suspended out of love. But if we succeed in this, there is no riddle at all. We can solve the riddle directly and say that the prophet is not really angry; out of his great love, he only suspends his love momentarily. There is no need for us to seek an explanation in the mystery of divine pathos which is so mysteriously experienced by the prophet as his very own state of the soul.

Let us now consider the biblical "proofs" for the religion of sympathy. Dr. Heschel interprets the concept of *daat E-lohim,* "usually rendered as knowledge of God," as sympathy for God. The passages he quotes to prove his point do prove the well-known truth that "in Hebrew *yada* means more than the possession of abstract concepts." *Yada* does certainly not mean merely intellectual knowledge. But Heschel's conclusion that it means sympathy, a sharing of an inner experience, is the fruit of imagination. We shall not deal with every one of the passages which he quotes. A few observations will suffice. Quoting the verse from Exodus: "You shall not oppress a stranger; you *know* the heart of a stranger, for you were strangers in the land of Egypt," Dr. Heschel remarks: "The correct meaning is: "You *have sympathy,* or a *feeling,* for the heart of a stranger." And now let us read the verse again, correcting at the same time the strange oversight of Heschel in dropping the English equivalent of the letter *vav* in front of the word *atem* of the Hebrew text. We get this: "You shall not oppress a stranger; for you have sympathy, you have feeling for the heart of a stranger, for you were strangers in the land of Egypt." No, certainly not. *To know* most definitely does not mean sympathy here. It does not make sense to command anyone not to oppress a fellowman, since he already sympathizes with him anyway. Neither does *to know* stand here for conceptual knowledge. It clearly means understanding gained by personal experience. You shall not oppress a stranger. You ought to know better. You ought to be able to appreciate his plight, since you experienced it yourself. You cannot say you are not fully aware of the significance of oppressing another man. You *ought* to feel with him, because you *know*.

Similarly, the passage from I Samuel, 2:12, where concerning the sons of Eli it is said: "They were base men; they knew not the Lord," can hardly be used in support of the thesis of sympathy. Dr. Heschel remarks: "Knowledge in the sense of information they must have had; what they lacked was inner commitment or an emotional attachment." The conclusion is a *non sequitur.* It is true that the passage shows that *to know* is not just to have information, which of course is no proof that it is inner commitment or an emotional attachment. In fact, it is most unlikely that it could be meant. Sympathy would be the highest form of religious life. To say, therefore: They were base men; they knew not the Lord, is stylistically about as appropriate as to say of a person: He was a villain; he was no saint.[34]

It is not our task to offer here a thorough discussion of the term *daat E-Lohim;* that was Dr. Heschel's responsibility. We shall only illustrate the central use *he makes* of the term in his interpretation of the prophet Hosea. Contrasting the prophets Amos and Hosea, he maintains: "To Amos, the principal sin is *injustice;* to Hosea, it is idolatry. Amos inveighs against evil *deeds;* Hosea attacks the absence of *inwardness."* [35] In order to underline the point, he juxtaposes a saying of Amos with one of Hosea. Amos said:

> I hate, I despise your feasts . . .
> I will not accept your sacrifices . . .
> But let justice roll down like waters,
> And righteousness like a mighty stream. (Amos 5:21-24)

Hosea, however, put it this way:

> For I desire love (*chesed*) and not sacrifice,
> Attachment to God [*Daat E-Lohim,* i.e., sympathy] rather than burnt offerings. (Hosea, 6:6)

This seems to show that whereas Amos contrasted a soulless, sacrificial form of cult to justice, Hosea held up before it the ideal of emotional attachment to God. According to Hosea then, God turns to the people and says to them: What I really want from you is that you love me, that you feel for me. No, no, no! The prophets are not like that! As is well known, *daat E-Lohim* is often associated with ethical action and social justice. Who does not remember the words of Isaiah?

> They shall not hurt nor destroy
> In all My holy mountain;
> For the earth shall be full of the knowledge of the Lord,
> As the waters cover the sea. (Isaiah 11:9)

In fact we have a prophetic definition of *Daat E-Lohim,* placed on record by no less a man than Jeremiah. It is found in chapter twenty-two of his book:

> Woe unto him that buildeth his house by unrighteousness,
> And his chambers by injustice;
> That useth his neighbour's service without wages,
> And giveth him not his hire;
> That saith: 'I will build me a wide house
> And spacious chambers' . . .
> Shalt thou reign, because thou strivest to excel in cedar?
> Did not thy father eat and drink, and do justice and righteousness?
> Then it was well with him.
> He judged the cause of the poor and needy;
> Then it was well.
> Is *not this to know Me?* saith the Lord. (Jeremiah 22:13-16)

It is exactly in this association with doing justice that Hosea himself uses the concept of *daat E-Lohim*. The words are:

> Hear the word of the Lord, ye children of Israel!
> For the Lord hath a controversy with the inhabitants of the land,
> Because there is no truth, nor mercy [*chesed;* love, in H.'s rendering]
> Nor *knowledge of God* in the land.
> Swearing and lying, and killing, and stealing, and committing adultery!
> They break all bounds, and blood toucheth blood. (Hosea, 4:12)

We see that in this passage not only does Hosea mean by *daat E-Lohim* the fruits of justice, but *chesed* for him is mercy and love between a man and his neighbor. The two passages quoted by Dr. Heschel to illustrate the distinction between Amos and Hosea prove the very opposite. It shows a point of exact agreement between the two. The love that God desires rather than sacrifice is not love for Himself but love and mercy practiced between man and man. And asking for "the knowledge of God," he is not pleading for sympathy with Himself, but exactly for those acts of justice which Isaiah and Jeremiah connect with the concept.

The words of Hosea:

For I desire love [*chesed*] and not sacrifice,
Knowledge of God rather than burnt offerings;

are the exact parallel to the words of Amos:

I hate, I despise your feasts, . . .
I will not accept your sacrifices . . .
But let justice roll down like waters,
And righteousness like a mighty stream.

We shall not continue with the detailed illustration of the inconclusiveness of Dr. Heschel's exegesis and its numerous misunderstandings. Jeremiah's exclamation, "I am full of the wrath of God" (6:11) does not mean that "his being filled with divine wrath was his sympathy with it." [36] Nor can his "For Thou hast filled me with indignation" (15:17) be interpreted as "the pathos that evoked in him an anger of sympathy." [37] His midrashic *diyuk* on the words, "Because of the Lord, and because of His holy words" (Jeremiah 23:9) is too thin to prove anything. Notwithstanding Dr. Heschel's dissertation on the meaning of the word *ruach,* the phrase, "But as for me, I am filled with power, with the *ruach* of the Lord" (Micah 3:8) definitely does not mean that "the prophet describes himself as a person filled with divine pathos." [38] *"Ruach* of the Lord" is as unlikely to mean divine pathos here as, for instance, in the case of the encounter between Samson and the lion, where it is said: "And the *ruach* of the Lord came upon him, and he rent him [the lion] as one would have rent a kid" (Judges, 14:6). There is no need for multiplying examples. Normally, *"ruach* of the Lord" in the Bible means strength, courage, authority. This is its meaning in Micah too. The full passage runs as follows:

But as for me, I am filled with power,
With the *ruach* of the Lord,
And with justice and might,
To declare to Jacob his transgressions,
And to Israel his sin.

It is not an easy matter to declare to a people its transgressions and sins. It requires strength, courage, authority. It is of these that Micah speaks and not of divine pathos that he made his own through sympathy.

It is not possible to conclude this part of our analysis without paying some attention to Dr. Heschel's interpretation of Hosea's marriage. God commanded the prophet: "Go, take unto thee a wife of harlotry and children of harlotry; for the land doth commit great harlotry, departing from the Lord" (Hosea, 1:2). Hosea did as he was commanded. He married such a woman and soon was betrayed by her. Normally, the marriage is understood as a symbol. It was meant to convey the idea of the people's faithlessness, of the temporary rejection of Israel, of God's abiding love for His people, who was taking them back in spite of their betrayal. Dr. Heschel rejects this interpretation and offers us a most original one. According to the imagery of Hosea's language, God is the Consort of Israel. The covenant between God and Israel is like that between a husband and his wife. Thus, Hosea, marrying "a wife of harlotry," went through an experience similar to the experience of God with Israel. By means of this marriage the prophet was able to feel the divine pathos; he and God shared in a common experience. Whereas the other prophets were able to feel God's feelings without the help of actual sympathetic experience, with Hosea it was different. He had to place himself into God's situation in order to be able to sympathize with God. In order to make sure that we do not misunderstand Dr. Heschel, we shall quote him:

> As time went by, Hosea became aware of the fact that his personal fate was a mirror of the divine pathos, that his sorrow echoed the sorrow of God. In this fellow suffering as an act of sympathy with the divine pathos the prophet probably saw the meaning of the marriage which he had contracted at the divine behest. . . . Only by living through in his own life what the divine Consort of Israel experienced was the prophet to attain sympathy for the divine situation.[39]

One cannot help wondering what concept of God a person must have in order to be able to appreciate this kind of an interpretation.

The God of Pathos

Although we have heard Dr. Heschel state that the relationship between the pathos of God and the essence of God is a mystery for man and the prophet is only concerned with God in his relatedness to man, quite obviously some concept of God must be implied in the God of pathos, in the God with whom the prophets sympathize. As we had occasion to observe earlier in our discussion, the pathos is significant because it is God's pathos; nor does the prophet sympathize with the pathos but with God. *Nolens volens* some concept of God is present here. We shall now inquire as to what kind of an idea of God must be associated with this theology of pathos and religion of sympathy. We have shown that what Dr. Heschel calls his theology of pathos does not deserve that name. Implied in his thesis is, however, a theology which he does not care to acknowledge explicitly.

A God of pathos, who is affected by man's behavior and responds to it emotionally—is he not a person? Dr. Heschel defends himself against such an interpretation of his theory by saying: "The idea of divine pathos is not a personification of God but an exemplification of divine reality, an illustration of His concern. It does not represent a substance, but an act or a relationship." [40] Similarly in his concluding remarks: "It is in this limited sense that we speak of God as a personal being: He has concern for nondivine being." [41] Yet, he also says with great emphasis: "God is all-personal, all-subject," [42] and with even greater intensity of conviction he insists: ". . . it is because God is absolutely personal—devoid of anything impersonal—that this ethos is full of pathos." [43] We maintain that this latter is the true position of Dr. Heschel, because only if we keep in mind that according to him, God in His essential nature is "all-personal," "all-subject," "devoid of anything impersonal," can he be understood.

When he is on the defensive, Dr. Heschel maintains that pathos has nothing to do with divine substance; it is an act, it is not an attribute. This, of course, he has to say in order to justify his other statement that God in His essence is not the divine reality given to the consciousness of the prophet. The fact, however, is that Dr. Heschel tells us much too much about the nature of God, for one who disclaims any comprehension of it. Pathos is at times identified as "God's inner acts." Of the prophets it is said that "they not only sense God in history, but also history in God." [44] Things are happening within God, *before* they are directed to man. We have heard him describe the transcendental aspect of inspiration as an event within God, consisting of the phase of decision and that of turning. Before it is directed to him, the prophet witnesses it as taking place within the divine life. Surely, if pathos were indeed nothing but a divine attitude in relationship to man, the nature of God itself remaining wrapped in mystery, it would be impossible to speak of history and events with God. If Dr. Heschel really meant to say that pathos was unrelated to divine essence, he could not have written as he did: "The decision to communicate is an event *in the life of God*. It arises directly from divine motivation; for it belongs *to the very nature* of God to declare His thoughts to the prophets. Inspiration as a crucial event is conditioned both by the history of man and by the *character of God*." [45] This is not just an attitude, an act *in* history in response to man. The Eternal's "inclination to tropos" is discovered beyond history, and beyond any relatedness, in the very nature of God. Dr. Heschel also calls pathos "the essence of God's moral nature," he speaks of "the *nature* or the *pathos* of God." [46] Most enlightening is what he has to say about justice. Discussing the meaning of divine justice in relationship to God's mercy and love, he declares: "No single attribute can convey the nature of God's relationship to man. Since justice is His nature, love which would disregard the evil deeds of man, would contradict His nature." [47] But if pathos is only a divine act, a changeable divine attitude,[48] how can the pathos of justice be called divine nature? We know of it only by the act of its manifestation in history. Why is it not, then, conceivable that it should not be manifested? Quite obviously, pathos does represent in all the passages quoted divine substance and it is indeed referred to in our last quotation as an attribute. In all these passages pathos is inseparable from the essence of the Divine Being and reveals it as "all-personal," "all-subject," "devoid of anything impersonal." These are not just occasional lapses of style. They are much too consistent, much too meaningful, and some of them occur in the key passages of Dr. Heschel's dissertation.

The truth is that possibility is, of logical necessity, an essential attribute of the Divine Being. We shall once again consider one of the most important statements on the meaning of pathos. It is maintained:

The prophets never identify God's pathos with His essence, because for them the pathos is not something absolute, but a form of relation. Indeed, prophecy would be impossible were the divine pathos in its particular structure a necessary attribute of God. If the structure of the pathos were immutable and remained unchanged even after the people had "turned," prophecy would lose its function, which is precisely so to influence man as to bring about a change in the divine pathos of rejection and affliction.[49]

One should note that what is said here applies only to "pathos in its particular structure," to pathos in its actual, specific manifestation. All pathos, revealed in the relation, has particular structure or specific quality. Actual pathos is always a response to human conduct of a particular nature and as such it is particular and changeable as man's behavior itself. But every form of actual pathos has its origin in an aspect of the divine essence itself, i.e., God's possibility. Human action may evoke pathos in its particular structure only because God is turned toward man, because He can be reached by man, because He can be affected by what man does. Pathos in its specific historic form, pathos in time, in a given situation, is always a response, it is a relation; but the relation comes about because God, prior to the moment of response in time, prior to all human action, makes Himself accessible for man, because He may be affected by man. This quality of God's possibility is timeless, is above all history; it is a genuine attribute of God, it is of the very essence of God, it is absolute. If God were not possible in His very essence, pathos could never arise, for He would never be affected by man. Only because pathos has its source in the very essence of Divine Nature may Dr. Heschel say, for instance:

> New is the prophetic conception that mercy or anger are not sporadic reactions, but expressions of constant care and concern. The divine pathos embraces all life, past, present, and future; all things and events have a reference to Him. It is a concern that has the attribute of eternity, transcending all history, as well as the attribute of universality, embracing all nations, encompassing animals as well as human beings.[50]

Only the specific form that pathos takes in specific situations is an act and not an attribute, changeable and not eternal, a divine situation and not representing divine substance. However, pathos in its historic and specific manifestations is due to the *constant care and concern* of God, which is not a response, but is timeless and universally unconditional, which is God's original approach to man, motivated altogether by His Divine Being. This is what makes God "all personal" and "all-subject."

How is this to be understood? Dr. Heschel knows the answer: "The fact that the attitudes of man may affect the life of God, that God stands in an intimate relationship to the world, implies a certain analogy between Creator and creature." [51] This, of course, is the cornerstone for the understanding of Dr. Heschel's position. If on one or two occasions he does mention that the difference between God and man is absolute, it is not to be taken literally. What he means is that although there is a certain analogy between God and man, yet God is still very much different from man. But the analogy remains. That is why God may be affected by man and that is why the prophet may feel the feelings of God, when God happens to be so affected. One may agree that a God conceived on the basis of a certain analogy to man may very well possess the attributes required by Dr. Heschel for his God of pathos. It is a God essentially shaped in the image of man. In order to escape the dilemma, Dr. Heschel occasionally resorts to the familiar idea of anthropomorphic theology of declaring that God is not anthropomorph, but man, theomorph. It is of little use. The idea, which is of kabbalistic origin, may have its proper place in a kabbalistic system of thought. In a nonkabbalistic context, however, a godlike man still implies a manlike god.

There is, of course, anthropomorphic and anthropopathic imagery in kabbalistic literature. Their true significance still awaits thorough investigation. Rabbi Hayim Vital, for instance, warns against all anthropomorphism and anthropopathy. In the *Shaar Hakadmut,* quoted in some editions of the *Eitz Chayim* in *Heikhal Adam Kadmon,* at the end of Chapter 1, he writes:

> It is well known that there is on high neither a body nor any bodily force. All these images and descriptions must not be taken literally, God forbid. They are expressions attuned to the human ear, so that man may grasp these supernatural spiritual realities, which otherwise could not be understood by or impressed on the human intellect. Only because of this is it permissible to speak in symbols and images as it is done in the Zohar. The verses of the Bible themselves testify to this method [of using anthropomorphic terminology to convey nonanthropomorphic meaning]. . . . If the Bible itself speaks in this manner, we too may follow its method.

A statement of this nature indicates that the great interpreter of Lurianic Kabbalah could never have called God a God of pathos. Such was also the position of Rabbi Moshe Hayim Luzzato. In *Choker u'Mekubbal* (p. 12, Mosad Harav Kook, 5712) he declares:

> Know that all the wisdom of the Kabbalah only clarifies His "law," blessed be He, and that He is One in ultimate true oneness, and that there is neither any change nor any bodily attribute within Him, God forbid.

In another passage again (p. 16):

> ... But know that we may only speak of His will, for that is nearer to us and it is permissible [to interpret it], because in this way we are not touching His blessed essence at all.

Luzzato elaborates his point of view in *Daat Tevunot:* At the conclusion of a striking passage (pp. 70-74; edition Mosad Harav Kook) he says:

> ... Perfection [God's] is utterly unrelated to these *Middot* (ways of God). These are specific *middot,* instituted by His will, finite and limited in accordance with the measure He wanted. However, since the Blessed One, who is perfect in His perfection, acts according to these *middot,* we call Him by these names and attributes [of the *middot*]. . . .

This is, indeed, a position not too far removed from that of Maimonides' attributes of action. There is little doubt in our mind that neither Vital nor Luzzato would ever have dared speak of God as being passible. Man's actions, according to the Kabbalah, do have an effect in the "higher world," but not on God Himself. If there is pathos in the system of Kabbalah, it is certainly below the world of *Atzilut,* in the realms of creation, finite emanations, and *Tzimtzumim.* It is most unlikely that any Kabbalist ever ventured to maintain, as Professor Heschel does, that "events and human actions arouse in Him joy or sorrow, pleasure or wrath. . . ."

Most important, however, is the consideration that Dr. Heschel does not give us a tractate on Kabbalah. He offers us a theology of pathos, outside the system of the Kabbalah. But apart from the concept of the various levels of the *Sephirot* and *Tzimtzumim,* a "God of pathos" is only tenable, if one can show how it may be philosophically and theologically reconciled with the idea of an infinite, perfect Being.

It is true that talmudic and midrashic tradition does speak of the *Galut ha'Shekhinah* (cf. *Megillah,* 29a), the exile of the *Shekhinah;* there is even a passage in the Talmud (*Sanhedrin,* 46a), which may indicate that the term *tza'ar ha'Shekhinah,* the sorrow of the *Shekhinah,* has a mishnaic basis. However, the very fact that the term *Shekhinah* is used, and not that of God, is in itself an indication how strongly rooted in the Jewish consciousness is the thought of God's impassibility. In other places, where the *Shekhinah* is not explicitly mentioned, anthropopathic expressions are introduced with the qualifying term, *keveyakhol,* "as it were." (Cf., e.g., the quotation from *Eikha Rabbati* in *Tosafot, Megillah* 45a, *Ani ve'Hu;* see also *Yalkut Shimoni,* on Jeremiah, ch. 40.) There are, of course, innumerable anthropopathic passages in the Aggadah and the Midrash of a similar nature. In themselves, they are even less to be taken as a theology of pathos than the numerous anthropomorphic phrases of the Bible. Theology demands meaningful interpretation. All these anthropopathic passages of the *Midrash* have found their kabbalistic interpretation, just as they are capable of interpretation within the context of the antianthropopathic tradition of Jewish philosophy and theology. (Cf. the remarkable interpretation of Maimonides in his commentary in the *Mishnah, Sanhedrin,* [6:5], in the phrase: *Shekhinah ma ha'lashon omeret.* . . . Even the well-known midrashic interpretation of the phrase in the 91st Psalm: "I will be with him in trouble," says no more than that God is near the man who calls on Him in times of trouble.) It is not permissible to take the metaphorical language of the *Midrash* literally and call it a theology of pathos.

Even less acceptable is Professor Heschel's concept of the religion of sympathy. Again, it would be a misunderstanding to compare it to the idea that one should feel the *tza'ar ha'Shekhinah,* so widely spread in all Hasidic literature. On the basis of what has been said about pathos in Kabbalah, it should be obvious that it is not possible to equate the "sorrow of the *Shekhinah"* with Heschel's "pain in the heart of God." The sympathy called for is with a finite manifestation of the divine in the world of creation. It is not sympathy with God, but, as it were, with the cause of God in the world. Most illuminating on this point is the teaching of the author of *Nefesh Ha-Chayim.* In keeping with kabbalistic principles he maintains that, because of the manner in which the various worlds of creation, the highest and the lowest, are connected with each other, all human action produces corresponding effects on high. Human failure is, therefore, a destructive action in "all the worlds" and is the cause of sorrow "on high." It is the task of man, when he approaches God in prayer, to think of the sorrow of the heavens over his failure, rather than his own tribulations. However, the term used is usually "the sorrow on high," but never feeling "the pain of God" (Cf. *Nefesh Ha-Chayim, Shaar* II, chapter 12). This is undoubtedly intentional, for in another striking passage the author insists on the impassibility of divine nature itself on all the levels even of its immanence. (Cf., *ib.,* chapter 6). The author interprets a midrashic statement, which compares God's indwelling in the universe to the soul's presence in every part of the body. The parallel is summed up in the words: "As the soul neither eats nor drinks, so is there neither food nor drink before the Holy One, blessed be He." The explanation offered is as follows: The soul does not partake of the food which keeps the body alive, yet on the food which sustains the body depends the connection between body and soul. Similar is the relationship between God and the worlds. All human action, all the commandments, the Torah and the divine service, *do not affect God Himself in the least.* It is in this sense that we say of Him that He "neither eats nor drinks." It is the will of God to remain in contact with the worlds according to the "sustenance" that man provides for the worlds through his deeds, performed in accordance with the Torah. This is just one among very many statements in a rich kabbalistic literature that are meant to preserve the idea of God's impassibility, notwithstanding His immanence in all creation. Only in their light may we try to interpret the meaning of kabbalistic sympathy with "the sorrow of the *Shekhinah* or "the sorrow on high."

We venture to maintain that not even in the most anthropopathic metaphors of the Kabbalah shall we find the kind of religion of sympathy that is offered by Professor Heschel. It is contrary to Jewish sensitivities to speak of "suffering together" with God, of "sharing an inner experience" with Him. Heschel's "emotional identification with God" is indeed shocking within the context of Jewish tradition, kabbalistic or theological. The Jewish awareness of God's reality must wince at the suggestion that a mere man, be he even a prophet, could be guided "not by what he but rather by what God feels." The suggestion that "in sympathy man experiences God as his own being" is alien to the heartbeat of Judaism.

Pathos, Sympathy, and Christian Theology

There is little doubt that in the context of Jewish thought and religious sensitivity, Dr. Heschel's position is most original. And yet, when he speaks of man's participating in "the inner life" of God and God's sharing in the life of man, there is a somewhat familiar ring about it. When he elaborates in innumerable variations on the prophet's feeling "His heart" and experiencing "the pain in the heart of God" as his own, or when he reveals the secret of sympathy as a situation in which "man experiences God as his own being," it does not take much perspicuity to realize that one has encountered these concepts in one's readings—in Christian theology.

Sympathy with the suffering of Jesus is one of the basic requirements of Christianity. To use Dr. Heschel's distinction between "feeling for" and having a feeling in common, it is no mere feeling for Jesus but actually sharing in his experience, feeling his feelings as one's own. According to Thomas à Kempis, a good Christian is Jesus' "companion in suffering." But while this concept is natural to a religion at whose focal point is the passion of a god incarnate, it is unheard of in Judaism, with its belief in the One God, who is in everything unlike man. Dr. Heschel, summing up what he has to say about the prophetic experience, declares:

> An analysis of prophetic utterances shows that the fundamental experience of the prophet is a fellowship with the feelings of God, a sympathy with the divine pathos, a communion with the divine consciousness which comes about through the prophet's reflection of, or participation in, the divine pathos. . . . The emotional experience of the prophet becomes the focal point for the prophet's understanding of God. He lives not only his personal life, but also the life of God. The prophet hears God's voice and feels His heart.[52]

In exactly the same words one could describe the religious experience of a good Christian in his relationship to Jesus. A Christian, however, would find no meaning in the thought of having sympathy, as defined by Dr. Heschel, with God as He is known in Judaism. Indeed, it makes no sense.

Seen from this angle, we shall take one more look at the theology of pathos. While it is utterly unknown to Judaism, it has a long history in Christian thought. Both Judaism and Christianity had to cope with the intellectual consequences of the confrontation with Greek philosophy and metaphysics. God as immutable, pure Being was not the God of the Bible. The dilemma, arising from the confrontation, was far less serious for Judaism than for Christianity. For Judaism it was a clash between metaphysical ideas and the biblical text. Solution could be found by interpreting the text. For Christianity, however, the conflict was between metaphysics and its faith in a god incarnate, who in human form walked this earth, suffered and died. Anthropomorphic text could be reinterpreted; the possibility of Jesus could not be explained away. It is the very essence of Christian faith that the divine is to be associated with emotions, that it is affected, that it suffers or rejoices, as the case may be. One of the Gifford lecturers expressed it succinctly: "The very truth that came by Jesus . . . may be said to be summed up in the passibility of God." [53] In Christianity, God does have pathos in exactly the same sense as Dr. Heschel understands the term—as an emotional affection of the deity. Because the confrontation between Greek metaphysics and Christianity was, indeed, much more serious than that between the Greek Absolute and Judaism, a genuine theology of pathos was produced by Christian theologians.

Already in the second and third century C.E., a theology of pathos was formulated in the Christian church which comes very close to that of Dr. Heschel. The anti-Trinitarians or Monarchians, holding onto the strict monotheism of Judaism, were puzzled by the fact that the immutable God should be passible. They reached the conclusion, quite logical on the basis of their assumptions, that God the Impassible became passible for the sake of man. They believed in the One God of Israel, but they considered him impassible and invisible in his concealment and passible and visible in his revealment. Because of their theory they became known as the Patripassians. [54] Strangely enough, it was Tertullian who most emphatically opposed this theology with the weapons of Greek metaphysics. He argued that the consequences of Patripassianism were that the "Incomprehensible" became comprehended, the Immortal mortal. And yet God could not have abandoned His own absoluteness and have remained at the same time the Invisible, the Incomprehensible, the Immutable and the Immortal." [55] Tertullian had a different solution for the problem. He found it in the Christian concept of Trinity. The first person of the Trinity is the Absolute, incomprehensible and immutable; passibility belongs to the second person in it.

This is, by the way, the solution which Thomas Aquinas adopted.[56] In a sense Dr. Heschel committed an act of intellectual injustice against Aquinas' excellence as a thinker. He evaluates his theology in the following terms: "To Thomas Aquinas, God is *actus purus,* without the admixture of any potentiality. Hence it is evident that it is impossible for God to change in any way. Passion, being a change, would be incompatible with His true Being." [57] How could Dr. Heschel write of one of the mightiest minds of the church that for him God's true Being was incompatible with passion, when—in truth—the passion of the God in whom he believed was at the very heart of his faith! Of course, Thomas Aquinas had a solution for his problem. He believed in a god incarnate.

It is neither our intention nor our task to indicate even in vague outline the various phases in the history of the theology of pathos in Christianity. Suffice it to say that having started in the second century, some of its rather interesting expressions border practically at our own era. The philosophical-metaphysical foundations of such a theology may be found in Hermann Lotze's major work, *Microcosmus.* He identifies the Infinite with Perfect Personality, that is God. He will not allow a mere personification of an idea, not even a personification of the *idea* of God. By the Personal God he means an actually living personality. It is most interesting to follow his argument. He explains that "we have a direct feeling of the wide difference there is between this personification of a thought and living personality." What is this hallmark of a living personality? In the words of Lotze "an essential condition of all true reality" is to be found "in the capacity for suffering." Personality has an "inner core" which cannot be conceptualized, "which cannot be resolved into thoughts, the meaning and significance of which we know in the immediate experience of our mental life, and which we always misunderstand when we seek to construe it—hence personality can never belong to any unchangeable valid truth, but only to something which changes, suffers and reacts." [58] Lotze's Personal God possesses, indeed, possibility; by his essential nature it is a God of pathos. It is, however, clear that his philosophy is oriented completely by the basic Christian affirmation concerning God. It is a late nineteenth-century metaphysics in support of second- and third-century Patripassianism. The metaphysics was paralleled by new voices in

theology. A. M. Fairbairn, for example, articulated it in the following
manner:

> Theology has no falser idea than that of the impassibility of God.
> If He is capable of sorrow, He is capable of suffering; and were He
> without the capacity of either, He would be without any feeling of
> the evil of sin or misery of man. . . . There is a sense in which the
> Patripassian theory is right. . . . The being of evil in the universe
> was to His moral nature an offense and a pain, and through His
> pity the misery of man became His sorrow. But this sense of man's
> evil and misery became the impulse to speak and to help. . . .[59]

Dr. Heschel uses practically the same terminology in his theology of
pathos. There is, of course, the difference that whereas in Fairbairn's
thought God's "impulse to speak and to help" leads to Jesus, with Dr.
Heschel it leads to the inspiring of the prophets.

If we now try to relate Dr. Heschel's position to the theology of
pathos in Christianity, the outcome will depend on whether we wish to
judge him by his explicit declarations or by the theology which is
logically implied in his thesis. According to the declaration, the relationship between God in His true Being, in His essential Nature, and
God in His relatedness to man, is a mystery. But the prophets never
refer to the Absolute or the Perfect. Their dealings are with God as
He reveals Himself by His pathos, with His earthly manifestations as they
are directed toward man. In His relatedness to the world they do
comprehend Him morally and emotionally. This position is very much
like that adopted by Tertullian: God, the Invisible, the Incomprehensible, the Absolute and Transcendent is impassible; the passibility
belongs to His earthly manifestation (as it was understood by the faith
of Christianity). And the same criticism that was levelled against
Tertullian also applies to Dr. Heschel: the earthly manifestation ob-
scures completely God in His true Being. It is as if there were two
gods: one wrapped in mystery, aloof and removed, inaccessible and un-
concerned; the other, the related one, comprehensible, loving and caring.
In what Dr. Heschel considers his theology of pathos the two aspects of
the divine reality, its true Being and its attitudes and acts remain unrelated to each other and thus, indeed, fall apart. The prophets are not
concerned with God in His essence. He might as well not exist as far
as the theology of pathos or the religion of sympathy are concerned.

We have shown that by the implicit logic of pathos and sympathy this
kind of separation is untenable, that pathos, even for Dr. Heschel, must

be understood to be an attribute of divine essence, that the God of pathos is "all-personal," "all-subject," "absolutely personal." Accordingly, God must be seen as being possible in his essential nature. This corresponds, as we have noted, to the position of the Patripassians in Christian theology.

One must, however bear in mind one important point in order to appreciate fully Dr. Heschel's position. The Christian theologian starts out with a faith whose central affirmation is that God is passible. Given that premise, a theology of pathos is unavoidable. The theology may be good or bad, the faith itself remains unaffected. In the context of Judaism, however, the situation is fundamentally different. Here we start out with a faith that abhors any form of "humanization" of divine nature; the theological climate is determined by a long tradition of affirmation of divine impassibility in face of numerous biblical texts to the contrary. Dr. Heschel, however, decided to take *some* anthropopathetic expressions in the Bible literally. In the light of his own interpretation of these passages he formulates a theology; in the light of his theology he then proceeds to offer us a God who is "all-personal" and "absolutely personal," who, since "the attitudes of man may affect the life of God," should be understood with the help of "a certain analogy between Creator and creature." From the Jewish point of view, these are alien and objectionable concepts. To have a faith in a passible God and to proceed from there in order to formulate an adequate theology is one thing; but to conceive of an "original" interpretation of biblical expressions and to proceed from there, by way of a questionable theology, to the formulation of the concept of a God of pathos is something entirely different. Given the Christian premise, a theology of pathos is an intellectual necessity; given the premises of Judaism, Dr. Heschel's theology of pathos and religion of sympathy seem to be offsprings of a theologically oriented fancy.

This episode of a "theology of pathos" in Judaism may, however, serve one useful purpose. It may point to the vital challenge that confronts contemporary Jewish theology. God is Infinite and Absolute and Perfect; yet, according to Judaism, the infinite, absolute, and perfect God is related to the world and cares for His creation. How are the two aspects of Divine Reality to be related to each other? The solution of the problem requires ontological investigations into the nature of Being, undertaken—perhaps for the first time—with specifically Jewish religious predilections and intellectual anxieties.

NOTES

NOTES

Hermann Cohen's Religion of Reason

All translations of quotations from the works of Hermann Cohen are by the author of this study.

1. Rosenzweig, Franz, "Einleitung" to *Jüdische Schriften*, C. A. Schwetschke und Sohn Verlag, Berlin, 1924, p. 63.
2. Hermann Cohen, *Die Ethik des reinen Willens*, B. Cassirer Verlag, Berlin, 1907, p. 61.
3. Ibid., p. 587.
4. Ibid., pp. 446, 450.
5. Cohen, *Der Begriff der Religion im System der Philosophie*, A. Toepelwanm Verlag, Giessen, 1915; p. 51.
6. *Ethik*, p. 7; cf. also, *Religion der Vernunft Aus den Quellen des Judenturns*, J. Kauffmann Verlag, Frankfurt a.M., 1919, p. 15.
7. *Der Begriff* etc., p. 52.
8. Ibid., p. 55; cf also *Die Religion der Vernunft*, p. 207.
9. *Ethik*, p. 299.
10. Ibid., p. 492.
11. *"Der Begriff*, p. 79.
12. *Die Religion*, pp. 18–20.
13. *Der Begriff*, pp. 45, 58, 62.
14. *Die Religion*, p. 12.
15. Ibid., pp. 20–22.
16. Cohen, Die *Logik der reinen Erkenntnis*, B. Cassirer Verlag, Berlin, 1902.
17. Cf. Immanuel Kant, *Kritik der Reinen Vernunft*.
18. *Die Religion*, p. 77.
19. For this presentation, cf. *Der Begriff*, 22–26; *Die Religion*, the chapter, "Die, Einzigkeit, Gottes." However, the basic idea of the uniqueness of divine Being is already present in the *Ethik*, p. 403.
20. *Die Religion*, p. 76.
21. Ibid., p. 77.
22. Cf., *Die Religion*, the chapter, *"Die Schöpfung."*
23. Ibid., p. 84.
24. Deuteronomy, pp. 4, 12.
25. Ibid., pp. 30, 14.
26. *Die Religion*, p. 98.
27. Ibid., p. 95.
28. Ibid., p. 104.
29. Ibid., p. 503.
30. *Der Begriff*, p. 106.

31. *Ethik,* p. 403.
32. *Die Religion,* p. 111.
33. *Der Begriff,* p. 106.
34. *Die Religion,* p. 188.
35. Ibid., p. 128.
36. *Der Begriff,* p. 79.
37. *Die Religion,* p. 171.
38. Ibid., p. 185.
39. *Der Begriff,* pp. 80–81, 84; cf also *Die Religion,* p. 188; *Ethik,* p. 403.
40. The two problems that ethics cannot solve, the response to the specific situation of human misery and the lifting of guilt from the human conscience, are treated in different sequences in the two works, *Der Begriff* and *Die Religion.* In the former, the problem of guilt is discussed first, then the social problem; in the latter the order is reversed. In our presentation we follow the sequence in *Die Religion.*
41. *Die Religion,* p. 222.
42. Ibid., pp. 238, 227.
43. Ibid., p. 251; see also *Der Begriff,* p. 64.
44. Ibid., pp. 470, 362.
45. Ibid., p. 48.
46. Cf. Ibid., pp. 114, 128, 442.
47. *Der Begriff,* p. 29.
48. Ibid., p. 37.
49. Ibid., p. 49.
50. Ibid., p. 50.
51. *Die Religion,* p. 187.
52. Ibid., p. 188.
53. *Der Begriff,* p. 45, also pp. 50–51.
54. Ibid., p. 60.
55. Ibid., p. 47.
56. Cf. for instance, Martin Buber's essay, "Religion and Philosophy" in his *Eclipse of God.*
57. *Die Religion,* p. 122.
58. Hermann Cohen, *Ethik,* p. 133.
59. Der Begriff, p. 47.
60. Ibid.
61. *Der Begriff,* pp. 63–64.
62. *Die Religion,* p. 383.
63. *Ethik,* p. 453.
64. *Guide for the Perplexed,* I. 47.
65. *Die Religion,* p. 73.
66. *Guide for the Perplexed,* II, 22.
67. Ibid.
68. *Die Religion,* 96.
69. See the *Guide* and *Emunot Ve'Deot.*
70. *Guide.*
71. *Hilkhot Y'sodei Hatora,* II. 2.
72. *Die Religion,* pp. 173, 296; *Ethik,* p. 495.
73. Ibid., p. 173.
74. Ibid., p. 306.
75. At a later time, Arnold Toynbee was to call the pale of enforced Jewish settlement in czarist Russia the natural condition for the Jew.

76. *Die Religion,* p. 511.
77. Ibid., p. 277.
78. Ibid., p. 517.
79. Ibid., p. 296.
80. Ibid., p. 445.
81. Ibid., p. 455.
82. See, for instance, this author's essay, "Jewish Universalism" in *History and the Idea of Mankind,* edited by W. Warren Wagar, University of New Mexico Press, Albuquerque, 1971.
83. *Logik,* p. 33.
84. *Die Religion,* p. 69.
85. *Logik,* p. 186.
86. Ibid., p. 104.
87. Ibid., pp. 131, 133.
88. *Die Religion,* p. 293.
89. Ibid., p. 360.
90. Ibid., p. 362.
91. Ibid., p. 354.
92. Ibid., p. 363.
93. Cf. also Cohen's rather tortuous elevation of love from a "second-grade" virtue allowing it to merge with respect, the "first-grade" virtue of ethics in *Der Begriff,* pp. 83–84.
94. *Die Religion,* p. 245.
95. Ibid., p. 175.
96. Ibid., p. 185.
97. Ibid., pp. 468–469.
98. Ibid., p. 104.
99. Ibid., p. 237.
100. Ibid., p. 383.
101. Ibid, p. 457.
102. Ibid., p. 442.

NOTES

For Franz Rosenzweig's Philosophy of Judaism

This study is based chiefly on Rosenzweig's *opus magnum, Der Stern der Erlösung,* Schocken Verlag. Berlin, 5690 A.M., which is usually quoted as *Der Stern.* The passages quoted in the text are translated by me, and my purpose was not so much literal exactitude as a correct rendering of the meaning in accordance with my own interpretation. This, I found to serve the general trend of my understanding of Rosenzweig better than the translation by William H. Hallo published under the title *The Star of Redemption* by Holt, Rinehart and Winston, (New York, 1970-71). This, however, should not be taken in any sense as implying any criticism of William Hallo's momentous undertaking. Corresponding references to his translation, quoted as *The Star,* are made in brackets.

1. *Der Stern der Erlösung,* [The Star, p. 419], Vol. III, p. 204.
2. Ibid., p. 55 [ibid., p. 303].
3. Ibid., p. 56 [ibid., p. 304].
4. Ibid., p. 110 [ibid., p. 346].
5. Ibid., p. 100 [ibid., p. 339].
6. Ibid., p. 55 [ibid., p. 303].

7. Ibid., p. 91 [ibid., p. 331–2].
8. Ibid., pp. 91–92 [ibid].
9. Ibid., p. 142 [ibid., p. 370].
10. Ibid., p. 85 [ibid., p. 327].
11. Ibid., p. 87 [ibid., p. 328].
12. Ibid., pp. 57, 87 [ibid.,]
13. Ibid., p. 91 [ibid., p. 332].
14. Ibid., p. 91 [ibid., ib.].
15. Ibid., p. 92 [ibid., ib.].
16. Ibid., p. 49 [ibid., p. 299].
17. Ibid., p. 50 [ibid., p. 300].
18. Ibid., p. 50 [ibid., p. 299].
19. Ibid., pp. 50–51 [ibid., p. 300].
20. Ibid., p. 175 [ibid., p. 396].
21. Ibid., p. 57 [ibid., p. 305].
22. Ibid., p. 115 [Ibid., p. 350].
23. Ibid., pp. 175–176 [Ibid., pp. 395–6].
24. Ibid., pp. 103–104 [ibid., p. 341].
25. Ibid., p. 115 [ibid., p. 350].
26. Ibid., p. 112 [ibid., p. 348].
27. Ibid., p. 190 [ibid., p. 408].
28. Ibid., p. 95 [ibid., p. 335].
29. Ibid., p. 200 [ibid., p. 415].
30. Ibid., p. 200 [ibid., pp. 415-6].
31. Ibid., p. 197 [ibid., p. 413].
32. Halevi, *Kuzari*, IV, 23; quoted in the *Stern*, p. 153 [ibid., p. 379].
33. Ibid., p. 154 [ibid.].
34. Ibid., p. 96 [ibid., p. 335].
35. Ibid., p. 140 [ibid., p. 369].
36. Ibid., p. 55 [ibid., p. 303].
37. Deuteronomy, 30, 19–20.
38. Leviticus, 18: 4–5.
39. Talmud Babli, *Yoma*, 87/B.
40. Leviticus, 19:2.
41. Isaiah, 38: 19.
42. *Der Stern*, vol. III, p. 188; cf. also what he says about the "Blessings," ibid., p. 60 [Ibid., p. 406; cf. also p. 307].
43. Talmud Babli, *Kiddushin*, 54/a.
44. *Bereshit Rabba*, 44; *Tanhuma, Sh'meenee*.
45. *Der Stern*, vol. III p. 50 [ibid., p. 299].
46. Ibid., p. 60 [ibid., p. 307].
47. Ibid., pp. 185–186, 204 [ibid., pp. 404, 419].
48. Ibid., p. 205 [ibid., p. 420].
49. Ibid., p. 159, vol. II, pp. 194–5 [ibid., pp. 383, 238].
50. Ibid., vol III, p. 50 [ibid., p. 299].
51. Ibid., p. 49 [ibid.].
52. Ibid., p. 104 [ibid., p. 341].
53. *Sh'mot Rabba*, 19, 4.
54. Micah, 4:5.
55. Op. cit., chapter 10.
56. Psalms 84: 12.

57. *Midrash T'hillim,* 1, 1.

58. Maimonides, *Yad Hahazaka, Melakhim,* 8, 11, based on *Talmud Babli, Sanhedrin,* 105/a.

59. Cf. this author's essay in *History and the Idea of Mankind,* ed. by W. Warren Wagar, University of New Mexico Press, Albuquerque, 1971.

60. *Emunot V'Deoth,* chapter III; cf. also this author's *God, Man and History,* chapter XI, *Israel.*

61. Cf., the edition of this correspondence in English under the title, *Judaism Despite Christianity,* Schocken, New York. All our references are to this edition.

62. Cf., letter of Oct. 30, 1916.

63. Talmud Babli, *Pesaḥim,* 25/B.

64. Op. cit., p. 126.

65. The essay is found in the "Smaller Writings," entitled *Zweistromland.* Philo Verlag, Berlin, 1926; the passage referred to on p. 256.

66. Rosenzweig, *Briefe,* Schocken Verlag, Berlin, 1935, p. 72.

67. Cf. *Judaism Despite Christianity,* p. 184.

68. Ibid., p. 138.

69. Ibid., p. 112.

70. Ibid., pp. 140–141.

71. Jeremiah 10:10.

72. Psalms, 31:6.

73. Cf. the author's, *Man and God, Studies in Biblical Theology,* Chapter 6, *Emeth, the Concept of Truth.*

74. Psalms 85:12.

75. *Mishnah, Abot,* I, 18.

76. Zechariah, 14:9–11.

77. Cf. this author's *Man and God, Studies in Biblical Theology,* the chapter, *Sedeq and S'daqah* especially conclusion of chapter.

78. Cf. R. Bultmann's essay, *History of Salvation and History* in his *Existence and Faith.*

79. This author has discussed this subject more thoroughly in an article, *The Death of a God,* published in *Judaism,* Winter, 1971.

80. Included in *Judaism Despite Christianity,* cf. p. 45.

NOTES

Martin Buber's Religion of the Dialogue

The following works by Martin Buber are either referred to or quoted in this essay:

Ich und Du, Im Insel Verlag, Leipzig, 1923.

I and Thou, translated by Ronald Gregor Smith, with a postscript by the author, Charles Scribner's Sons, New York, 1958.

As a rule the references in the text are to the German text. The corresponding references to the English translation are given in brackets. Literal quotations are, as a rule, from the translation, in which case the corresponding reference in the German original is not given.

Dialogisches Leben, G. Müller Verlag, Zurich: 1947. The essays, *Das Problem des Menschen, Zwiesprache, Die Frage an den Einzelnen* are found in this volume. When they are quoted in the Notes, the reference is always to it.

Die Schriften Über das Dialogische Prinzip, L. Schneider Verlag, Heidelberg:

1954. The essay, *Elemente des Zwischenmenschlichen* is found in this volume. The book is quoted as *Die Schriften*.

Urdistanz und Beziehung, L. Schneider Verlag, Heidelberg: 1960.

Eclipse of God, Studies in the Relation between Religion and Philosophy, Harper & Brothers, New York: 1952, quoted as *Eclipse*.

Between Man and Man, translated by Ronald S. Smith, Beacon Press, Boston: 1957.

Israel and the World, Essays in a Time of Crisis, Schocken Books, New York, 1948; quoted as *Israel*.

Moses, East and West Library.

1. *Ich and Du*, p. 77.
2. Ibid., pp. 12–17, 117; 113 [I And Thou, pp. 6–10, 101, 96–7].
3. Ibid., p. 10 [ibid., p. 4].
4. Ibid., pp. 9; 18, 91; 70–71; 65, 118, 133, 137 [ibid., pp. 3, 11, 77, 58–59, 54, 102, 115, 119].
5. Ibid., p. 39; 24, 31; 40–41; 43; 77 [ibid., pp. 31, 16–17, 32–33, 33–34, 65].
6. *Eclipse*, p. 61, 95 [ibid., pp. 80–81].
7. *Ich and Du*, pp. 118–119, 124; 94 [ibid., pp. 102, 107, 80].
8. Ibid., pp. 93, 124–125; *I and Thou*, pp. 78, 79 [ibid., pp. 78–79].
9. *Ich and Du*, p. 116 [ibid., p. 100].
10. *Israel*, p. 209; cf. also Postcript to *I and Thou*, p. 135; *Eclipse*, pp. 61, 127, 35.
11. Ibid., pp. 51, 54; *Israel*, pp. 49, 51, 16; cf. also Postcript, *I and Thou*, pp. 136–137.
12. *Israel*, pp. 16, 33.
13. Ibid., pp. 27, 22, cf. also ib., p. 98.
14. *Eclipse*, p. 50.
15. *Ich and Du*, p. 134 [ibid., pp. 116–117]; *Israel*, p. 98.
16. *I and Thou*, p. 109; *Ich and Du*, pp. 126–129; cf. also ibid., p. 125.
17. *I and Thou*, p. 53.
18. Ibid., pp. 62–69. [ibid., pp. 51–58].
19. Ibid., 111–112 [ibid., p. 96].
20. *Eclipse*, p. 92.
21. *I and Thou*, p. 82.
22. *Ich and Du*, pp. 95–98 [ibid., pp. 81–83].
23. *I and Thou*, p. 87.
24. *Ich and Du*, pp. 109–110; cf. also the essay, "Religion and Reality," in *Eclipse*.
25. *I and Thou*, pp. 114–115.
26. *Ich und Du*, p. 132 [ibid., p. 115].
27. Ibid., p. 56 [ibid., p. 45].
28. Ibid., [ibid.].
29. *I and Thou*, p. 117.
30. *Ich und Du*, p. 137 [ibid., p. 119].
31. Israel, 51.
32. Ibid., p. 209.
33. Eclipse, p. 46.
34. Ibid., p. 61.
35. See the essay, "Religion and Philosophy", in *Eclipse*.
36. *Eclipse*, p. 28.

37. Ibid., p. 129.
38. Ibid., p. 139.
39. Ibid., p. 141.
41. Ibid., p. 32.
41. Ibid., p. 111.
42. Ibid., p. 33.
43. Ibid., p. 34.
44. Ibid., pp. 166–167.
45. Ibid., p. 167.
46. Postscript, *I and Thou,* p. 137.
47. Ibid.
48. *Israel,* p. 82.
49. Ibid., p. 27.
50. In one passage of his work, *Dialogisches Leben,* pp. 232-236, Buber is fully conscious of the fact that there is no objective standard by which the validity of the response in each situation may be tested. The certainty is only a "personal" one, an "uncertain certainty." This, indeed, is the essence of his teaching about the meaning of truth. Every person has his own proper, though inadequate, truth, which may find an entirely different maturing in another human situation. Cf. also *Urdistanz* und *Beziehung,* pp. 30–31, and *Die Schriften,* p. 275. Yet, most of the time Buber seems to overlook that he is offering his readers his own personal uncertain certainties.
51. *Israel,* p. 85.
52. Ibid., p. 87.
53. Ibid., p. 142.
54. *Eclipse,* p. 129; cf. also *Israel,* p. 142.
55. *Eclispe,* p. 130.
56. *Israel,* pp. 31, 73.
57. *Eclipse,* p. 173.
58. *Dialogisches Leben,* p. 229.
59. Ibid., p. 234.
60. Cf. Buber's writings, *Das Problem des Menschen, Urdistanz und Beziehung, Elemente des Zwischenmenschlichen.*
61. *Between Man and Man,* 35.
62. Ibid., 16.
63. As is well known, Heidegger reinterprets the Christian dogma of original sin as the fundamental guilt of being. It consists in man's inability to free himself from the impersonal and thus to understand as well as to embrace his own authentic self-being. As against this, Buber declares: "Original guilt consists in remaining with oneself." (*Between Man and Man,* p. 166). A man who does not go out to meet the present is guilty. It would seem to us that the issue at hand will not be decided by bandying about affirmations. Both Heidegger and Buber miss the point. No matter how we interpret the nature of being or of man's being, our statements concerning it will only be statements of fact. There may indeed be a distinction between authentic and unauthentic being, as Heidegger would have it, as there may be one between man's being-with-himself and his being-with-others, as Buber maintains; but being itself, in whichever way one may understand it, does not carry in itself any obligation for man to be. This would seem to us elementary.
64. *Between Man and Man,* 14–15.
65. See "Nachwort," *Die Schriften,* p. 301; our own, not literal, translation.
66. *Between Man and Man,* 50–54.

67. In order to strengthen his point, Buber quotes the famous sentence from the *Journal*, "Had I had faith I would have stayed with Regina." Interpreting it one way first, Buber continues: "But while meaning this he says something different, too, namely, that the Single One, if he really believes, and that means if he is really a Single One, can and may have to do essentially with another [than God]." Now, anyone who is as familiar with Kierkegaard's *Fear and Trembling* as Buber must be, should on no account impute such an idea to the author of the *Journal*. For Kierkegaard, the man who had faith was Abraham. He gave up Isaac unquestioningly and without any hope of ever regaining him. But because he had faith, he was allowed to stay with Isaac in the end. Similarly, had Kierkegaard had the faith of Abraham, he would have been permitted to stay with Regina, even though he had renounced her. In this passage, Kierkegaard is not doubting the correctness of his decision to sacrifice his "Isaac." What he means to say is that the outcome of the sacrifice, so very different from that of Abraham's, proves that he was lacking in faith.

68. *I and Thou*, p. 136.

69. Ibid., p. 95.

70. Ibid., p. 39.

71. Ibid., p. 49.

72. *Ich und Du*, pp. 56, 132 [ibid., pp. 45, 115].

73. Ibid., pp. 57–60 [ibid., pp. 47–51].

74. The subject of the community is taken up again and again in Buber's writing; Cf. *Zwiesprache, Die Frage an den Einzelnen, Das Problem des Menschen*. Whatever he says in criticism of collectivism is most pertinent and valid. But nowhere has he gone beyond his original statement in *Ich und Du*. So that the problem of the community, as it arises from his concept of I-Thou remains unresolved.

75. *Israel*, p. 248.

76. Ibid., pp. 169, 199.

77. Ibid., p. 186.

78. Ibid., p. 169.

79. Ibid., p. 127.

80. Ibid., p. 98.

81. Ibid., p. 193; Cf. also Buber's *Moses*, p. 31, where the fact is mentioned that "this 'Israel' understood as a divine charge something that was potential within him."

82. In Buber's work, *Moses*, there is no sign of the idea that the people as a people encountered God and experienced revelation. There, the encounter and the experience are all Moses'. On the strength of what was revealed to him, Moses endeavors to form the tribes into a people and to formulate for them the laws of God.

83. *I and Thou*, III.

84. In a note to the Postscript, *I and Thou*, reference is made to a work, *We: Studies in Philosophic Anthropology*. At the time of the writing of this study, June 1961, this volume does not seem to have been published as yet. However, careful consideration has been given to Buber's *Das Problem des Menschen*, described by him as a prelude to his philosophical anthropology, as well as to the short essays, *Urdistanz und Beziehung*, and *Elemente des Zwischenmenschlichen*, which are to be included in the above-mentioned work. On the basis of these available writings, it would seem to us that Buber is not at all aware of the seriousness of the problem. His I-Thou just does not yield a We in the sense of a

community. We shall quote only one passage to illustrate what we mean. In *Das Problem des Menschen,* Buber says: "The special character of the We is shown in the essential relation existing, or arising temporarily, between its members; that is, in the holding sway within the We of an ontic directness which is the decisive presupposition of the I-Thou relation." (*Between Man and Man,* 175–176) The "essential relation" and the "ontic directness" are the foundation of all I-Thou relations. They indicate the unreserved encounter in the wholeness of personal existence between being and being. Buber has not gone one iota beyond his thesis in *Ich und Du.* The problem is still the same. Since the essential relation, as well as the ontic directness, are of necessity exclusive, how can a multitude of people stand in such a relation to each other at the same time? How can there ever be a true community?

85. *Israel,* 95.

86. Deuteronomy, 5:21–22.

87. Ezekiel I:28; cf. also other related passages.

88. Daniel, X:8–9.

89. Ezekiel, II:2.

90. Daniel, X:10–11.

91. Song of Songs, 5:6.

92. Psalms LXVIII: 10; for the entire quotation see *T. B., Shabbat,* 88b, *Cf.* also *Sh'mot Rabba,* Ch. 29.

93. *I and Thou,* p. 82.

94. Cf. Postscript, *I and Thou.*

95. *Eclipse,* p. 93.

96. *Israel,* p. 85.

97. *Eclipse,* p. 46.

98. *Israel,* p. 49.

99. Nor is faith the only area where freedom and responsibility are vital. They have their appropriate function within the realm of the revealed law itself. The will of God for man, as expressed in his law, is established; but it is for man to implement the law in the concrete situation of his life. We fully agree with Buber that "in spite of all similarities every living situation has, like a new-born child, a new face, that has never been before and will never come again. It demands of you a reaction which cannot be prepared beforehand." (*Between Man and Man,* 114.) Buber, of course, cannot show how a situation may make demands on man that have to be met in responsibility. Once, however, the law is established, the demand is made to apply the law to the living situation. This is a demand to the human conscience which one can answer only in freedom and responsibility. Because every situation is indeed unique, one has to go back continually anew to the law and inquire of its meaning again and again. The meaning is then revealed afresh, in relationship to the new situation, for the one who inquires in responsibility and decides in the freedom of his conscience. It is indeed in this spirit that the great Rabbinical teachers of the oral tradition have taught the application of the law to every new situation. Whoever is familiar with their teaching and their method knows well that the law often reveals unsuspected levels of meaning as it is being applied to a new situation. In keeping with prophetic tradition, the Rabbis insisted that one should approach the contents of God's revelation as if it had been revealed to man every day anew. (See *T. B. Berakot,* 63b.) In the task of applying the law to every specific situation man's responsibility is tested. Of course, he has the law before him; but it is man who interprets, it is he who makes the decision and is responsible for his action. As is well known, the Rabbis, on one

occasion, went so far in their affirmation of their responsibility to interpret and to decide in the freedom of their conscience that they defied heavenly signs which demanded a different decision. (See *T. B. Baba Metsia*, 59b.)

100. *Between Man and Man*, p. 97.
101. Ibid., pp. 96, 23, 22; cf. also p. 29 and the essay, *Urdistanz und Beziehung*, pp. 34–36.
102. *Between Man and Man*, p. 170.
103. *Ich und Du*, p. 92 [Ibid., p. 78].
104. *Israel*, p. 49.
105. *I and Thou*, p. 27.
106. Ibid., p. 18.
107. Ibid., p. 25.
108. Ibid., p. 101.
109. Ibid., p. 116.
110. Postscript, *I and Thou*, p. 126.
111. *Ich und Du*, p. 118. [Ibid., p. 102].
112. *I and Thou*, p. 101.
113. *Ich und Du*, p. 75 [Ibid., p. 63].
114. *I and Thou*, p. 80.
115. Ibid., p. 96.
116. Ibid., p. 95.
117. Ibid., p. 23.
118. *Between Man and Man*, p. 175.
119. *Urdistanz und Beziehung*, p. 11.
120. *Dialogisches Leben*, p. 419.
121. *Die Schriften*, p. 276.
122. Ibid., p. 277.
123. *Eclipse*, p. 25.
124. *I and Thou*, p. 135.
125. *Moses*, pp. 7–8.
126. *I and Thou*, p. 107.
127. *Die Schriften*, p. 292.
128. Ibid., pp. 299–230.

NOTES

Mordecai Kaplan's Reconstructionist Theology

Quotes from *The Meaning of God in Modern Jewish Religion* by Mordecai M. Kaplan have referred to as *Meaning of God*. Quotes from *Meaning of God* are from the 1947 edition (Behrman House, N.Y.); from *Judaism without Supernaturalism* from the 1958 edition (Reconstructionist Press, N.Y.).

I. The Theology of Reconstructionism

1. Cf. subtitle of *Judaism without Supernaturalism*, Reconstructionist Press, New York; 1958.
2. Ibid., *Judaism without Supernaturalism*, Reconstructionist Press, New York; 1958. p. 18.
3. Ibid., p. 16.

4. *Judaism without Supernaturalism,* Reconstructionist Press, New York; 1958. p. 98, *Meaning of God,* p. 25.

5. *The Meaning of God in Modern Jewish Religion,* Berhman House, New York, 1947. p. 26.

6. Ibid., pp. 25–26.

7. Ibid.

8. Ibid., p. 294.

9. Ibid., p. 29.

10. *Judaism without Supernaturalism,* pp. 10, 111.

11. Ibid., p. 10.

12. Meaning of God, p. 325.

13. Ibid., pp. 244–245.

14. *Judaism without Supernaturalism,* p. 120.

15. Ibid., p. 119.

16. Ibid., pp. 101–102.

17. Ibid., p. 110.

18. Meaning of God, p. 118.

19. Ibid., pp. 160–161.

20. *Judaism without Supernaturalism,* pp. 48–52.

21. *Meaning of God,* p. 323.

22. Ibid., p. 295.

23. Ibid., p. 110.

24. Ibid., p. 226.

25. Ibid., p. 167.

26. Ibid., p. 27.

27. Ibid., p. 29.

28. Ibid., p. 54.

29. Ibid., p. 245.

30. Ibid., pp. 64, 73, 76.

31. Ibid., p. 272.

32. Ibid., p. 76.

33. Ibid., ibid.

34. Ibid., p. 327.

35. Ibid., pp. 12–13.

36. Ibid., p. 110.

37. Cf., ibid., pp. 26, 113, 120, 161, 245, etc.

II. Criticism

38. *Meaning of God,* pp. 26, 88.

39. Ibid., p. 76.

40. Ibid., p. 137.

41. Ibid., p. 269.

42. Ibid., p. 20.

43. Ibid., p. 62.

44. Ibid., p. 282.

45. Ibid., pp. 270–271.

46. Ibid., p. 273.

47. Ibid., p. 274.

48. Cf. Kant's discussion of the problem, for instance, in *Kritik der reinen Vernunft, Elementallehre,* II. Teil, II. Abt., II. Buch, II. Hamptstuck, III.

49. *Meaning of God*, p. 62.
50. Ibid., pp. 281–282.
51. *Judaism without Supernaturalism*, p. 27.
52. *Evolution and Ethics*, 1893–1943, by T. H. Huxley and Julian Huxley, The Pilot Press, London, 1947, p. 175.
53. See above, note 16.
54. *Judaism without Supernaturalism*, pp. 101–102, *Meaning of God*, pp. 177, 213, 244–245, 316.
55. T. B. *Berakhot*, 33/b.
56. *Meaning of God*, pp. 270–271.
57. *Judaism without Supernaturalism*, p. 119.
58. *Meaning of God*, p. 173.
59. Ibid., p. 177.
60. Ibid., p. 177.
61. Spinoza, *Ethics*, III, Preface.
62. Ibid., IV, Preface.
63. Cf. *Die Religion der Vernunft aus den Quellen des Judentums*, J. Kauffmann Verlag, Frankfurt A.M., 1919., p. 484.
64. See the discussion of this subject by W. R. Sorley in his Gifford Lectures, *Moral Values and the Idea of God* (Cambridge, University Press, 1935), p. 387. Cf. also the position of Hermann Cohen in his *Ethik des Reinen Willens* and in *Der Begriff der Religion im System der Philosophie*.
65. *Meaning of God*, p. 75.
66. *Judaism without Supernaturalism*, p. 77.
67. Hermann Cohen, *Die Religion der Vernunft*, pp. 278, 471, 517.
68. Max Scheler, *Vom Eurigen in Menschen*, Franche Verlag, Bern, 1954, pp. 107–108.
69. T. B. *Sanhedrin*, 38/a.
70. *Judaism without Supernaturalism*, p. 221.
71. Ibid., p. 120.

III Evaluation

72. *Meaning of God*, p. 176.
73. Ibid., p. 89.
74. Ibid., p. 83.
75. Cf. the discussion of the subject by Joseph Needham in his *Time, The Refreshing River*, George Allen & Unwin Ltd., London, 1944, the chapter, "Evolution and Thermodynamics."
76. *New Pathways in Science*, Cambridge, University Press, 1935, p. 309.
77. *Meaning of God.*, p. 27.
78. Ibid., ibid.
79. Psalms, 8:4–6.
80. *Meaning of God*, p. 29.
81. Ibid., p. 89.
82. Ibid., p. 148.
83. Ibid., p. 135.
84. *Judaism without Supernaturalism*, p. 33.
85. *Meaning of God*, p. 83.
86. *Judaism without Supernaturalism*, p. 216.
87. *Meaning of God.*, p. 7.

88. Ibid., pp. 30, 335; *Judaism without Supernaturalism*, 110–111.
89. Ibid., pp. 110–111.
90. Ibid., p. 68.
91. Sir James Jeans, *Physics and Philosophy*, Cambridge, University Press, 1943, p. 145.
92. See the discussion in *New Pathways in Science*, pp. 300-332.
93. *Science in the Modern World*, Cambridge, University Press, 1943, pp. 4–5.
94. Ibid., p. 16.
95. Ibid., p. 56.
96. *The Bases of Modern Science*, Pelican Books, 1928 (published by Penguin Books Ltd., Harmondsworth, Middlesex, England), p. 11.
97. Ibid., p. 186.
98. Cf. A. S. Eddington, op. cit., p. 262.
99. Ibid., pp. 313–314.

NOTES FOR DR. A. J. HESCHEL'S THEOLOGY OF PATHOS

1. *For Dr. A. J. Heschel, The Prophets*, Harper & Row, New York, 1962, p. 226.
2. Ibid., pp. 284, 230, 320.
3. Ibid., pp. 223–224.
4. Ibid., pp. 229.
5. Ibid., pp 219, 232, 226.
6. Ibid., p. 228, 219.
7. This presentation of the thought of sympathy based on ibid., **pp.** 34, 308–9, 319, 311, 314.
8. Ibid., p. 271.
9. Ibid.
10. Ibid., p 319.
11. Ibid., p. 312.
12. Ibid., pp. 219, 226, 232, 276.
13. Ibid., p. 227.
14. Ibid., p. 271.
15. Ibid., p. 259.
16. Ibid., pp. 282–284.
17. Ibid., p. 294.
18. Ibid., p. 312.
19. Ibid., p. 277, see also pp. 286, 294.
20. Ibid., p. 295.
21. Ibid., p. 294.
22. Ibid., p. 485.
23. Ibid., p. 232.
24. Ibid., for this analysis of the divine event of inspiration cf. pp. 432–438.
25. Ibid., cf., pp. 255–8, 260–262.
26. Ibid., p. 274.
27. Ibid., p. 484.
28. Ibid., pp. 231, 272.
29. Ibid., p. 257.
30. Ibid., p. 276.
31. Heschel is not unaware of the risk to which he exposes himself. In his discussion of anthropopathy, and in obvious reference to his own endeavor, he says: "A sacred venture is always in danger of ending in a blasphemy. The sacred

venture of conveying more than what minds could visualize or words could say is always in danger of being a failure" (loc. cit. 273–274.) It is to be regretted that Professor Heschel has succumbed to the dangers of the path on which he ventured out.

32. Ibid., p. 341; for the references to Hosea and Jeremiah, cf. pp. 49–50, 125.
33. Ibid., p. 310.
34. For this part of our discussion see ibid., pp. 57–8.
35. Ibid., p. 60.
36. Ibid., p. 115.
37. Ibid., p. 116.
38. Ibid., p. 317.
39. Ibid., p. 56.
40. Ibid., p. 273.
41. Ibid., p. 486.
42. Ibid., p. 218.
43. Ibid., p. 225.
44. Ibid., p. 277.
45. Ibid., p. 437.
46. Ibid., pp. 225 and 310.
47. Ibid., p. 297.
48. Ibid., p. 231.
49. Ibid.
50. Ibid., p. 277.
51. Ibid., p. 229.
52. Loc. cit., p. 26.
53. A. M. Fairbairn, *The Place of Christ in Modern Theology,* N. Y. 1893., p. 483.
54. *Cf.* F. Loofs, *Dogmengeschichte,* Halle, 1906, p. 185, W. G. T. Shedd, *History of Christian Doctrine,* New York, 1863, pp. 254–5, 402–4.
55. M. Werner, *The Formation of Christian Dogma,* London, p. 240.
56. Cf., *Summa Theologica* III, XIV, 1.
57. Loc. cit., p. 262.
58. *Microcosmus,* English Translation, N. Y., 1856; Book IX, chapter IV, cf. pp. 682–682.
59. *Fairbairn,* op. cit., p. 483,ff.

INDEX